American Dove

Zachary C. Shirkey argues that the United States is overly reliant on the active use of force and should employ more peaceful foreign policy tools. Force often fails to achieve its desired ends for both tactical and strategic reasons and is relatively nonfungible, making it an inappropriate tool for many US foreign policy goals. Rather than relying on loose analogies or common sense as many books on US grand strategy do, *American Dove* bases its argument directly on an eclectic mix of academic literature, including realist, liberal, and constructivist theory as well as psychology. Shirkey also argues against retrenchment strategies, such as offshore balancing and strategic restraint. He argues such strategies lack a moral component leaving them vulnerable to hawkish policies that employ moral arguments in favor of action and that US withdrawal would weaken the existing liberal international security, economic, and legal orders—orders that benefit the United States. Rather, the book argues the United States needs an energetic foreign policy that employs passive uses of force, such as deterrence, and nonmilitary tools such as economic statecraft, international institutions, international law, and soft power. Such a policy leaves room for a moral component, which is necessary for mobilizing the American public, and would uphold the existing international order. Last, Shirkey argues that to be successful, doves must frame their arguments in terms of strategy rather than in terms of costs and must show that dovish policies are consistent with national honor and a broad range of American values. *American Dove* offers a framework for US grand strategy and a plan for persuading the public to adopt it.

**Zachary C. Shirkey** is a Professor of Political Science at Hunter College and The Graduate Center, City University of New York (CUNY).

# American Dove

## US FOREIGN POLICY AND
## THE FAILURE OF FORCE

## Zachary C. Shirkey

University of Michigan Press
Ann Arbor

First paperback edition 2023
Copyright © 2020 by Zachary C. Shirkey
All rights reserved

For questions or permissions, please contact um.press.perms@umich.edu
Published in the United States of America by the
University of Michigan Press
Printed and bound by CPI Group (UK) Ltd, Croydon, CR0 4YY


A CIP catalog record for this book is available from the British Library.

*Library of Congress Cataloging-in-Publication data has been applied for.*

First published in paperback January 2023

ISBN: 978-0-472-13217-1 (Hardcover : alk paper)
ISBN: 978-0-472-12723-8 (ebook)
ISBN: 978-0-472-03929-6 (paper : alk paper)

*To the people of Michigan and New York, without whose wisdom and support this book could not have been written*

# Contents

Digital materials related to this title can be found on
the Fulcrum platform via the following citable URL:
https://doi.org/10.3998/mpub.11644328

# Acknowledgments

I would like to thank Lina Benabdallah, Nicole L. Freiner, Stuart Gottlieb, Jeff Izzard, Jeremy Kennedy, Michael Lee, Cynthia A. Roberts, Ivan Savic, Erin Shirkey, Linda Coleman Shirkey, Robert Shirkey, Alex Weisiger, Mike White, and Kezia C. Shirkey Zakem for their helpful comments, encouragement, and advice. Any mistakes are my own.

# Introduction

## The Need for a More Peaceful US Foreign Policy

We could make no more tragic mistake than merely to concentrate on military strength. For if we did this, the future would hold nothing for the world but an Age of Terror.

PRESIDENT DWIGHT D. EISENHOWER.[1]

In recent years, a quip has circulated around Washington about American policy failures in the Middle East. Richard Fontaine, advisor to both John McCain's and Jeb Bush's presidential campaigns as well as a former National Security Council and State Department staffer, told it this way:

> In Iraq, we toppled the government and did an occupation and everything went to hell. In Libya, we toppled the government and didn't do an occupation and everything went to hell. In Syria, we didn't topple the government and didn't do an occupation and everything went to hell. So, broadly this is the Middle East. Things go to hell.[2]

The quip misses the point. It deftly, albeit deceptively, shifts the responsibility for US policy failures from Washington to the Middle East itself. It also creates a false sense of equivalence between the three outcomes as far as the United States is concerned. While current conditions in all three countries range from challenging to dire—the costs to the United States could not be more different. The United States paid dearly in Afghanistan and Iraq. As of late 2019, 2,438 Americans have died in Afghanistan and another 4,886 have died in Iraq. The number of wounded service personnel is far higher: 20,516 and 32,337 in Afghanistan and Iraq respectively.[3] At its peak, the troop demands of the Iraq War severely strained the US military's manpower.[4] On top of this, the US invasion of Iraq helped to create the monstrosity that is ISIS (Islamic State in Iraq and Syria) thereby exacerbating the Syrian and Libyan conflicts. The wars were also costly in monetary terms. Direct US military costs in Iraq (2003–2011) came to $1.06 trillion.[5] The same figure for Afghanistan (2001–2019) is at $975 billion and counting.[6] These numbers dwarf the much smaller direct costs of military intervention in Libya and Syria where the combined US military fatalities are in the single digits as of late 2019.[7] The monetary costs have also been much lower, though they are hardly small. The Libyan War cost US taxpayers about $1.1 billion, while ongoing operations in Syria and Iraq to fight ISIS have averaged roughly $15 billion per year.[8]

The one true, though buried, element of the quip is that it illustrates the ineffectiveness of recent American uses of force. And the United States has used force a lot lately. Since al Qaeda's attacks on September 11, 2001, the United States has been engaged in a series of conflicts around the world. Including covert operations, the US military has fought in Afghanistan, Iraq, Libya, Somalia, Syria, Yemen, Niger, and Pakistan. Even in the 1990s, the United States was engaged in almost four dozen military interventions including conflicts in Somalia, Iraq, Bosnia, and Kosovo.[9] In other words, the US military has been exceptionally busy over the past thirty years and many believe it will remain just as busy for the foreseeable future.

In some ways, this is understandable. The world is full of dangers, and US foreign policy must protect against threats posed by foreign countries and terrorist groups. Yet, this recurrent use of force has failed to make the world a safer place for the average American. The United States would benefit from a more dovish, in other words a more peaceful, foreign policy. Such a policy would better secure US interests, protect American allies, and do so at a reduced cost.

Doves, as opposed to hawks, are skeptical about the use of force, by which I mean actually waging war or otherwise actively engaging in hostilities. Outside of their views on the use of force, doves come from a wide range of political orientations. They may be liberal or conservative. They may be Democrats, Republicans, Libertarians, Greens, or independents. Some favor free trade, while others favor protectionism. Some doves are internationalists; others are isolationists. In sum, dovishness is not a foreign policy, nor an overall political philosophy. Rather it is an orientation toward the use of force. Whether doves come to that deep skepticism about the use of force through moral or practical concerns also varies, but this shared outlook means that all manner of doves can come together on one of the most important questions that any country faces: When should it engage in violence and war?

This book focuses on the practical argument for a dovish foreign policy: force is ineffective. In short, force fails to achieve its desired ends, is overly costly, and often makes things worse rather than better.[10] Force fails for several reasons. One, it is incredibly difficult to control the battlefield and bring about desired tactical results. Two, even if tactical military successes are achieved, they don't guarantee the accomplishment of policy ends. For example, the United States and its allies have won a great many battles in Afghanistan, but they have not been able to create a stable Afghan government that can stand on its own. Nor have these battlefield successes ensured that terrorist groups cannot base themselves in Afghanistan—either in ungoverned spaces or those controlled by the Taliban.[11] It is possible to win the battles and lose the war. Three, the frequent use of force saps military morale and reduces the amount of money available for research and development of new military hardware.[12] Four, many US foreign policy goals are unconnected to force. Force can do little, for instance, in the realms of international trade or finance. Last, the frequent use of force sets negative precedents that allow other countries, such as Russia, to use force more freely. It is very hard for Washington to criticize Russian interventions in Syria, Georgia, and Ukraine without sounding hypocritical. This is not to condone those Russian actions. They should be condemned. Nor is it to claim those actions were caused by US military actions. They were not. But American complaints ring hollow when US forces are engaged in multiple conflicts around the world.

Despite the failures of force, its frequent use has bipartisan backing. Like someone that owns only a hammer and believes every home improvement project looks like a nail, Americans have come to see far too many foreign policy problems in exclusively military terms.[13] President Bush's 2003 invasion of Iraq, which even hawks such as Eliot Cohen now admit was a mistake, is but the largest example of the recent American embrace of force.[14] President Obama's foreign policy was also quite hawkish despite his philosophy of "don't do stupid stuff."[15] Under his watch, the North Atlantic Treaty Organization (NATO) used airstrikes to facilitate the overthrow of Muammar Gaddafi in Libya and authorized 540 drone strikes in Pakistan, Yemen, and Somalia.[16] The Obama administration's actions reflect a broader trend in which the Democratic Party has become more supportive of the active use of force in recent decades.[17] Likewise, President Trump, while far less internationalist than his predecessors, has also shown strong hawkish tendencies.[18] Though he has not expanded the geographic footprint of US military operations, he has sent more troops to Afghanistan, deepened US involvement in Somalia, continued ongoing US military actions in Iraq, increased the rate of drone strikes in Yemen, used drones to kill a leading Iranian general, and authorized cruise missile strikes against Syria.[19] He has also threatened military action against Venezuela and has opposed Congressional attempts to limit US involvement in Yemen.[20] Hillary Clinton, Donald Trump's opponent in the 2016 presidential campaign, was also quite comfortable with hawkish positions.[21] As President Obama's Secretary of State, she repeatedly advocated for the use of force—most infamously in Libya.[22]

These recent uses of force are not a departure from traditional US foreign policy. Rather, they fit within a general pattern of the extensive American use of military force since the Spanish-American War and especially since the end of the Cold War.[23] The United States has had military forces in combat in 57 of the 122 years from 1898 through 2019. The rate since the Berlin Wall fell in 1989 is even higher, with US forces being in combat in twenty-four of the thirty years of the post-Cold War era.[24] Clearly, hawks are winning the argument with doves.

Simply avoiding large-scale uses of force is insufficient. Smaller uses of force such as in Somalia, Yemen, or Libya are as apt to go wrong as larger ones such as in Iraq. While it is certainly possible to have an overly ambitious foreign policy, the limitations and drawbacks listed above are inherent to all uses of force regardless of scale. Further, in many ways the United States should continue to aim high and have expansive foreign policy goals. As will be shown in chapter 2, withdrawal from the world is not in America's interests. Specifically, the United States should continue to uphold and strengthen the existing international security, legal, and economic orders. The United States should continue to advance its interests and promote its values. It just should rarely use force to achieve those goals.

Instead, the United States would be wise to emphasize nonmilitary tools—economic might, diplomacy, international institutions, and moral authority—to advance its goals. Many other countries around the globe, including rising powers like China, use nonmilitary tools to great effect. The United States has also benefited from the use of nonmilitary tools in the past. Many of America's greatest foreign policy successes during the Cold War, such as the Marshall Plan that rebuilt Europe after World War II, used non-military tools.[25] Yet, today, they are underused. Instead, Washington over relies on the military. Failure to use these other tools amounts to conducting foreign policy with one arm tied behind America's back.

What is needed is a US foreign policy that greatly reduces the American use of force while still protecting US interests and advancing American ideals. Such a foreign policy would recognize that the United States, due to its large population, immense wealth, and powerful military, must play a major role in the world. The United States must be prepared to fight if necessary but be reluctant to do so except when compelled to defend American soil or that of US allies. At the same time, any US foreign policy must acknowledge the very real limits of what the United States can do. It is impossible to reshape the world in the United States' image or to squelch all potential threats.[26] In other words, the United States can neither reform nor hide from the world.[27]

A dovish foreign policy is able to do all of this. It would be just as hard-headed and realistic as more hawkish foreign policies. Indeed, it would be more realistic as hawks often are overly optimistic about what force can achieve, while doves are more aware of the real limits to and costs of the use of force. It would advance American interests and values. In short, such a foreign policy would be wise, moral, honorable, and vigorous.

This is not an argument for pacifism or a claim that force never works. One can recognize that the world is a dangerous place and that there is, at times, a need for the use of force while remaining deeply skeptical about the frequent use of force. While the United States should use force very rarely, it must remain prepared to defend itself and its allies if needed.[28]

Furthermore, force has worked at times. The United States' participation in World War II was both wise and necessary. On a smaller scale, the Gulf War (1990–1991) successfully drove Iraqi forces out of Kuwait, though tellingly it did not solve the problem that was Saddam Hussein's Iraq. Indeed, it was the recognition of the limits to the use of force—marching on Baghdad would have been unwise—that sets the Gulf War apart as a success when compared to the grinding counterinsurgency operation that emerged from the 2003 invasion of Iraq.

There are in fact several arguably successful American uses of force in the post-Cold War years. Most of them, however, ring hollow upon closer inspection. For example, the United States restored Jean-Bertrand Aristide to the Haitian presidency in 1994 through threats of force, and the US military landings were central to the successful delivery of food in Somalia in 1992.

However, Haiti continues to be plagued by political violence, and, of course, the US intervention in Somalia quickly soured. The United States withdrew following the 1993 Black Hawk Down incident, and US actions failed to prevent decades of civil war in Somalia.[29] US involvement in Liberia in 2003 was more productive, though it was mostly limited to protecting US diplomatic personnel in Liberia and avoiding a humanitarian crisis during the terminal stage of that country's civil war.[30] Certainly, such small, short run actions to protect lives will at times be appropriate, but they say little about broader uses of force. The removal of Charles Taylor and longer term peace in Liberia were a result of broader international pressure and events within the country, rather than the 2003 US military mission. Yet, as will be seen in the following pages, even these qualified successes are exceptions, not the rule. In short, force does work at times, but these occasions are rare and the successes are often narrow in scope.

Similarly, this is not a criticism of US military personnel. If recent wars and military engagements have failed to deliver, the fault lies not with those that faithfully execute their orders but with those that issue the orders: US-elected officials and, ultimately, the Americans who choose those officials. US servicemen and women are brave, highly skilled, and dedicated. They have repeatedly done all that has been asked of them and done it well. But think about what is asked: To be separated from their families for long stretches. To kill. To risk being killed or maimed. To see things no one should have to see. And yet, they serve willingly and honorably. At the very least, when they are asked to go off to war, they are owed that their sacrifices actually advance US interests. They are owed far more than that; but at a bare minimum, they should not have to risk their lives carrying out self-defeating policies.

The remainder of the book builds off of existing social science research to show how and why a more dovish foreign policy would benefit the United States. In other words, the book does not test hypotheses but rather synthesizes existing findings to generate and defend policy recommendations. The book is laid out as follows. Chapter 1, "Why Hawks and Doves Continue to Clash," explains why the debate between hawks and doves remains unresolved. The chapter also looks at a number of tactical mistakes doves have made in the past, such as focusing on costs and blaming the United States for the ills of the world, which have greatly reduced doves' ability to out argue hawks.

Chapter 2, "Defending the International Order," offers a blueprint for a dovish foreign policy. It argues the United States should strive to preserve and strengthen the existing international security, legal, and economic orders. This can be done by maintaining existing US alliances, keeping but reforming global economic arrangements, and using international organizations and international law when possible. The key to such a strategy is recognizing the very real limits of US power and not overreaching in an attempt to remake the world in the United States' image. Following a dovish strategy would make the world a safer and more prosperous place, as well as create an environment where American interests can more easily be advanced. It would also allow the United States to harbor its resources and avoid wasteful wars.

Chapter 3, "Doves as Pessimists: Why Force Fails," shows why the tactically successful application of force often fails to achieve desired political objectives. This happens because there is often a disconnect between force and policy aims and because it is very difficult to exercise control of the battlefield. Further, the use of force sets precedents that make it easier for countries hostile to the United States to also use force. The chapter concludes by examining why force remains seductive despite these failings.

Chapter 4, "Doves as Optimists: How the United States Can Succeed without Waging War," argues the United States can better achieve its goals peacefully than through war. In particular, economic levers, international institutions, international law, the appeal of American ideals and culture, and old-fashioned diplomacy work better than force the majority of the time. Furthermore, these tools are far cheaper than force, both in terms of money and lives, making them more efficient as well.

Chapter 5, "Competing Strategies for Confronting Adversaries," looks at how hawkish and dovish policies have addressed the foreign threats that the United States faces: hostile countries and international terrorism. Hawks have relied on preventive uses of force and a mix of regime change and nation-building to deal with hostile countries and foreign terrorist groups. These policies have failed when compared to the dovish solutions of deterrence and counterterrorism policies that rely on a combination of intelligence gathering and police work.[31]

Last, chapter 6, "How Doves Win," offers some thoughts about how ordinary Americans can advocate for a more dovish US foreign policy. In particular, it discusses how arguments are best framed to sway others and contends that doves cannot wait until war is imminent to advance their position.

Each of these elements is important to understanding why the United States would benefit from a more dovish foreign policy, what such a policy might look like, and how doves can convince others to support such a policy. If dovish strategies are superior both in theory and in practice, why do hawks continue to win the day? What are doves doing wrong? The next chapter takes up these questions.

# CHAPTER I

# *Why Hawks and Doves Continue to Clash*

For arms are of little value in the field unless there is wise counsel at home.

MARCUS TULLIUS CICERO[1]

Americans are a martial people but also have deep dovish traditions.[2] Debates about war and peace are as old as the republic itself. Questions about how to respond to British and French naval provocations during the Napoleonic and French Revolutionary Wars roiled both Congress and the public at large. US responses ranged from President Jefferson's economic embargo, to the Quasi-War with France, and to the War of 1812 with Britain. Such debates about war and peace continued through the Mexican-American War, Spanish-American War, and World War I to the present.[3] Questions have always swirled as to what US aims should be, how involved the United States should be in world affairs, and the effectiveness and morality of military actions. This chapter explores why those debates have continued and why doves have usually lost them.

These continuing debates between hawks and doves present something of a puzzle. Why doesn't someone win the debate and the other side concede its own errors? Even accounting for factors like pride, which may prevent an individual from admitting error, over time, one would expect future generations to gravitate toward the "correct" answer. Yet this clearly does not happen in foreign policy debates—or indeed in many debates about public policy both in the United States and abroad. What is going on? To understand why hawks and doves continue to clash, it is necessary to think about the different types of policy debates. In turn, this illuminates how doves can win these debates.

## THE NATURE OF POLICY DEBATES

Generally, advocates of policy—whether inside or outside of government—
argue that their policy would best achieve some shared goal. In other words,
they have the correct answer and those that disagree are mistaken. While this
is a powerful rhetorical tool, only one of at least four possible types of policy
debates—disagreements over strategy—actually fits this description. Many
disagreements are not about strategy but instead are debates about or between
goals. Such policy debates include distributional disagreements, what trade-
offs to make between two goods, and disagreements about what is in fact a
positive outcome. Each type of debate has distinct implications for how it can
be resolved and the possibility for compromise. Beginning with debates over
strategy, each of the four types of debates will be covered in turn.

*Debates over Strategy*

Debates over the best strategy to achieve a shared goal are common. In foreign affairs, such debates include how to defeat al Qaeda, how to confront
the Soviet Union during the Cold War, or how to reduce the global incidence
of poverty and disease. The vast majority of Americans share these aims. The
question is how to best achieve these goals. Crucially, such debates have a
correct answer. However, with the information currently available, it may be
impossible to know for certain what that answer is. Still, this means such
debates theoretically are resolvable. As evidence comes in, people should
begin to rule out certain policies and potentially converge upon a shared
answer *given sufficient evidence.*[4] In other words, as various arguments are
proven wrong, they should be abandoned, and arguments confirmed by evidence should be embraced. Given sufficiently static conditions, the correct
answer may even be found.[5] Yes, egos may make people reluctant to admit
errors, hence physicist Max Planck's quip about knowledge advancing one
funeral at a time,[6] but disproven strategies shouldn't find new champions. In
other words, eventual agreement is possible.
    Of course, changing conditions—new challenges and problems always
arise—mean that there is no shortage of these sorts of debates. There is no
manual of right answers to guide the government now and forevermore.
Still, there should be certain lessons learned about what works and what
doesn't. Whether the ever-rising new dilemmas and challenges are analogous to those of the past would, of course, be debated. Even so, as long as it is

accepted that humans can learn—and there is every reason to believe that is true—something else must be going on if debates about strategy are never resolved.

An example of such an endless debate comes from economics: What should governments do to fight recessions? Economists largely agree that the best solution to reduce the severity of recessions is to increase aggregate economic demand using a mix of fiscal stimulus through deficit spending and monetary stimulus through lower interest rates and more exotic policies to create easy money.[7] Of course, there would always be a need for some variation to meet specific conditions, but the basic underlying principles are widely agreed upon within the economics profession. Yet, policy makers and pundits continue to debate core questions about how to confront recessions and often reject policies that are supported by decades of research and practical experience. What explains this?

This tendency for debates to never be resolved despite logically having a correct answer suggests that the disagreements are not really about the best strategy. Because policies often have other effects beyond the shared goal, individuals that oppose those ancillary outcomes may oppose the optimal strategy to achieve the shared goal. For example, fiscal and monetary stimuli not only help end recessions but they also redistribute wealth and expand the government. So individuals may oppose stimulus measures to avoid those ancillary outcomes. Yet, it is politically difficult to argue widespread economic suffering must be prolonged to advance one's parochial or ideological interests. It is more politic instead to claim what we in fact know about fighting recessions is incorrect. People may also come to believe that their own narrow interests are aligned with those of the commonweal as that is psychologically more comfortable. Thus, while their arguments would be false, they might not be deliberately so. Thus, the debate appears to be about strategy even though it is not. This is fairly common. Many debates are in fact not about strategy but rather are one of the following types of debate masquerading as debates about strategy for rhetorical reasons.

*Distributional Debates*

Among these is the second type of debate: fights over how the costs and benefits of a policy are to be distributed across the populace. A distributional debate can most clearly be thought about as two people having to decide how to divide a dollar between them. Each would like the full dollar. How the dollar is ultimately divided will depend upon the bargaining power of each side, any rules or structures already in place to determine how the dollar is to be divided, and whether outside parties could influence the bargain. Such distributional debates are part and parcel of everyday politics. Domestically, debates over tax rates and social programs have clear distributional implications. Changes to programs benefit some and harm others.

Foreign policy debates can also be distributional in nature. How should a contested piece of territory be divided? Should the US government pay for military actions through borrowing or increased taxes (and on whom should the burden of those new taxes fall)? The US Army and US Navy frequently contend with each other for a greater share of the US defense budget. Likewise, the Defense Department clashes with the State Department for foreign policy dollars, and NATO members debate how much they should each contribute to the alliance's military capabilities.

Distributional debates have two seemingly contradictory characteristics: they are never-ending and compromise is eminently achievable. Though this appears to be a paradox, it is not as will be seen momentarily. Such debates are never-ending because there is no correct answer, only bargains between interested parties. It is impossible to strike a bargain that can never be renegotiated provided both parties continue to exist.[8] For example, tax rates can always be changed; social programs can always be expanded, curtailed, or ended; budget allocations can always be altered; and constitutions can be amended. The closest to permanence that can be achieved are so called self-enforcing bargains—those bargains, given current conditions including third party enforcement, in which none of the parties sees fit to renegotiate given the expected costs and benefits.[9] Politics always goes on, and the bargains struck at any given time hold only as long as the underlying power structures that led to them remain in place or the costs associated with renegotiating the bargain exceed the expected gains any party would get.

Even though such debates are effectively endless, compromise is possible because it is very rare that any party realistically expects to get the whole good at stake. I am not likely to be able to get a mix of taxes and social programs that takes all of your money and gives it all to me. Nor are you likely to be able to achieve the inverse. Even bloody conflicts with unrestrained bargaining, such as wars, usually end in negotiated settlements.[10] Even wars that end in so-called "unconditional surrender" usually have implicit conditions.[11] For instance, the Germans "unconditionally" surrendered in World

War II with the understanding that the lives of average Germans would be spared and most of their remaining economic infrastructure preserved.[12] In other words, compromise happens because it is expected and necessary to get the other side to accept the bargain even if it is done with ill-humor.

Of course, some things are indivisible—though in practice most political goods are in fact divisible.[13] Even King Solomon's classic example of the indivisibility of a child[14] has been proven wrong by the modern creation of joint custody. Still, there may be things that are impractical to divide even though division is theoretically possible. To take another example from divorce, it is impractical for a divorced couple to continue to share their house. Yes, one person could live upstairs and the other downstairs, but as a practical matter, that solution would be inconvenient and unpleasant at best. Side payments and issue linkage, however, can solve such issues. One person might keep the house with the other receiving monetary compensation. Or if there are multiple homes or other goods that are difficult to divide, say cars, one party could receive one good and the other party another. Last, the house could be sold and the proceeds divided.

Similar deals are struck in politics. For example, food stamps and farm aid are usually linked so that a wide range of Americans and areas of the country benefit from the same bill.[15] Similarly, in 1819, the United States acquired Florida from Spain in return for $5 million and the establishment of an agreed upon border with Spanish-held territories in the Southwest.[16] The first example illustrates issue linkage while the second involves not only linkage but also side payments and the division of a good. Thus, compromises should be attainable in distributional debates.

When it comes to foreign affairs, current debates over trade policy exhibit a number of these elements. While it is widely agreed that freer trade increases efficiency and the global economic output, it also has distributional consequences. For instance, more of the benefits of free trade may accrue to one country than to another. Similarly, cheaper imports help consumers but hurt industries that compete with those imports. Likewise, tariffs on steel help the US steel industry by raising the price of steel but hurt US automakers who use steel. By raising the cost of one of their major inputs, steel tariffs force US automakers to raise the cost of their cars, making them less attractive when compared to foreign-built cars.[17] Thus, trade policy creates winners and losers within the United States regardless of whether the country as a whole receives a net benefit or a net loss.

*Debates over Trade-offs*

The third type of policy debate is disagreement about how to make trade-offs between two agreed upon goods.[18] This sort of debate is closely related to distributional debates. The difference is mostly one of framing. Take the previously mentioned debate about how much money should go to the US Army versus the US Navy. From the perspective of individuals serving in either military branch, this is a distributional debate. Both are fighting over the same good: budget allocations. Yet, from the perspective of US citizens who are not in either military branch, it is a debate about trade-offs. Both land and naval forces are goods, but people may disagree about how much of each the United States should possess resulting from different beliefs about which sort of military force adds the most to US security. Further, in this example, there is also a trade-off between using money to fund the military and using that money for some other purpose entirely.

Perhaps the clearest example of a trade-off debate is the one between economic growth and environmentalism. Most people prefer a robust, vibrant economy to a weaker one and also prefer a cleaner environment to a dirtier one. Yet, there are heated disagreements about how much of one good should be sacrificed to achieve gains in the other. Certainly, societies should strive to be at the Pareto frontier—the point at which neither good can be improved without harming the other. If gains in one good can be achieved without losses to the other, it only makes sense to achieve those gains. Usually, however, choices and trade-offs must be made.[19]

Many such debates exist in the international realm. How much money should be spent or how many lives should be sacrificed to achieve a given policy goal? How do you make trade-offs between the lives of US servicemen and women and those of foreign noncombatants?[20] How much security does one give up to maintain liberty and vice versa? How hard should the United States push authoritarian allies to democratize or improve their human rights records if such moves undermine the stability or allegiance of those regimes? Reasonable people can easily disagree about the appropriate trade-offs. For instance, two people who are willing to sacrifice some economic gains for cleaner air may disagree about how much they would pay for say 10 percent cleaner air.

In other words, it is not a question if both goods are valued—they are—but what their relative values are given their current levels. Most people will, of course, prefer some of both goods but may well disagree on the preferred mix. They may also disagree about which good to obtain more of given different initial endowments of the goods. Wealthy countries, for instance, may be willing to sacrifice more economic growth to achieve environmental gains than would poorer countries. This is not because they absolutely value the environment more but rather, given their comparative abundance of wealth, losing some wealth hurts less than losing that same amount of wealth hurts people from a poorer country.

As with distributional debates, compromise should be possible. Each side is able to see the value in the other side's preferred good as they also value it. Much as with distributional debates, neither side expects, or in this case even wants, the outcome to totally favor their preferred good. This doesn't mean that fights about how much of one good to sacrifice to obtain the other won't be intense. They will. Yet at the end of the day, compromise on such issues is both possible and common.

*Debates about What Is a Positive Outcome*

The last type of debate is disagreement about what is a positive outcome. An example from domestic politics would be if same sex marriage should be allowed. Is allowing that positive or negative? People fundamentally disagree. Foreign policy provides other examples. Is the use of torture ever acceptable?[21] Does national honor matter? If it does—and repeated polling has shown most Americans believe that it does[22]—what contributes to or detracts from national honor? Did leaving South Vietnam to face the North alone harm national honor or did intervening in the first place? Such questions do not boil down to one of strategy, distribution, or trade-offs. They are not questions about what is a sufficiently positive outcome but instead rest on basic conceptions and value structures about what is positive and what is ill. This makes compromise difficult and perhaps impossible.

## DEBATES BETWEEN HAWKS AND DOVES

In the real world, the exact nature of the debate may be unclear. Actual policy problems may have elements of a variety of debates, including questions of strategy, the distribution of costs and benefits, trade-offs between goods, and even what is a positive outcome. For instance, debates about the Obama administration's "Pivot to Asia" could be framed as strategic debates (what is the best way to secure the United States and its allies) or a trade-off between goods (how many resources should be devoted to Asia versus to Europe and the Middle East).

In general, debates between hawks and doves have elements of several of the debates. Clearly, they have elements of debates over strategy. That is how this book is framed. It was argued above that these sorts of debates should be resolvable. Yet, this requires conditions to remain reasonably constant—something that is definitely not the case in foreign policy. Thus, prior to the 2003 invasion of Iraq, doves cited the successful containment of the Soviet Union during the Cold War and the lessons of Vietnam as reasons to not invade. Hawks, on the other hand, cited the Gulf War (1990–1991) as a reason to invade and questioned the applicability of the doves' Cold War analogy. These constantly shifting conditions make it harder to settle on an agreed policy. Still, if the debate was only of this nature, one would expect some convergence at least for long periods of time. Yes, conditions change, but the overall utility of force is unlikely to shift that much. Nor do the challenges that the United States faces shift constantly, though of course they do change over time. Yet, near the end of the Cold War, even after decades of reasonably stable conditions, debates between hawks and doves still raged about how to confront the Soviets. The lack of convergence, even after a long period of reasonably stable conditions, suggests that other types of debates may be at play.

Distributional debates play only a limited role when it comes to debates among Americans over the use of force. Certainly, in other international relations issues, such as trade policy, distributional debates are front and center. In the security realm, however, such concerns should be muted. There are certainly distributional debates between the United States and other countries in the security realm, but within the United States itself, the costs and benefits of security policies should fall fairly evenly across the population with the important exception of military personnel and their families. Clearly, the cost of the use of force falls far more heavily on military personnel and their families than on the rest of the country, but most doves are not personally connected to the military nor are military personnel necessarily doves.[23] Besides, there would be very few doves if they only came from military families as the US military burden currently falls on a very narrow segment of the population. In practice, hawks and doves are found in both groups. Outside of military personnel and their families, it is very unlikely that gains in security could be withheld from some Americans while being given to others. National security is largely a public good—one's benefit from it doesn't diminish another's benefit, and it is very hard to exclude people from benefiting from it while providing it to others. Actions that make Texas safer also make Wisconsin safer and vice versa. It's hard to imagine a modern scenario short of total or nuclear war where sacrificing one US state or region would save others.

It is possible to think of situations where sacrificing certain individuals might save others. For instance, a number of historians claim that in World War II the British learned from their codebreaking efforts that the Germans were going to bomb Coventry. Yet, Winston Churchill opted to not warn the citizens of Coventry so as to keep the Germans from knowing their code was broken. The idea being that keeping secret that the code was broken would allow the British to win the war more swiftly and ultimately save more British lives than it cost. While there are serious debates among historians about whether the British actually knew Coventry was the target of the coming bombing run and if Churchill really did deliberately sacrifice Coventry to protect British codebreaking efforts,[24] the example serves as a useful illustration about when distributional debates would matter. Importantly, such decisions would necessarily happen quickly and without public debate. Thus, they don't have much bearing on the current discussion. This is not to say that hawks and doves don't debate costs and benefits of actions. They do, but in the mainstream, these debates rarely focus on who benefits or pays but whether the country as a whole benefits or not. Those are strategic debates or debates over trade-offs, not distributional debates.

Debates between hawks and doves, however, do involve questions of trade-offs between goods. How many lives and how much money should be sacrificed to protect an ally or remove a repugnant regime? No one would argue that lives and money are not valuable, and most agree that protecting allies and the removal of brutal dictatorships is positive holding all else equal. But clearly, Americans disagree about the relative values of these goods and how they would trade them off. Still, as suggested above, compromises about these sorts of trade-offs should be able to be struck. Yet, this is rarely done—at least not explicitly. This may be because people are loath to consciously put a value on a life, yet of course all military actions do this. To wage war is to assume that the policy gains are worth the lives lost. There may be a reluctance to admit that soldiers, sailors, and airmen were sacrificed for limited objectives if those objectives were limited for reasons of domestic political compromise rather than for reasons of international strategy.[25] Thus, compromises about trade-offs between goods, while eminently possible, are often done implicitly rather than explicitly. In practice, when such debates do happen explicitly and publically, they become debates about which good is favored in the absolute: lives and money or security. This framing puts doves at a significant disadvantage as many people value security highly and in an immediate, visceral way and are willing to bear significant costs to obtain it. Further, seeking security may feel more immediate and concrete (even if its actual attainment is not) when compared to anticipated but uncertain future costs.

Last, debates about what is a positive outcome may matter. Some in Congress opposed the Obama administration's nuclear deal with Iran out of a concern that it would not work (a debate about strategy). Others were concerned with halting the spread of Iranian influence in the Middle East and thus believed that concessions related solely to the nuclear program were insufficient (a debate about trade-offs between reducing Iran's regional influence versus curtailing Iran's nuclear program). Yet another group, however, opposed the deal out of a sense that any agreement with the regime in Tehran was unacceptable.[26] In other words, for this last group, a deal, any deal, with the Iranian regime was inherently bad. It wasn't just that the deal on the table was insufficiently favorable from a US perspective or failed to strike the right bargain between various goods, but rather it was inherently wrong to strike *any* deal with the Islamic Republic of Iran. One can see a similar dynamic at work in regards to the Cuban embargo. Few argue that the embargo is likely to cause the Cuban regime to collapse. Yet, many still favor retaining the embargo because they believe it is better to punish the Cuban regime rather than shift to a policy that would benefit both the American and Cuban economies.[27] These sorts of fundamental disagreements are not resolvable. While additional Iranian concessions would have brought many opponents of the Iranian deal on board, others would never have accepted a deal regardless of its contents. Only the collapse of the Iranian regime or unremitting hostility toward it would have been acceptable. Thus, once debates take on this frame, it is exceedingly difficult to change the minds of opponents.

Two conclusions can be drawn from the above discussion. First, the frame debates between doves and hawks takes in turn influences who wins those debates. Debates over what is a positive outcome lead to deadlock. Neither hawks nor doves are likely to budge on arguments about honor or morality. Thus, framing debates in those terms is unlikely to win converts. Similarly, debates about trade-offs go badly for doves. Arguments pointing out the high cost of the use of force are unconvincing if the public finds the underlying justification for the use of force compelling. Arguments that war is too expensive in terms of money and lives fall on deaf ears if hawks have already successfully argued that the threat is real and force is the best way to remove it.[28] Hawks and many fence-sitters are willing to pay large costs in return for obtaining security objectives. In other words, if Americans are willing to make this trade-off between two goods, pointing out the trade-off does little to change anyone's mind. This is especially true during crises where security threats are immediate, but costs won't be paid until the future. Instead, they must be convinced that force would not obtain those security objectives. As will be shown below, historically, doves have fallen into this trap of emphasizing costs and framing debates as trade-offs. True, after a war is launched and mounting costs become tangible, doves fare better in such debates, but it is too late at that point. It is far easier to get into a military quagmire than it is to get out.

Given that public distributional debates are rare when it comes to the use of force, that frame is usually unavailable. This means doves' best chance for winning others over to their point of view is to frame debates in terms of strategy. Doves should emphasize that force fails, not that it is wrong or costly. Doing so doesn't require doves to abandon their views on the costs or morality of the use of force. Nor does it mean that morality or costs should never be raised—there is no need to concede these points. While pointing out high costs is reasonable, doves should not make it the central plank of their argument. Rather, when trying to convince non-doves, arguments that focus on strategy and show that force won't achieve American aims are the ones that are most likely to be effective. As will be shown below, in the past, doves have often neglected strategic arguments.

The second conclusion is that debates over US foreign policy are likely to continue. There are enough changes in the international environment to allow strategic debates to continue. Further, debates over the distribution of goods, trade-offs between goods, and what is a positive outcome do not lead to an inevitable resolution. Likewise, the heterogeneous and ever-changing nature of American society—in terms of interests, ideologies, ethnicities, religions, and circumstances—means US foreign policy will always be contested.[29] This is neither surprising nor discouraging. As stated above, US foreign policy has always been debated, going back to debates between Hamilton and Jefferson during Washington's administration. Such debates are part and parcel of a healthy, robust democratic society.[30] In fact, given doves' beliefs that their ideas are superior, ongoing debate should in theory be encouraging to doves.

Much classical liberal theory holds that open and free debates should result in better policies. Building off of John Stuart Mill, theorists argue that free competition between beliefs and policies in "the marketplace of ideas" ought to result in the better policies winning out.[31] Thus, doves should welcome such debate. Yet, in practice, democracies do in fact adopt foolish policies even given robust debate. Further, factually erroneous beliefs are held by both elites and the mass public in open societies. In other words, the marketplace of ideas can fail and even fail badly.[32]

This can happen for several reasons. One, voices do not enter into the marketplace of ideas with equal power. Elites—especially the President of the United States—have far more power to shape public debate than do ordinary citizens or those in the political minority.[33] Media reporting often reflects these power dynamics and thus cannot be counted on to make sure all views get a fair hearing.[34] This means who advocates a position, not just the quality of that position, matters.[35]

Also, open and free debate does not imply quality debate. The marketplace of ideas, unlike courts of law or scientific journals, has no clear standards of evidence by which to judge ideas.[36] Given how uninformed much of the American public is on foreign policy, the public may lack the necessary knowledge with which to judge policies. The result can be foreign policy debates that are dominated by clever quips, weak evidence, and loose analogies.[37]

Last, Mill himself was not nearly as optimistic about the marketplace of ideas as some later writers make him out to be.[38] While Mill argued that open debate should be an ally of truth, he clearly stated that truth does not always win out.[39] Rather, Mill argued that silencing dissent hides true opinions and also prevents the sharpening of good ideas by having them challenged.[40] In other words, we cannot possibly arrive at truth without open contestation. Thus, preventing contestation harms society.[41] This means open debate provides an *opportunity* for better ideas to prevail but in no way guarantees that outcome.[42]

Mill put forward several reasons why better ideas might lose even in the absence of active government repression. First, social pressures, even in an open society, can keep people from speaking their mind. More broadly, minority opinions may not get a fair hearing even if they are voiced.[43]

Because of this, Mill argued for the active support and encouragement of minority opinions[44]—something that of course rarely happens even in open societies. Second, partisanship can prevent the emergence of truth even in free discussion. As Mill put it,

> [T]he tendency of all opinions to become sectarian is not cured by the freest discussion, but is often heightened and exacerbated thereby; the truth which ought to have been, but was not, seen, being rejected all the more violently because proclaimed by persons regarded as opponents.[45]

Further, Mill argues how ideas are presented, not just the substance of those ideas, matters.

> [F]acts and arguments, to produce any effect on the mind, must be brought before it. Very few facts are able to tell their own story without comments to bring out their meaning.[46]

In short, doves cannot simply trust that their ideas will win out, especially in the near term. Not everyone is open to persuasion. Also, who advances those positions, how much attention they get, and how they are argued all play a large role in whether doves can persuade others of the merits of a more peaceful foreign policy. As will be seen, historically, doves have done a poor job in confronting these realities and in framing their arguments.

WHY DOVES LOSE

This means that doves must be prepared to debate and debate well. They must realize that the debate will never be permanently won nor permanently lost. Rather, it will be necessary to engage and win the same debates over and over again, albeit in different circumstances and with different specifics. Unfortunately, dovish arguments have often failed to carry the day in these debates. For instance, 57 percent of Americans supported President Trump's cruise missile strikes in Syria.[47] Most clearly, doves utterly failed in the run up to the 2003 Iraq War. Public support for invading Iraq in 2003 consistently ran above 55 percent in the months leading up to the war and jumped to 76 percent in the war's first days.[48] This failure was not due to a lack of trying. Doves engaged in widespread efforts to oppose the war. International relations scholars took out a full page ad in the *New York Times* prior to the 2003 US invasion of Iraq warning quite correctly that it was folly.[49] Of course, that effort failed. A small group of professors carries little weight in national debates, and the letter was not deemed newsworthy by the media, meaning the scholars' arguments received little attention.[50] The same message, however, also went unheeded when it was delivered by more notable persons such as former US National Security Advisor Brent Scowcroft.[51] Likewise, large-scale, anti-war protests did little to slow the march to war.[52] Why have doves failed to win political debates about war and peace?

In part, this failure is a result of how difficult it is to change individuals' minds about any political preference.[53] Research has shown that even attempts at correcting factual errors are often ineffective and fail to change most people's minds.[54] Attempts to persuade individuals to change aspects of their political beliefs can even result in backlashes where the individuals cling all the more tightly to their original views and deepen their hostility toward opposing ones.[55] This is an especially likely outcome if opponents are told they hold mistaken views because of psychological biases.[56]

Studies, however, have found that correcting misperceptions and changing policy views is possible.[57] Success requires frequent repetition of the corrective message, and the message must come from a variety of sources. Information coming from elites that share an individual's ideological commitments is especially important for two reasons. One, individuals are more likely to accept information from sources they believe share their goals. Two, since many Americans are uninformed on foreign policy, they are quite likely to base their foreign policy preferences on cues from trusted political elites.[58] When arguments and information are presented by a variety of sources, especially trusted ones, many individuals do in fact change their views.[59] Only those most ideologically committed to their prior position remain impervious to the new information, and the aforementioned backlash is also limited to these intensely committed partisans.[60] In other words, doves can persuade many Americans but are unlikely to be able to change the minds of die-hard hawks. That is okay. Unlike a public health campaign where the ultimate goal is to have 100 percent participation, to change foreign policy in a democracy it is only necessary to secure a stable majority. Thus, not everyone needs to be won over for doves to succeed. Nevertheless, it is clear that political persuasion is quite difficult. This makes doves' past failures both unsurprising and unexceptional. Political persuasion is unlikely to succeed unless it is done in a wise and strategic manner.

Unfortunately, doves have often gone about this task of persuasion in suboptimal ways. As suggested above, doves have focused on the costs of the active use of force, rather than on its effectiveness at achieving national aims. This rhetorical strategy has repeatedly proven unsuccessful for doves as it frames debates in terms of trade-offs between goods rather than debates about strategy. The same is true of arguments that focus on international legalities or Congressional procedures for declaring war.[61] Likewise, arguments that focus solely on morality and ignore US interests are unpersuasive.[62] Americans want to decide serious questions of war and peace on the merits of those actions, not on if all the i's have been dotted and t's crossed. This isn't to say that costs, international law, and Congressional procedure are not important—they are—but rather that arguments based on those principles have repeatedly failed to avert war in US history.

Doves have also failed to make their arguments in ways consistent with several core American values. This results in doves' arguments being rejected. Many Americans have deeply held beliefs and values that result in them favoring the use of force, especially once a crisis occurs.[63] One of these values is honor.[64] National honor requires that the country should respond promptly when wronged.[65] While honor does not necessarily demand that response be military in nature, it is easy enough to see how people would believe such a response would be natural or proper—especially if those that oppose force do not show how peaceful responses are also consistent with honor. While a belief in the importance of national honor is hardly unique to the United States—many countries have borne significant costs to uphold their honor[66]—examples from US history are easy to come by. President Wilson cited honor to justify his policy toward Germany during World War I.[67] So did President Kennedy in defending his strategy during the Cuban Missile Crisis.[68] Similarly, public opinion polls in 1969 found that Americans who favored staying in Vietnam cited "national prestige" as a major reason to do so.[69] Likewise, National Security Advisor Henry Kissinger claimed the requirements of honor kept the United States trapped in Vietnam.[70] These are not isolated incidences but part of a repeated pattern of US leaders and the American public citing honor as a reason for using force.[71]

Glory, too, is an important American value that leads individuals to favor using force. Glory is the belief that competition is productive and that being number one is important. As the nineteenth-century US statesman Henry Clay put it, "Of all human powers operating on the affairs of mankind, none is greater than that of competition."[72] Cross-national studies have found that Americans are far more focused on competition than are people from most other countries.[73] Americans' love of sports—especially the focus on winning championships—reflects this belief that competition is important. Likewise, Americans frequently discuss economics in terms of competition, winners, and losers. This emphasis on winning translates over into the international arena. Americans believe that international prestige is important.[74] They want the United States to be seen as the best country in the world and as an international leader. While striving for success certainly has virtues, a desire to win can also make cooperative outcomes more difficult as the focus becomes which side gains more, not just if the United States does well.[75] Much as with honor, though a pursuit of glory does not mandate the use of force, it can push Americans in that direction.

Such collective beliefs and values are visceral and emotional rather than intellectual in nature. This makes them exceptionally resistant to change. They can even become unquestioned.[76] Information that contradicts such deeply held values is rejected or ignored. This doesn't mean it is impossible to change such views, just that doing so is exceptionally difficult.[77] Only exceptionally persistent or powerful inputs can get individuals to question and ultimately change such deeply held beliefs. Even people who argue that efforts to change these beliefs are worthwhile suggest that any change would be quite gradual. For instance, one such scholar, Christopher Fettweis, points to younger generations of Americans being less hawkish than their forbearers as a source of optimism.[78] In other words, he is essentially conceding that older Americans are unlikely to change their views. Thus, dovish efforts that focus solely or mainly on changing deeply held beliefs are at a minimum conceding decades worth of foreign policy debates to their adversaries. Doves should strive for more immediate results. Yet, dovish arguments that either ignore or are contrary to these underlying values will be rejected.

Doves, however, have failed to account for these values when presenting their arguments. As suggested by Mill above, how policies are sold to the public matters as much as what the policies are. Yet, doves often advance their arguments in ways that are unlikely to persuade hawks and instead are likely to alienate many Americans. Doves must make their arguments within the confines of American nationalism and values, including those of honor and glory.[79] Arguments that "blame America" by accusing the government of being a bunch of warmongers, of having created the problem in the first place through unwise policies, or of acting immorally are bound to fail. Such arguments are seen as unpatriotic and giving aid and comfort to the enemy, especially during crises or in wartime.[80] Likewise, arguments that impugn the overall US political structure or blame the military-industrial complex are more likely to turn off Americans than elicit their support.[81]

To be clear, aligning dovish rhetoric with these values is necessary but insufficient to persuade Americans to adopt dovish policies. While better salesmanship is vital, more than that is needed. Dovish policies must also be consistent with Americans' foreign policy preferences. Even if the public is convinced about the limits of force, it must also be persuaded that a more peaceful foreign policy advances US interests and values. Doves must show how their policies preserve American leadership. Dovish policies must be vigorous and exhibit strength rather than weakness. In other words, the content of dovish policies matter, and those seen as inconsistent with American ideals and interest will be rejected even if convincing arguments are made about why force fails. As will be shown in chapter 2, this is why doves should commit to engagement with the world, the advancement of American values, and US leadership of the West. The case for such an assertive, yet dovish, foreign policy will be made in the next chapter.

Doves also put themselves in an unfavorable position by waiting until the danger of war looms to make their arguments.[82] Research both in the United States and abroad has shown that the popularity of hawkish policies rises when hostile countries make threats and often leads to doves losing office.[83] Thus, the atmosphere of a crisis disposes people to favor hawkish arguments. Research has shown that psychological biases that push people to favor military action (see chapter 3) become stronger as the possibility of war draws closer.[84] Also, a president who favors military action can speak directly to the American people at times of crisis, putting doves at a serious rhetorical disadvantage. Worse, a hawkish president could create a *fait accompli* by deploying troops or authorizing military strikes.[85] Once fighting has begun, even strong Congressional opponents of the conflict are unlikely to take actions such as cutting off funding for the troops that would force the president to end the conflict.[86] Yet, doves often wait until crises occur to advance their arguments.

Likewise, prior to the outbreak of war, media coverage largely reflects elite opinion. Only after the fighting starts does media coverage become more independent and critical. Thus, if there is not significant elite opposition to the use of force, dovish arguments won't be reflected in the media's coverage.[87] Given the tendency of members of the president's party to rally around the White House's policy and of the minority party being reluctant to challenge a popular president over the use of force prior to a debacle, it's not uncommon for there to be little elite opposition to the use of force prior to the outbreak of war. These features of American public discourse mean dovish arguments don't get a full hearing until after a conflict has begun. This limits the effectiveness of dovish arguments as it is far harder to get out of a quagmire than to avoid getting sucked in.

Last, doves are often divided amongst themselves making it difficult to advance a consistent argument against the use of force.[88] Internationalist doves may rankle at the arguments advanced by isolationist doves. Doves focused on moral arguments may be left cold by arguments based on national self-interest. These divisions are especially deadly when they are partisan in nature. Dovish Republicans may have a hard time working with dovish Democrats and vice versa. Unless elites across the political spectrum advocate for dovish policies, calls for a more peaceful foreign policy are easily dismissed by hawks as nothing more than partisan politics even when the arguments are made in a nonpartisan manner. Given doves are rarely an overwhelming majority, such internal divisions are lethal to doves' ability to carry the day.

## THE LIMITS OF DEFEAT

Thus, doves face an uphill battle, but historically, they have made that hill steeper than it needs to be. Internal divisions, waiting until crises occur, and advancing arguments that are poorly framed or inconsistent with American values have all made it much harder for doves to win policy debates. Happily, these are correctable errors. None of them are inherent to human nature or the American political system. Doves can craft better arguments and deliver them at more opportune times. They can also overcome internal divisions and form pragmatic alliances with others that share their views on the use of force even if they differ on other political questions. Last, given that these debates are eternal, past defeats do not condemn doves to future failures. The battle can always be rejoined.

Provided doves learn from their past mistakes and advance their best arguments in an optimal manner, there is every reason to believe doves can win future debates. While examples of how doves can do this will be raised in the book's conclusion, the first step toward crafting better dovish arguments is outlining what doves hope to achieve in foreign policy. This is necessary so that doves can argue on the basis of strategy, rather than on the basis of trade-offs between goods or what counts as a positive outcome. It is also necessary to place dovish policies within a grand strategy that is consistent with American values. This allows arguments for peace to be in alignment with, rather than in opposition to, values such as honor and glory that so often have been exploited by hawks to their advantage. With this in mind, the next chapter outlines the fundamental realities any US foreign policy must contend with and provides a template for a dovish foreign policy to follow.

# CHAPTER 2

## Defending the International Order

Of course it is far easier to diagnose what is wrong or what will not work than to forge and implement a policy that is both right and feasible.

RICHARD BETTS[1]

What goals should Americans set for their country's foreign policy? While many dovish foreign policies are possible, outlining a specific set of goals is necessary before discussing why the frequent use of force fails or how nonmilitary tools can succeed. This is because without a set of goals, it is impossible to know what success or failure would entail. Of course, not all doves will agree with these goals. This is inevitable, but it is unnecessary for doves to completely agree on US foreign policy goals to remain united against the frequent, active use of force.

In arguing for a set of overarching US foreign policy goals, I do not attempt to provide specific solutions to current foreign policy challenges such as Syria or North Korea. Such a laundry list of problems and solutions would quickly become dated and irrelevant. New problems, opportunities, and challenges will arise. Foreign policy is always a work in progress with no end point. This means that thinking about long-term goals is vital for day-to-day foreign policy. If short-term solutions are not placed within an overarching framework or strategy, foreign policy suffers. It can drift aimlessly as appears to currently be happening in the Trump administration.[2] It can also lead to playing Whac-A-Mole, à la President Clinton during his first term, where the government tries to address every problem as it arises with no particular sense of which ones are most important or how they fit into a long-term strategy.[3] Stephen Hadley, former National Security Advisor in the Bush administration, understood this problem well, stating,

> When you have a series of crises and . . . all you end up doing is crisis manage-
> ment . . . then all you're going to get is more crises because you're not going to
> be shaping events and the future direction of our interests.[4]

Foreign policies must draw distinctions about what is vital, important, less
important, and trivial.[5] Such distinctions outside of national survival are
neither objective nor self-evident,[6] hence the need for an overarching framework to serve as a source for determining and prioritizing those interests.

Setting priorities also helps avoid wasting resources on unimportant
objectives or blundering into unnecessary wars.[7] By hewing closely to the
main goals of US foreign policy, the United States can resist the temptation
of trying to fix every problem in the world. While the United States' significant power gives it a great deal of influence over events, it cannot control
them. Others always have a say, and US power, vast as it is, is grossly insufficient to dominate the world.[8]

Foreign policy also involves trade-offs in which improvements in one
area can lead to setbacks in another. For instance, the United States would
like good relations with both India and Pakistan, and yet, due to their rivalry,
improving relations with one often hurts relations with the other. Indeed,
foreign policy is often a choice between poor and worse options. The key is
to limit costs and advance core interests at the expense of less important
goals. This is frustrating and even dissatisfying, but much as in a game of
cards, it is impossible to win every trick or even every hand. The idea is to
play the cards you are dealt as best as you can so as to achieve what is most
important. It is often necessary to accept small defeats in order to achieve the
main objective and conserve resources for future challenges. So how can
proper American foreign policy goals be determined?

## AMERICAN POWER, POSITION, AND PREFERENCES

In determining and prioritizing its foreign policy goals, the United States
must take into account several underlying realities about itself and its place
in the international system. The first of these realities is that the United
States is the most powerful nation in the world. It has the largest economy,
the most powerful military, and the globe's third largest population.[9] Even
as China continues to gain power through economic growth, the United
States will remain one of the preeminent global powers. This immense

strength means that the United States cannot remain aloof from international politics.[10] This has been true since the early twentieth century.[11] President Teddy Roosevelt realized this, declaring,

> In foreign affairs we must make up our minds that, whether we wish it or not,
> we are a great people and must play a great part in the world. It is not open to
> us to choose whether we will play that great part or not. We have to play it. All
> we can decide is whether we shall play it well or ill.[12]

This is even truer today. The existing international order reflects, in large
part, US preferences, and its continued existence is very much dependent
upon the exercise of US power.[13] Retreating into isolationism or even significant retrenchment would seriously disrupt the global order by creating
power vacuums that would in turn spark regional arms races and conflicts.[14]
Indeed, Sigmar Gabriel, the former German foreign minister, is already
warning that the Trump administration's reduced attention to Europe is creating an opening for the Russians and Chinese to fill the void.[15] The dangers
of American isolationism can be seen from past US attempts at retreating
from the world. Acting unilaterally worsened the Great Depression through
the Hawley-Smoot Tariff, and refusing to participate in the Versailles settlement that ended World War I created a power vacuum that contributed to
the rise of Nazi Germany.[16] Military and economic realities today make a
withdrawal from the world just as foolish as it was in the 1930s.

The need for engagement is perhaps clearest in the security realm. Modern military power projection—the ability to quickly deploy military forces
across the globe—has made isolationism an untenable position since the
start of the twentieth century.[17] The Japanese attack on Pearl Harbor in 1941
showed American isolationists that distance alone could no longer protect
the United States.[18] Senator Arthur Vandenberg of Michigan, up until then
one of the leading isolationists in Congress, became convinced of the need
for an internationalist foreign policy as a result of that attack. He realized the
United States could not again withdraw from the world and that US security
was linked to the security of other likeminded countries. Near the end of
World War II, he said, "I have always been frankly one of those who has
believed in our own self-reliance . . . But I do not believe any nation hereafter
can immunize itself by its own exclusive action."[19] After the war, Vandenberg
became a champion of the United Nations, NATO, and the Marshall Plan to
rebuild Europe. He credited this change of beliefs directly to Pearl Harbor

saying, "In my own mind, my convictions regarding international cooperation and collective security for peace took firm hold on the afternoon of the
Pearl Harbor attack."[20]

Likewise, the United States has economic ties and connections around
the globe that cannot be easily severed without harming the US economy.
These economic ties mean that political connections to and complications
with other countries are necessary and unavoidable. American shipping and
trade inevitably drew the United States into political difficulties with Europe
during the Napoleonic Wars and World War I. Similarly, in the nineteenth
century, US trade in the Mediterranean resulted in conflict with the Barbary
pirates.[21] At the beginning of the twentieth century, trade with China
embroiled the United States in diplomatic disputes with Japan and the European powers through the Open Door Policy.[22] Attempts to avoid these disputes by halting US commerce, such as President Jefferson's embargo on
trade with Europe (1807–1809), were deeply unpopular political and economic disasters.[23] The United States is tied to the rest of the world whether
Americans desire it or not.

Even critics of American foreign policy excesses acknowledge the need to
play an important part. George Kennan, a preeminent American diplomat
and architect of the US strategy of containment during the Cold War, during
a 1984 speech in which he was highly critical of US overreach and involvement in the developing world during the Cold War stated,

> This is not a plea for a total isolation, such as our grandfathers and great-
> grandfathers cultivated. It is only a request, if I may put it that way, for a
> greater humility in our national outlook, for a more realistic recognition of
> our limitations as a body politic, and for a greater restraint than we have
> shown in recent decades in involving ourselves in complex situations far
> from our shores. And it is a plea that we bear in mind that in the interactions
> of people, just as in the interaction of individuals, the power of example is far
> greater than the power of precept, and that the example offered to the world
> at this moment by the United States of America is far from being what it could
> and ought to be.[24]

Indeed, at the beginning of the Cold War, Kennan had feared the United
States would repeat its mistake of the interwar period and withdraw from
Europe and again retreat into isolationism. He rightly warned that such a
move would have let the Soviets dominate Europe, thereby endangering US

security.[25] Similarly, modern critics of the overuse of American force, such as political scientist Donald Snow, recognize that it is impossible to be deeply involved in the global economy and isolationist politically. He quite rightly points out that this was the major US mistake of the interwar period.[26]

Remarkably, the eventual greater American involvement in the international system was seen early on in the republic's history. President Washington, in his Farewell Address, a pronouncement often seen as the foundation of American isolationist sentiment, anticipated an internationalist US foreign policy. He said,

> If we remain one people, under an efficient government, the period is not far off, when we may defy material injury from external annoyance; when we may take such an attitude as will cause the neutrality, we may at any time resolve upon, to be scrupulously respected; when belligerents nations, under the impossibility of making acquisitions upon us, will not lightly hazard the giving us provocation; *when we may choose peace or war, as our interest, guided by justice, shall counsel.*[27]

In other words, Washington's warning wasn't that the United States should be isolationist, but that America was too weak to benefit from becoming involved in European quarrels. Washington realized that the United States would eventually be strong enough to not have to remain above the fray. His warning about entangling alliances in the same address wasn't advice for all time. Rather, it was sound policy for the immediate circumstances of the late eighteenth and early nineteenth centuries when American weakness meant that any alliance would bind the United States to more powerful countries that could exploit America for their own benefit. President John Quincy Adams reminded Congress of the section of Washington's address quoted above in 1826 when he advocated forming a league with the independent states of Latin America. Adams felt that United States was already strong enough to form permanent alliances without running the risk of being at the mercy of its allies.[28] Certainly, the United States has possessed the power Washington envisioned as necessary for such an internationalist foreign policy for at least the last 125 years.

Even Washington, while avoiding binding alliances, did not pursue isolationism. He had an active foreign policy that resulted in the Jay Treaty with Britain and Pinckney's Treaty with Spain. (The two treaties required the British and Spanish to evacuate forts in the Great Lakes region and American

South respectively, normalized trade relations with Britain, and ensured the free navigation of the Mississippi River through Spanish-controlled New Orleans).[29] Washington also commenced the construction of the US Navy. His nineteenth-century successors also shunned isolationism by backing the Monroe Doctrine, which opposed the recolonization of Latin America, and by regularly deploying the navy to the Mediterranean and Far East. Nor were Washington and Adams alone in supporting an active US foreign policy. Writing in *The Federalist* during the debates over the ratification of the US Constitution, Alexander Hamilton, John Jay, and James Madison all anticipated and urged an active US foreign policy.[30]

Thus, American involvement in the world is unavoidable and also necessary for US safety and interests. This has been long recognized by American leaders and foreign policy experts. Isolationism, though seductive, fails. Any US foreign policy must accept this reality in order to be successful.

The second reality is the United States is blessed with a highly favorable strategic position. North America is a very safe place, as is the Western Hemisphere more generally.[31] As of late 2019, with the 2016 peace agreement in Colombia, there are no wars, civil or interstate, anywhere in the hemisphere. While that deal could unravel or new civil wars could emerge in places like Venezuela or Haiti, such conflicts would pose little danger to the United States.[32] When wars break out in the world, whether or not the United States ultimately becomes involved, they usually happen far from home. Further, there are no countries in the hemisphere that can rival the United States in power. The closest in population is Brazil, a geographically distant, less wealthy, and friendly power. For immediate neighbors, the United States has two oceans, Mexico, and Canada.[33] The United States is on generally good terms with Mexico, and Canada is America's closest ally, recent trade disputes notwithstanding. The economies of all three countries are tightly integrated, and international cooperation between all three is routine. The United States has no serious territorial disputes with either country, and neither Canada nor Mexico can rival the United States in economic or military might.[34] This means the United States is able to avoid many of the dangers of war-prone regions such as armed rebel groups crossing its borders. It also doesn't have to deal with arms races between its immediate neighbors or provocative military exercises in close proximity to its borders.

On top of the lack of immediate security threats, the United States has an abundance of arable farmland; vast water resources; and a large and diverse mix of minerals, metals, oil, and natural gas resources.[35] Much of America's climate is relatively mild, and the United States possesses many good harbors. These highly favorable circumstances directly contributed to making the United States a world power.[36] They also reduce American vulnerabilities to being cut off from international trade. While, as argued above, this doesn't mean that the United States can safely retreat into isolationism—not only would it create a dangerous power vacuum, the United States would also have to sacrifice many valuable, international economic ties—it does mean the United States is far more economically secure than the average country is.

Added to these highly advantageous natural features, the United States' security is greatly strengthened by its alliance network.[37] The United States is allied with Canada and most of Europe through NATO. Likewise, many countries in the Western Hemisphere are allied with the United States through the Rio Pact.[38] The United States is also allied with Japan, South Korea, the Philippines, Australia, and New Zealand[39] and has close, albeit often informal relations, with many other countries. No other country has or has ever had anything like this vast alliance network.[40]

Importantly, many of the world's strongest countries in both economic and military terms, such as Britain, France, Germany, and Japan, are US allies. This means many of the countries that on paper could pose threats to the United States are in fact allies who help protect it and advance many of its interests.[41] The idea that war could break out between the United States and its Western European allies or Japan in the foreseeable future is absurd.[42] Few, if any, great powers have ever enjoyed such close and peaceful relations with so many of their potential rivals. This alliance network greatly enhances American diplomatic and economic leverage and also significantly strengthens US security.[43] This advantage is further enhanced by the United States' dominant position in international organizations and its "far-reaching cultural and ideological influence."[44] This allows Washington to set much of the global agenda and many of the rules by which international interactions occur.

Thus, even before considering the powerful US military and America's large nuclear arsenal, the United States is unusually well-protected from military threats and dangers.[45] The US military, especially the combination of the US Navy and US Air Force, further insulates the United States from threats. The US military controls the international commons: sea lanes, air routes, and space—something any US grand strategy should strive to maintain.[46] This puts the United States in a unique position. In order for America's enemies to attack the United States, they first must go through the US military, which can confront them far from home. And given US naval superiority, no country can deploy military assets across the open ocean if the United States moves to prevent it. Only the United States has the ability to truly project military power across the globe.[47] The result of this is that since World War II, when Americans have gone to war, they have done so out of choice rather than necessity.[48] This is quite different from many other countries that face far less favorable security environments and are forced to counter immediate, local threats. This is why Americans focus so heavily on nuclear threats and international terrorism.[49] The United States is quite safe from conventional military threats.

The third reality is Americans insist on a moral component to US foreign policy.[50] A majority of Americans believe that the United States should help solve the world's problems, the United States should promote American values abroad, and US actions and institutions should reflect those values.[51] Likewise, polling found that 72 percent of Americans believe that moral principles should guide US foreign policy.[52] This belief that the United States can and should be a powerful force for good is reflected in President Lincoln's claim that the United States was the "last best hope of Earth" and former Secretary of State Madeline Albright's proclamation that the United States is the "indispensable nation."[53] Unsurprisingly, a wide range of American presidents, such as, but not limited to, Jefferson, Wilson, both Roosevelts, Truman, Kennedy, Reagan, both Bushes, Clinton, and Obama, have engaged in moral appeals to build support for their foreign policies.

The American experience shapes how Americans see the world and their place in it. While individual Americans of course do not all hold the same beliefs, it is possible to talk about collective American beliefs. Collective ideas are distinct from individual beliefs in that they are intersubjective.[54] This means they are shaped and created through the interactions and discussions individuals have with each other. They are as much beliefs about what convictions others in society have as about one's own, personal beliefs. These collective beliefs, in turn, shape policymakers' worldviews and act as a significant domestic constraint on the actions of those leaders.[55]

This American desire for a moral foreign policy has two major sources: faith and ideology. Americans are remarkably religious for citizens of a wealthy, developed country.[56] This religiosity has shaped American foreign policy since the founding of the republic and led Americans to think about foreign policy in moral terms.[57] The effect of ideology on foreign policy may be even greater than that of faith. Americans are more ideological than they themselves generally realize, in part because their most deeply held ideals are widely held across the American political spectrum. Since the beginning of the republic, Americans have held an uncritical attachment to the Lockean values of individual liberty; democracy; and open, rules-based economic markets.[58] Americans do not joke about the ideals of the Founding Fathers and believe in the superiority of their values, institutions, and traditions.[59] These ideals, rather than ethnicity, historically have defined the American community.[60] Of course, American actions and institutions often fall short of these ideals, but they remain real aspirations nevertheless. Unsurprisingly, Americans want US foreign policy to reflect these values.

Active involvement is needed to uphold these values. Retreating from the world like a cloistered monk may keep one's hands clean, but it also does nothing to improve the world. It simply is resignation. The United States must engage with the world in order to improve it and yet have sufficient moral fortitude to avoid the temptation to foist American views on others or resort to force out of frustration with the state of the world.

The relationship between these broad values and support for specific policies is not straightforward. What actions those values and morals imply is often hotly debated. Some have concluded from these values that America is exceptional—that the United States is different in character from the other countries in the world and uniquely suited to champion Lockean values.[61] Certainly, these values do not necessarily imply either a dovish or hawkish foreign policy. Many Americans have seen wars as moral crusades, but others have engaged in contentious objection to military service while citing similar values.[62] Likewise, while Americans have generally supported democracy and self-determination abroad, they have also, without a sense of irony, become deeply involved in other countries' internal affairs to promote those same values.[63] Finally, voters may support or oppose policies based on partisanship rather than the content of the policy itself. Even so, policies that embody Lockean values should be more able to garner broad support than those that do not embody those values.

Many foreign policy theorists who argue for a more restrained US foreign policy miss this crucial role of faith and ideology in American foreign policy.[64] Leveraging these values is necessary to mobilize ordinary Americans to support US foreign policy efforts.[65] Americans often respond enthusiastically when presented with a clear, singular, moral challenge,[66] though this can also lead to overreaching. Arguments that the United States should retrench—i.e., pull back from the world—out of its own self-interest will fall flat if they do not show how the United States can still promote its values abroad. Such amoral approaches are unlikely to gain traction with the public and are easy targets for overly ambitious but value-laden foreign policies.[67] Advocates of retrenchment also miss that other countries have come to expect the United States to act in accordance with American values.[68]

These realities mean that the United States needs a foreign policy that is internationalist, yet limited, and that maintains popular support by reflecting American values and morals. Americans will not support a foreign policy that fails to reflect their values as well as their interests.[69] This combination of values and interests can best be advanced by upholding the US-led international political, legal, and economic orders established after World War II. These orders are based on the rule of law, the renunciation of the use of force to redraw international borders, support for democracy and human rights, and open, although preferably regulated, economic intercourse between countries.

Since 1945, the United States and its allies have worked to expand, deepen, and entrench this order. For most of that time, US foreign policy has been quite successful,[70] albeit with important exceptions and blunders. It won the Cold War, fostered international economic growth, and led to the proliferation of democracy.[71] The world has grown more peaceful as well.[72] There are both fewer interstate and civil wars than in past decades or centuries.[73] In other words, the order has materially benefited the United States and advanced American values. Abandoning this US-created international architecture would make addressing current global political and economic challenges more difficult.[74]

A policy aimed at upholding this order would recognize that the United States must play a significant role in world affairs given its political and economic power. It would also reflect in its broad outlines, if not always its specifics, the values of elites and everyday Americans across the political spectrum. For instance, polling has shown that a majority of Americans believe the US government is obligated to follow international law and that the United States should enter into a wide variety of new legal agreements including joining the International Criminal Court and the Comprehensive Test Ban Treaty, which would outlaw the testing of nuclear weapons.[75] Majorities also favor remaining in the Paris Climate Accord and support strengthening the United Nations.[76] Last, Americans have expressed that while they favor the United States playing a leading role in global affairs, they prefer the United States act multilaterally rather than unilaterally.[77]

Such an overarching policy would have four main pillars: maintaining existing US alliance structures (US-led security order), supporting and strengthening the international legal order, maintaining while reforming the global economic order, and recognizing the limits of US power so as to not overreach in an attempt to remake the world in America's image. By following these four pillars, the United States can help stabilize the world, increase peace and prosperity, and avoid frittering away its resources—both material and moral. Each of these pillars will be addressed in turn.

## MAINTAINING THE SECURITY ORDER

The first pillar of upholding the US-led international order is maintaining the existing American-led alliance structures.[78] These include NATO, a variety of bilateral alliances in the Pacific (e.g., with Japan, South Korea, Australia, New Zealand, and the Philippines), and the Rio Pact with much of Latin America. This can be done through deterrence, which is the threat of retaliation in response to an unwanted action by another country. As long as potential aggressors believe that the United States would respond to attacks on its allies with military force, such aggressors will be deterred and active force will be unnecessary. Of course, this also requires limiting the size of the US alliance network to countries Americans would truly fight and die for. (How and why deterrence works will be covered in detail in chapter 5.)

Limiting the use of force to deterring attacks on the United States itself and its allies is consistent with the notion that the United States should threaten the use of force only to secure the most vital of interests.[79] There is no reason to be overly alarmed about hostile, minor powers that are located in strategically unimportant regions because no matter how much they wish to harm the United States, there is little they can actually do.[80] Also, the reality is the United States is sufficiently secure that it has time to react to threats as they arise. It can act with forbearance and rely on deterrence rather than striking first.[81] Relying on deterrence would greatly reduce the odds that the United States would be sucked into the sort of counterinsurgency campaigns that have so frustrated American foreign policy in recent years.[82] This strategy is also consistent with an acknowledgement that force does, at times, work. The key is to strictly limit its use to protecting vital US interests.

Such a strategy would also help rein in military spending as it sets clear and limited goals. Defense expenditures would reflect what is necessary to deter attacks on the United States and its allies and control the commons. In other words, US military spending would be proportionate to the threats faced. Such spending would reflect what US enemies are capable of doing rather than their unrealistic dreams and desires. Likewise, spending based on enemy capabilities would make more sense than arbitrarily benchmarking military spending to a certain percentage of GDP or to Cold War levels as threats do not expand in proportion to economic growth and the Soviet Union posed a threat far greater than America's enemies do today.[83]

Additionally, by backing allies, the United States can stabilize these regions.[84] The American presence reduces uncertainty and current political settlements in those regions are predicated on American power.[85] This benefits the United States because secure allies feel less of a need to engage in military buildups to defend themselves. For example, if Japan and South Korea were not under the US security umbrella, they would have to engage in significant military expansions that would threaten their neighbors, including China, North Korea, Russia, and potentially each other. This would destabilize Northeast Asia, prompt arms races including nuclear proliferation that would threaten the United States itself, and could even lead to regional armed conflicts.[86] A militarized, nuclear-armed Japan is not in the United States' interest. Nor is a fully remilitarized Germany. These countries have smaller militaries than one would expect for a great power. US leadership and security guarantees have allowed them to do without large militaries,[87] which in turn makes their neighbors feel safer. The stability provided by US security guarantees makes a forward policy of upholding the alliances superior to withdrawal or retrenchment. In other words, by limiting regional security competition abroad, the United States itself is more secure.[88]

Further, US security guarantees have allowed security communities—groups of countries for which the use of force between them is unthinkable—to develop, especially in Western Europe.[89] An example of a security community familiar to most Americans is the relationship between the United States and Canada. The idea that these two countries would go to war with each other is absurd—so absurd that it once was the premise of a Hollywood comedy.[90] Once security communities form, they are quite stable—they are more likely to endure than are their opposite number: international rivalries.[91] (Rivalries are relationships in which pairs of countries, such as India and Pakistan, repeatedly engage in military conflict as a result of their enmity and political disagreements). In other words, once countries establish deep trust in each other, that trust is likely to endure as it is more robust

AMERICAN DOVE

than even deep-seated hatreds. Thus, helping to create and maintain security communities is one of the best and most enduring ways to reduce the amount of war in the world.

These benefits are recognized by US allies who generally welcome the American presence in Europe and East Asia.[92] They understand that US security guarantees prevent unrestrained regional security competitions and stabilize once war-torn regions like Europe and Northeast Asia. Of course, the United States should not pick up the entire tab for defending its allies. Washington should encourage American allies, especially those in Europe, to take up a greater share of the collective defense burden.[93] This is, however, difficult to achieve. Credible US security guarantees—the very basis of these alliances—undermine the need for our European and Asian allies to defend themselves. US protection creates an incentive for these countries to free ride and have Washington pick up a disproportionately large share of the collective defense tab.

While it would be better if US allies paid their fair share, the cost is worth it to the United States. Preserving these alliances is very much in the United States' interest and is one of the core elements of its strength. They ensure that most of the rich and powerful countries in the world work with rather than against the United States. Also, by directly controlling the largest share of these alliances' military assets, the United States obtains more leverage in discussions of war and peace. When added to the increased stability in Europe and Asia, the net benefits outweigh the costs. US public opinion surveys reflect this conclusion. While Americans naturally want US allies to pick up their fair share of the security burden, Americans also indicate they want the United States to remain engaged with the world. Surveys show that Americans prefer acting in concert with allies and burden sharing over both isolationism and unilateral US action.[94]

Nor is there a significant danger of the United States being drawn into wars it does not want to fight by these allies. This danger, known as entrapment or entanglement, has long worried American isolationists. Yet, the historical record shows that entrapment as a result of alliances is quite rare for both countries in general and the United States in particular. This is because alliances can be carefully constructed to limit the situations for which the United States would be required to fight for its allies. This helps avoid problems posed by allies pursuing overly adventurous and reckless foreign policies. Indeed, carefully constructed alliances that narrowly specify US obligations and the scenarios that would invoke those obligations can help restrain

US allies from undertaking reckless gambles in the first place. In the past, the United States has been able to construct such treaties and avoid fighting wars that were contrary to US interests.[95] Yes, the United States would be obliged to defend its allies if they were directly attacked, but presumably such wars would be in the United States' interest as it would only form alliances with those countries it wants to defend. Also, as will be shown in chapter 5, these alliances likely would deter such attacks from occurring to begin with, further reducing the odds the United States would have to wage wars on behalf of its allies. Thus, the United States should strive to maintain the current international security architecture.

## UPHOLDING THE LEGAL ORDER

The United States should also work to maintain, deepen, and improve the international legal order. The international legal order is the set of rules about how countries are to behave both internationally and domestically. It sets limits on how countries interact with each other and with individuals. The legal order provides a framework for determining which actions are legitimate and for resolving disputes. It directly bears on human rights and also intersects with both the security and economic orders.

The United States and its allies created this order after World War II.[96] Though it largely developed in the West, the legal order has subsequently been influenced by and extended to the rest globe since the end of the Cold War. It is characterized by multilateral decision-making, cooperative security efforts, broad compliance with international laws and rules, and strategic forbearance on the part of the United States.[97] Governance of the system is widely, though not equally, shared with different countries performing different functions to stabilize the international security, legal, and economic orders.[98] This results in a high level of international interdependence, with countries benefiting from their political, economic, and social connections to each other. At its core, the US-led legal order is a group of countries acting in concert to advance liberal values.[99] Not liberal in the American partisan sense of the term that indicates someone left of center on the political spectrum, but in the international sense of the term. In this sense liberalism is "the tradition of liberty and democracy, and by extension, the open rules-based international and economic and political system."[100] In sum, liberalism reflects the Lockean values central to American political ideologies traditionally embodied in the platforms of both the Republican and Democratic parties. These shared values help preserve, legitimize, and stabilize the international order.[101] As a result of this order, the United States is not simply the most powerful country in the world but also serves as the central hub of a far-reaching international order characterized by liberal values.[102] This stems from the fact the order was constructed by the United States, and therefore, unsurprisingly serves US interests and embodies the shared values of the United States and its democratic allies.[103]

Even given the benefits that accrue to the United States, other countries accede to the order because they too gain from the services the United States provides, such as security, free navigation of the seas, and economic stability.[104] In many ways, such global governance is similar to governments providing public goods in a domestic context. These international services often go little noticed, as they are uncontroversial, but they are crucial to getting countries to support an order that broadly benefits the United States.[105]

Americans should not take the existing international order for granted. The three-quarters of a century that the order has endured is long enough for most people to assume its inevitability, as few people alive today were born prior to its existence. Thus, almost no one has experience with alternative orders. Yet, while the order has proved to be remarkably durable,[106] its existence is not inevitable for several reasons. First, it is quite dissimilar from the international orders that preceded it. It did not just pop into being but was deliberately forged by the United States and its allies. This was done both to win the Cold War and to create a durable, stable peace so as to avoid a replay of the world wars.[107]

Second, the order is faced with a number of challenges that have stressed and could ultimately undermine it. Rising powers such as China, India, and Brazil often advocate for changes to the order to reflect their increased power.[108] While not entirely hostile to the current order—these countries have benefited from the rules, which have encouraged international trade and investment and the lack of great power wars[109]—these countries do seek modifications to the order. They naturally want an order that better reflects their interests and gives them a greater say in the system's governance. They want their international status within the order to reflect their increased economic power. Many of the most important international institutions were created when these countries were weaker and the institutions' rules reflect international power distributions from a bygone era. While there are many shared preferences between the United States and these rising powers, there are also important divergences of interests and varying understandings of sovereignty, human rights, and even territorial claims. This requires making compromises and adjustments to manage these conflicts—such as granting rising powers a greater say and more status within international institutions—while maintaining the core features of the order.[110] This certainly is doable but requires careful, difficult diplomacy.

Also, many in the West have become disenchanted with the fruits of the order. Some of this stems from the inherent tensions and trade-offs between the values embodied in the order—such as sovereignty, self-determination, individual liberties, and stability.[111] Naturally, not everyone is pleased when choices are made that favor one value over another. Likewise, others have become dissatisfied with political outcomes within Western democracies.[112] Movements hostile to the existing international order can be found throughout the West.[113] Nationalism, too, is reinvigorated creating opposition to international institutions and supranational organizations like the European Union. These grievances have reduced support for investing resources to maintain the current global order and have led to the rise of leaders in the West who seek to undermine that order.[114] This has already resulted in skepticism about embracing newer aspects of this order. For instance, the United States has not joined and is not subject to the International Criminal Court (see chapter 4). If such skepticism further results in the United States or its allies refusing to play by their own rules, the international order would be undermined.[115]

When combined, these challenges indicate there is a crisis of authority in the international system. It must be addressed if the current international legal order is to endure. A new bargain within the old order is required. This should be possible as the general principles of openness, stability, and democracy that undergird the order are broadly, though not universally, accepted both in the developed and developing world.[116] Further, difficult trade-offs between competing values are not new. Humanity has struggled with such trade-off since antiquity.[117] Ultimately, though, the order must deliver on its promises to maintain elite and popular support.[118]

The United States should reembrace this order and exercise its power through its rules and institutions for several reasons.[119] Most importantly, the international legal order as currently structured lowers the level of threat faced by the United States and its allies. It does this by reducing the number of empires by promoting self-determination, reducing the incentives for aggression by emphasizing that territorial changes imposed by force are illegitimate, and by using international institutions and law to promote a rules-based order thereby giving the global system a semblance of governance.[120] It also creates an international environment that is more propitious for the emergence and survival of democracies, though of course it does not guarantee democratization as the internal characteristics of countries also play an important role in whether democratization occurs.[121] Additionally, by acting multilaterally through international institutions in accordance with international law, the United States is able to cloak, legitimize, and enhance its own power.[122] The exercise of power is cheaper when it is seen as legitimate and more likely to be complied with.[123] This means working within the constraints of this legal order. While frustrating at times, over the long run, this allows the United States to obtain its preferred outcomes with less effort.

To preserve this order, the United States must respect the rules—rules the United States helped write. Essentially, Washington must commit to following certain processes while advancing American interests. It must follow international law the vast majority of the time, consult with its friends and allies before acting, and act multilaterally when possible.[124] International law is shaped not only by treaties but by how countries, especially powerful ones, act.[125] In other words, American actions help determine what the rules of the international order are and the nature of that order. Such moderation and a willingness to work through established legal and institutional settings grants US actions legitimacy, which in turn reduces resistance to US policies.[126] It also makes US power less threatening to other countries, which again lessens opposition to US initiatives.[127]

Further, such a commitment to multilateralism and legal processes gives US allies a stake and a say in the order without giving them a veto. This encourages them to support US foreign policy efforts while still largely maintaining US freedom of action. This commitment to multilateralism can also save us from ourselves. If the US government cannot convince American allies to support a particular action nor get international institutions to work with the United States, US leaders should double check their thinking and make sure their intended course of action is indeed wise. This is similar to when friends and family members warn us that we are making a mistake. Certainly, we have a right to seek our own council and proceed as we wish, but more often than not we would be wise to heed the well-intentioned advice we are getting. Conversely, acting alone alienates allies and places the entire cost of action on the United States.[128] While the US government should always retain the right to use force unilaterally to uphold and defend US interests, that does not mean it is wise to regularly practice unilateralism—especially on issues of limited importance.

The United States should also allow rising powers a greater say in revising and implementing the rules of the legal order. An order with broad input and that is adaptable to the needs and beliefs of many countries is more legitimate and stable. Such accommodations increase the odds rising powers, such as China, will accept the existing order rather than seek to undermine it.

Last, the US government must work to advance and uphold human rights. Even some self-described isolationists argue that the United States should advance human rights abroad as long as the means remain limited.[129] This is not a call to impose an American or Western vision on the world as that is beyond the United States' abilities.[130] Obviously, not all countries have the same notions of human rights. Yet, many basic human rights, such as those enshrined in the United Nations' 1948 Universal Declaration of Human Rights and the 1993 Vienna Declaration, are widely shared and yet are still frequently violated.[131] Steps can be taken to pressure offending regimes to alter their behavior and to alleviate the plight of the aggrieved. This should be done primarily through modelling exemplary behavior and working multilaterally with other countries and through international institutions. The use of economic, diplomatic, and legal tools—all of which will be covered in chapter 4—can pressure offenders into modifying their behaviors. Indeed, research has shown that military force is generally a poor tool for improving human rights when compared to economic, legal, and diplomatic tools.[132] Much as with more narrow political objectives, force should only be used in very rare circumstances such as in the case of genocide. For example, using force in Rwanda in 1994 to halt the genocide there would have been both moral and wise. Such occasions are quite rare but do occasionally occur. Again, doves are not pacifists. Force is sometimes, though rarely, the correct policy.

In sum, by working to uphold the international legal order, the United States can advance its own interests. An order that promotes human rights, the rule of law, self-determination, and even democracy while dissuading the use of force is an order less likely to spawn empires or countries seeking territorial conquests. Such an order is safer for status quo countries like the United States and its allies. Likewise, by promoting the settlement of disputes through regularized legal channels, the order provides stability and predictability, which in turn undergird both peace and economic prosperity. In short, the legal order strengthens the aforementioned security order and also the international economic order, which is covered below.


## REFORMING THE ECONOMIC ORDER

The United States should also work to maintain and strengthen the global economic order that it and its allies have constructed over the course of the post-World War II period. This order has enabled goods and capital to move around the world, aiding both American and global economic growth. Much as with the global legal order, disenchantment with the global economic order is also on the rise. The Great Recession and growing economic inequality in developed countries have led many to question the benefits of international economic openness.[133] Likewise, as with the legal order, rising powers and developing countries want a greater say in the economic order's governance. While the order is far from perfect and its flaws must be addressed—unemployment, economic instability, and inequality have resulted from unfettered international economic exchanges[134]—it has largely benefited the United States and the world as a whole. Also, open, market-based, and rules-based economic orders, despite their faults, have provided more economic prosperity over the long run than have other economic orders. Greater openness is not needed, but maintaining the existing order is important. Obviously, this is a vast topic, which many books have taken as their main subject. It, therefore, cannot be addressed in any sort of comprehensive manner here, yet it is important to discuss briefly, as economic aims are an important part of any foreign policy.

The collapse of the international economic order would disrupt and destabilize countries' domestic economies including that of the United States. Countries are deeply connected to each other through trade, supply chains, and investments. While it is possible to imagine a less interdependent global economic system, the transition to such a system would be very costly. Investments have been made based on assumptions that interdependence will continue. Those investments would lose much of their value if trade barriers were erected. In turn, that would cause unemployment and job dislocations just as the movement from a less international system to a more international system did in the first place. And the short-term pain would not bring any long-term benefits because a less integrated international economic system would be less efficient overall, meaning the world would be somewhat poorer. Thus, the US government must work to maintain and reform the open, rules-based international economic order.

While the United States has had the greatest hand in its crafting and governance—US leadership is especially apparent in global economic institutions and in ensuring the free navigation of the seas[135]—the system is overwhelmingly multilateral.[136] The United States is not nearly powerful enough to dictate its preferred policies in the economic arena. This means other countries already have a significant say in what the international economic order looks like. It also means that many countries contribute to the order's governance and success. These countries' participation in the order's maintenance and the nature of the order itself have lowered US costs and helped stabilize the global economy. Likewise, its clear rules reduce the need for repeated renegotiation of the terms of economic exchange.[137] In other words, the order is a partnership, which has made US economic leadership more legitimate. This is necessary because while the United States is dominant in the military realm, power is far more diffuse in the economic realm.[138] This makes cooperation vital. It is impossible for countries to address global recessions or currency crises without significant international economic cooperation and coordination.[139] Further, the economic ties that the order has forged between countries have bound them closer together, which has in turn promoted peace between those countries.[140]

To maintain and improve this beneficial order, the United States must do two things. First, it must respond to the demands of rising powers such as China, India, and Brazil. Ideally, the United States would find ways to satisfy these countries within the existing order. They have benefited from international trade and investment and, therefore, have a stake in maintaining the order. By giving these countries more voting power and responsibilities within existing institutions such as the International Monetary Fund, World Bank, and World Trade Organization, it should be possible to keep and strengthen the existing open, rules-based, multilateral order and also to reduce US burdens. Doing so is better than the alternatives: the creation of a rival order by such countries or the unraveling of the international economic order.

Second, Washington must address the very real issues of inequality and destabilization that have crept into the order. Individuals harmed by trade must be compensated through social welfare systems. Historically, the United States has done a poor job at this. When this is not done, workers harmed by international trade quite naturally insist on protectionist measures and a more closed economy. Yet, protectionism raises the cost of goods for the poor and middle class, and in practice, tariffs are often structured so as to secure sweetheart deals for politically connected corporations.[141] Likewise, the order must regulate the flow of capital to avoid financial crises such as that those that hit Europe in the 2000s and East Asia in the late 1990s, both of which were caused in part by such flows.[142] While an order that allows capital to move internationally is largely beneficial, rapid influxes and exoduses of capital can destabilize economies and cause recessions. Real, but modest, controls on the flow of capital can significantly mitigate these dangers.[143] Much as with trade, if these reforms are not undertaken, countries destabilized by hot capital flows would quite naturally seek to undermine and attack the order.

The key is that any changes to the economic order must be done in a manner consistent with the existing rules and processes of that order. Unilateral actions by the United States would undermine others' confidence that the order is truly rules-based and not just a reflection of the interests of powerful countries. Such actions would also give other countries the green light to break the rules. Yes, the United States should strongly pursue modifications that would help the American economy in general and specifically those Americans who have been harmed by the current international economic order. It just must do so within the existing mechanisms for modifying the rules of international economic exchange. If this is done, it would both strengthen other countries' faith in US leadership and Americans' belief that an open, rules-based, economic order can provide prosperity.

To be sure, the Chinese are likely to demand an increasing say in the international economic system. Countries are already being drawn toward Beijing to maintain or gain access to China's growing economy. Yet, there is little reason to believe most countries would prefer Chinese economic leadership to American leadership, provided the United States recommits to playing within the existing rules of the system. The United States still has the world's largest economy in terms of nominal GDP, shares democracy with most of the world's largest economies, and, for much of the past seventy-five years, has shown itself to be a reliable economic partner. Indeed, the formation of the Comprehensive and Progressive Trans-Pacific Partnership by Pacific Rim countries—some of those most likely to benefit from connections to the Chinese economy—is an illustrative case. The United States was originally supposed to join the deal, while the Chinese were not invited.[144] This demonstrated that the Pacific Rim countries were eager to foster other economic connections, including ones with the United States, to avoid Chinese economic domination. Washington's withdrawal from the treaty, however, undermined this purpose and also put into question whether the United States was willing to commit to new, longer term economic cooperation. While the United States is still invited to join in the future, China is now also invited.[145] Thus, by withdrawing from economic arrangements, the United States cedes some of its leadership to others. Instead, by reinvesting in, while simultaneously reforming, the existing rules-based economic order, the United States could preserve its leadership and continue to prosper economically through international connections. It would be wise to do so.

## THE LIMITS OF AMERICAN POWER

Last, the United States must avoid overreaching. Overactive countries uselessly squander their resources and weaken themselves.[146] Unnecessary wars, like the 2003 invasion of Iraq, waste lives, squander money, and sap willpower. Overreach also scares other countries and pushes them to oppose the United States.[147] Overweening exercises of American power lead to fear, frustration, and resentment in other countries.[148] While the United States must stand against injustice, it cannot solve every problem. Perhaps the most famous American formulation of such a policy came from John Quincy Adams. In a Fourth of July oration during his tenure as Secretary of State, he said of the United States,

> Wherever the standard of freedom and independence has been or shall be unfurled, there will her heart, her benedictions and her prayers be. But she goes not abroad in search of monsters to destroy.[149]

This need for forbearance is particularly acute as truly global orders and an international society are emerging for the first time in history.[150] While regional orders and societies have existed in the past and countries have interacted globally within an international system for centuries,[151] the attempt to construct overarching sets of rules and standards of behavior for the entire international system is new. This makes agreement more difficult and increases the odds that American values will be at odds with the values of at least some other societies within this order. In other words, pushback against American values is to be expected. Thus, attempts to spread our values—while certainly important—should be done cautiously and without hubris. Further, US behavior can threaten international order by making too many demands without providing enough benefits to justify countries' acquiescence to American preferences.[152] US attempts to be a global humanitarian cop generate foreign resentment and also lack the deep domestic support necessary to sustain any resulting military missions. While there is broad support to do something, there is also a preference to keep costs limited.[153] This means diplomatic and economic efforts would be better received both at home and abroad than military ones.

In particular, the United States should be reluctant to become deeply involved in efforts to remake other countries' societies or regimes.[154] State-building is slow, irregular, and rarely imposed from the outside.[155] Violent conflicts associated with state-building are especially likely to turn into guerrilla wars and become intractable quagmires.[156] Outcomes in civil wars often depend more on political factors internal to that country, rather than on outside military factors.[157] Unsurprisingly, outside interventions into other countries' conflicts in the post-World War II era have failed more often than they have succeeded.[158] Further, outside intervention into another country's domestic politics is never impartial. It always harms or hurts one faction or another and thus sucks the intervener deep into the politics and conflicts of the country in question.[159] This is true even of attempts to end conflicts. As political scientist Richard Betts puts it, "making peace is to decide who rules."[160]

Finally, US military efforts should be restricted to key regions: North America, Europe, and East Asia—areas where the United States has important allies to protect. US interests outside of those regions are especially unlikely to justify the returns to force. US force has been particularly ineffective in the Middle East.[161] Crucially, no country in the Middle East can project substantial power outside of the region, meaning they cannot threaten the overarching global order. Nor is it only doves who recognize the wisdom of limiting the geographic scope of American uses of force. As then Secretary of Defense William Gates said in a speech to West Point cadets,

> In my opinion, any future defense secretary who advises the president to again send a big American land army into Asia or the Middle East or Africa should "have his head examined" as General MacArthur so delicately put it.[162]

Even threatening the use of force in such regions can be problematic as it can lead to having one's bluff called. President Obama's 2012 "red line" on Syrian chemical weapon use is a good example. He ultimately was not willing to go to war over Syrian actions and ended up looking irresolute when it became obvious he would not carry out his threat.[163] A dovish foreign policy is less likely to write such bad checks as it would be reluctant to use or threaten force except in limited circumstances. This means the resolve to follow through would be more likely to exist. In other words, given the high costs of force, the difficulty making force effective, and limited US willingness to pay the necessary costs, military threats must be reserved for protecting US allies and vital interests in key regions.

As articulated above, none of this is a call for isolationism. American leadership is necessary—and even expected by other countries, if not always liked.[164] Without US leadership, these orders are likely to change significantly. Yet, Americans have developed a mistaken view of leadership equating it narrowly with the use of force and with the United States doing the majority of the heavy lifting. These orders can endure and prosper without the frequent use of active force. The current overreliance on the active use of force ignores deterrence and nonmilitary tools of statecraft, both of which are sufficient for maintaining these orders as will be shown in chapters 4 and 5. Further, the current understanding of US leadership in Washington fails to recognize that true leadership is mobilizing others to work toward a common goal[165] and "finding opportunities for mutual gain."[166] Happily, the United States has many allies and friends with reasonably similar preferences to the United States. There is no need to do all of the work. Military officers or the captains of sports teams who did all of the work for their troops or fellow players would be poor leaders indeed. Instead, they should strive to motivate others to work with them and to bear many of the costs. As President Eisenhower said, leadership is,

> [T]he art of getting someone else to do something that you want done because he wants to do it, not because your position of power can compel him to do it, or your position of authority. A commander of a regiment is not necessarily a leader. He has all of the appurtenances of power given by a set of Army regulations by which he can compel unified action. He can say to a body such as this, "Rise," and "Sit down." You do it exactly. But that is not leadership.[167]

Similarly, Washington can mobilize other countries to work with the United States by allowing them to partially shape the strategy and goals. A good example of this is the sanctions that were placed on Iran's nuclear program. By abstaining from using force and making clear that the United States would accept a halting of the weapons program as sufficient (as opposed to dismantling the entire Iranian nuclear power program or insisting on regime change), the United States was able to lead a group of Western European countries, China, and Russia in placing additional sanctions on Iran. These multilateral sanctions ultimately culminated in a deal to suspend Iran's nuclear enrichment.[168] Of course, there are debates about the benefits of the deal and the United States has since abandoned the agreement, but it was only achievable in the first place by working with others under overarching US leadership. Decades of unilateral American sanctions failed to bring Iran to the bargaining table or halt the Iranian nuclear program. Nor would the multilateral sanctions that brought Iran to the table have been implemented if the United States had remained on the sidelines. Thus, US leadership can often result in multilateral actions that are more effective than unilateral US actions.

In sum, the United States is a secure, generally status quo power. It has no territorial ambitions, is geographically removed from the most dangerous regions in the world, and is well-protected by both its conventional military and nuclear arsenal. This makes it tempting to retreat from the world. Yet, the United States is too powerful and has too many interests—economic and political—to remain aloof from international politics. The existing international order is dependent upon US involvement and power. Also, the world would not let America alone if it hid. Thus, the United States must remain active in foreign affairs, both to preserve its interests and prevent the world from changing for the worse.

In many ways, this argument is consistent with the school of thought known as liberal internationalism. (Again, liberal in the sense of promoting Lockean values, not in the US domestic sense of the term). The overlap is strongest in urging an active and internationalist foreign policy and wanting to largely maintain the existing international order. It is also consistent with liberal internationalism in believing that economic tools, international law, and international organizations can be effective tools of US foreign policy. (These will be covered in greater detail in chapter 4). However, the argument differs from liberal internationalism, at least as practiced by the Clinton, Obama, and to some extent the George H. W. Bush administrations,[169] in several crucial ways. To start, the United States should be more conservative in its hopes and goals about what its efforts can achieve. Liberal internationalists, at times, have become unduly optimistic about what can be achieved and have often overreached. Also, the argument is for a far more dovish foreign policy than liberal internationalists have practiced in recent decades. American uses of force should be limited to key regions—North America and the Caribbean, Europe, and the Asia-Pacific. Focusing on key regions is similar to early conceptions of containment in the Cold War that would have limited US efforts to Europe and possibly Northeast Asia, thereby avoiding conflicts like Vietnam.[170] Further, uses of force in those regions should be limited to protecting US territories, deterring attacks against US allies, and defending those allies if need be. Force should not be used to bring about regime change or promote human rights except in cases of genocide. Thus, the argument is for a restrained, dovish, liberal internationalism and, therefore, departs significantly from liberal internationalism as recently practiced by Washington.

This argument for a dovish foreign policy also differs from arguments that fall under the umbrella of "strategic restraint." While such arguments agree with the dovish view that the United States should restrict the use of force substantially,[171] the general strategic outlook varies in important ways. The starkest difference is that strategic restraint arguments—much like isolationist arguments—argue for pulling back from the United States' alliance structures and position of global leadership. Since US allies have often failed to carry their fair share of the Western security burden, advocates of strategic restraint argue that the United States would be better off without these allies.[172] They argue Washington should dismantle NATO and its bilateral agreements with Pacific Rim states.[173] Yet, doing this would be throwing away some of America's best strategic assets: its powerful friends. Further, while the argument that doing so would prompt these European and Asian states to spend more on their own defense is probably true,[174] a fully rearmed Germany and a possibly nuclear Japan are not in the interests of the United States. Also, by focusing on narrow US self-interests, a policy of strategic restraint would encourage other countries to act likewise, undermining Washington's ability to cooperate productively with them on non-security issues, and would undermine the multilateral institutions that undergird the international security, legal, and economic orders.[175]

The dangers of US withdrawal also apply to offshore balancing strategies, which, like a policy of strategic restraint, would encourage the United States to pull out of or greatly reduce its commitment to NATO and its Asian allies.[176] Such strategies argue the United States should only become involved if another country or countries threaten to significantly alter the world order. Yet, as with strategic restraint, such a US withdrawal makes those threats more likely to occur in the first place. Stephen Walt, a political scientist, even trumpets US foreign policy in the early twentieth century as an example of successful offshore balancing[177] as though allowing the rise of Nazi Germany and Imperial Japan and being forced to fight World War II—a war that US engagement after World War I might well have prevented—should be counted as a success! Such a general withdrawal would be dangerous and is not necessary. Likewise, withdrawal ignores that the United States has significant economic and political interests throughout the globe and that the preservation of the existing security, legal, and economic orders helps to keep the United States safe.[178] Arguments that the only alternative to withdrawal is a militarized attempt to force American views on the world present a false choice.[179] It is quite possible to limit US actions without engaging in such an extreme withdrawal from international affairs.[180] As this chapter has shown and as will be returned to in chapters 4 and 5, peaceful alternatives to disengagement exist.

Further, strategic restraint arguments and offshore balancing arguments are often heavily based on the logic of amoral self-interest and the economic costs of the use of force.[181] Some go so far as to argue that as long as other great powers exist, no country can safely pursue advancing a moral agenda[182] even though countries have had moral components to their foreign policies for centuries.[183] As such, these arguments can leave Americans cold. Yes, like all peoples Americans want their government's foreign policy to advance their own and their fellow citizens' interests. They also, however, want to believe that their country's foreign policy is moral and is advancing something larger than material interests narrowly defined.[184] This is true of Americans with a wide range of political beliefs: progressives, conservatives, neoconservatives, libertarians, internationalists, and isolationists. Attempts to have a Machiavellian foreign policy à la Henry Kissinger in the 1970s that hews closely to US interests but lacks a moral element will be ultimately rejected by the American public as Kissinger himself has acknowledged.[185] This is true whether those policies are hawkish or dovish. Likewise, as argued in chapter 1, arguments that emphasize costs and trade-offs are unlikely to persuade hawks and fence-sitters of the benefits of a more peaceful foreign policy.

Amoral policies also needlessly throw away a potential source of strength: American ideals. Ideals and interests are not always in conflict with each other. The two can be productively combined when crafting foreign policy.[186] As discussed above, American ideals justify and support the existing international legal order. By promoting liberal ideals, American foreign policy shapes what is seen as acceptable behavior by countries. This in turn reduces countries' incentives to engage in illiberal behaviors—such as empire building—which would be detrimental to American interests.[187]

Crucially, material self-interest *alone* fails as a way to check American overreach and the use of force. Restraint must have a moral component to serve alongside material self-interest. As historian Robert Osgood said in the early years of the Cold War,

> [A] rational calculation of the imperatives of American power is needed to moderate and guide the nation's idealistic impulses; but it would be foolish to suppose that a concern for America's power interest could, by itself, suffice to check the impulsiveness of American foreign policy; for it is, to a large extent, that very concern which, under the stress of continual fear, tends to distort reason and destroy moderation. Once more the lesson is clear: unless national self-interest is sought within the context of ultimate moral values transcending both egoistic and idealistic impulses, it must be self-defeating. Unless contemporary Realists in seeking to counter utopianism take into account the interdependence of ideals and self-interest in international relations, they will spread little enlightenment by opposing one kind of oversimplification with another....
>
> A view of international relations which imagines that nations can in the long run achieve a stable and effective foreign policy solely by a rational calculation of the demands of national self-interest is based upon an unrealistic conception of human nature, for it is certainly utopian to expect any great number of people to have the wit to perceive or the will to follow the dictates of enlightened self-interest on the basis of sheer reason alone. Rational self-interest divorced from ideal principles is as weak and erratic a guide for foreign policy as idealism undisciplined by reason. No great mass of people is Machiavellian, least of all the American people. Americans in particular have displayed a strong aversion to the pursuit of self-interest, unless self-interest has been leavened with moral sentiment.[188]

Without a moral rationale upon which to base restraint, Americans become tempted to fix or reform the world through the use of force. When these hawkish policies fail or the inherent moral contradictions become apparent, Americans become tempted to reject the world and seek an impossible isolationism. In other words, arguments lacking a moral element lose to those containing one even if such arguments are inconsistent and unwise. This can result in a pendulum of embracing and then rejecting engagement and force.

Dovish internationalism is well suited to meet these challenges. Dovishness can provide this joint moral-material check on the overuse of force. Dovishness can advance American values through nonmilitary tools thereby maintaining popular support for an active, vigorous, and honorable foreign policy. Acts by other countries that contravene US interests and values can be countered with diplomatic pressure, economic tools, and deterrence. Dovishness also avoids overreach and unnecessary bloodshed that often backfires and pushes many Americans toward isolationism. It would also keep the United States from making demands it cannot enforce. In short, doves are not only pessimistic about force but optimistic about other sorts of solutions to international problems. This pessimism about force and optimism about nonmilitary tools is the focus of the next two chapters.

# CHAPTER 3

## *Doves as Pessimists*

### Why Force Fails

Never, never, never believe any war will be smooth and easy, or that
anyone who embarks on the strange voyage can measure the tides and
hurricanes he will encounter. The statesman who yields to war fever
must realize that once the signal is given, he is no longer the master of
policy but the slave of unforeseeable and uncontrollable events.

WINSTON CHURCHILL[1]

Hawks accuse doves of being naïve, pie-in-the-sky dreamers. Hawks argue
that if one understands the world, it becomes obvious that the frequent use
of force is wise and necessary. Yet, a hardheaded analysis of the effectiveness
of the use of force shows it is hawks that are overly optimistic, while doves are
the ones with a levelheaded, accurate assessment of the nature of the world
and the use of force in particular.

Doves oppose the use of force in part because force is very costly. Most
clearly, force is especially costly when it fails. Countries suffer far more damage to their reputations when they lose wars than when other policies fail.
They also risk losing territory and even political independence—outcomes
the United States has been spared because of its favorable location and
strength even in defeat. Even in victory, the direct costs of war are tremen-
dous. There is perhaps no more costly action for a society to undertake in
terms of both blood and treasure than war. Force must produce exceptional
results to justify those costs.[2]

Yet, force often fails. This is true even if costs are not taken into account.
As General Martin Dempsey, then Chairman of the US Joint Chiefs of Staff,
said in an August 2013 interview on the Syrian Civil War, "Simply the appli-

cation of force rarely produces—and in fact, maybe never produces the outcome that we seek."[3] Perhaps most obviously for every side that wins a war, the other side must lose. And of course, many wars such as the Iran-Iraq War (1980–1988) go badly for both sides. Still, given the United States' military prowess, it could be argued that it is unlikely to lose wars. The United States, however, is not omnipotent.[4] Other countries and groups can successfully resist the United States through strategies, such as guerilla warfare, which limit and counter American technological advantages on the battlefield.[5] Unforeseen events, accidents, and randomness also undermine the successful employment of force. Last, as American experiences in Vietnam, Iraq, and Afghanistan demonstrate, even the successful tactical application of force does not guarantee a successful political outcome.[6] One can win battles and lose the war. This means force—including American force—often fails.

WINNING BATTLES, LOSING WARS

The effectiveness of force as a policy tool is vastly overstated. It is not enough for the US military to defeat the opposition's military for force to be an effective political tool. The belief that victory on the battlefield is sufficient to achieve foreign policy goals is a common mistake. Foreign policy goals are inherently political and cannot be reduced to military maneuvers.[7] Strategy is needed to connect military results to political goals.

This is quite difficult. For example, in 2003, the US military easily defeated Saddam Hussein's forces in Iraq and overthrew his government. However, the American goal of a stable, nonthreatening Iraq was not achieved. Similarly, in 2011, NATO's air campaign easily toppled Muammar Gaddafi's regime, but the result was a chaotic mess. Ultimately, both Iraq and Libya became breeding grounds for jihadist groups like ISIS. Further, the removal of Gaddafi a decade after his regime ended its nuclear weapons program in response to Western pressure has caused the North Korean regime to question whether it would be safe if it surrendered its nuclear weapons.[8] In other words, the removal of Gaddafi by force has made containing nuclear proliferation in the rest of the world more difficult. Last, the disorder in Iraq allowed Iran to greatly increase its influence there—both through direct ties to the government and through newly empowered Shia militias.[9] In both cases, battlefield successes did not produce the policy outcome Washington sought.

Nor are these isolated incidents. Since 1945 when the United States has lost wars, it has won most of the battles.[10] Likewise, the disconnect between military and political success is not exclusively an American problem. It is a problem for all countries. American technological superiority does little to solve this problem as it is inherently political and not technical in nature.[11]

Why doesn't tactical success guarantee strategic success? First, many goals are only partially tied to the successful tactical use of force.[12] Yes, military victory is a requirement, but it's insufficient. Defeated enemies can always regroup and continue their resistance. Repeated tactical victories over the Viet Cong and North Vietnamese army did not end the Vietnam War, just as repeated victories over the Taliban have not made Afghanistan secure. There are seemingly always more terrorists to capture or guerillas to fight.

Worse, tactical successes can harm the overall strategy.[13] If operations alienate populations through the killing of many civilians or if they draw other countries into the war, they actually reduce the odds of overall success despite local, tactical victories. For example, when drone strikes have succeeded in killing leaders of terrorist groups, those groups have become less discriminating in their attacks and have shifted from military to civilian targets—hardly a desired outcome.[14] Further, the strikes are a feature of terrorist recruitment propaganda, meaning the terrorists themselves believe the strikes motivate individuals to join those groups.[15] Thus, battlefield success must be combined with policies that dissuade opponents from continuing to take up arms as it is impossible to kill or capture all of America's opponents.

Second, in cases where force is used to overthrow a hostile regime, securing long-term successes requires replacing the overthrown regime with a stable, acceptable alternative—something that is generally beyond the ability of an outside power to impose even given years or decades of ongoing commitment.[16] For instance, success in Afghanistan as defined by the Bush, Obama, and Trump administrations necessitates the creation of a stable, self-supporting government that does not aid anti-American terrorist groups. This in turn requires political and economic policies to construct such a government as well as defeating the Taliban on the battlefield. Yet, after nearly two decades of American efforts, the Afghan government is still unable to stand on its own.[17] In sum, tactical battlefield successes often fail to translate into policy successes.

## LIMITED BATTLEFIELD CONTROL

Of course, even obtaining battlefield success is difficult. Knockout victories leading to a quick cessation of hostilities are especially rare.[18] This stems from difficulties in controlling what happens on the battlefield. As noted in the Churchill quote at the beginning of the chapter, war is never fully controllable.[19] It is a complex process involving a great many people, institutions, and equipment. Surprises, both good and bad, are common.[20] Because of this, wars always have significant elements of randomness. Events in war are contingent on multiple factors, making connections between actions and outcomes unclear.[21] The inherent limits of human cognition mean keeping all of these moving parts and their connections to each other in mind is impossible.[22] Pre-war estimates of risks, costs, and the odds of victory are inherently uncertain and vague.[23] In other words, even the best strategy with the most capable military cannot come close to dictating or even fully understanding the likely outcome of a war. Much of this stems from factors that Prussian General Carl von Clausewitz identified as inherent to war in his classic book, *On War*.[24]

One, the battlefield is covered in the fog of war. This means it is very difficult to know where the enemy is, what they are doing, and even at times where your own troops are and what they are doing. This results in mistakes and suboptimal strategies. Even though modern technology—such as satellites delivering real-time battlefield information—helps reduce the fog of war, the problem remains. For example, since the mid-1990s the United States has accidentally bombed the Chinese embassy in Belgrade,[25] bombed a Doctors Without Borders hospital in Afghanistan,[26] and killed US soldiers in incidents of "friendly fire."[27] And these are simply the most egregious mistakes as buildings don't move and knowing where your own forces are is much easier than knowing where the enemy is. Even drones—which have an unusually high ability to view the battlefield—make mistakes.[28] Like any use of force, they kill civilians and don't always hit their targets. At times, it is not even clear who was killed in a particular drone strike.[29]

These examples demonstrate not any unusual failing of the US military, but that the chaos, complexity, and uncertainty of war make precision impossible and ensure that unintended consequences will occur. Advances in technology cannot do away with the fog of war—there will always be unknowns.[30] Perhaps most clearly, in every war, noncombatants are killed—

even if they are not deliberately targeted and great caution is taken to avoid killing them. Any use of military force will be messy and imprecise in its effects.

Two, things go wrong because of what Clausewitz calls friction. Errors and mistakes creep into even the best laid plans for reasons beyond anyone's control. In war, such events are common. Soldiers tire, get lost, or fail to act out of fear. Orders are misunderstood or even deliberately disobeyed. Severe weather spoils attacks. Machinery—even sophisticated modern machinery—breaks down.

Examples of friction abound in US military history and indeed in the histories of all militaries. The April 1980 attempt to rescue the American hostages in Iran failed because several US helicopters became inoperable due to hydraulic failures and the ingestion of sand.[31] Likewise, during the successful raid to kill Osama bin Laden, one of the US helicopters became inoperable and had to be abandoned.[32] Finally, in June 1944, General Mark Clark, an excellent commander, contrary to his orders, opted to occupy Rome rather than cut off the retreating German army. This allowed the Germans to escape and fight another day.[33] Thus, Robert Burns' aphorism about the "best laid schemes of mice and men"[34] going awry applies fully to the use of force.

Three, Clausewitz argues that wars tend to the absolute. This does not mean that all wars become total fights to the finish like World War II, but rather the mutual hatred and animosities that build up during wars push them toward escalation. Clausewitz argues that only skillful leadership can keep wars limited to their original aims and scope. This tension between escalation and limitation means wars often cease to be about the narrow political goals for which they were originally launched. Each side continues to escalate in an attempt to win when more limited uses of force fail. Emotions also take over, leading to cycles of violence and counter-violence. This escalation makes the use of force far more costly. It also detaches the use of force from its original political goals, making force less likely to achieve those goals. This process whereby limited uses of force escalate into more extreme forms has been noted by students of post-World War II US foreign policy.[35] Vietnam is perhaps the best example of runaway escalation, but it is hardly the only one.

Thus, the very nature of war makes the successful application of force difficult. It means that human agency—the ability of individuals to influence the world around them—is limited. No matter who is president, no matter how capable American diplomats and generals are, these inherent limits on what can be achieved remain.[36] Wise officials recognize these limits and realize that force often fails and rarely justifies its exceptionally high costs compared to other policy options.


## NEGATIVE PRECEDENTS AND THE USE OF FORCE

Another drawback to the frequent American use of force is that it sets dangerous moral and legal precedents for the rest of the world.[37] Recurrent US military actions make it far harder for Washington to criticize the use of force by other countries. Calling the Russian interventions in Ukraine illegitimate, while simultaneously engaging in military interventions in Libya, Iraq, Afghanistan, Somalia, and Syria, rings of hypocrisy. Yet, Vladimir Putin's actions in Ukraine are illegitimate and must be condemned. US actions that undermine such condemnations are, therefore, problematic. In other words, frequent American uses of force legitimize the use of force in general, making it difficult to effectively critique the international use of force. If the world's most powerful country and a self-proclaimed champion of democracy and human rights can use force, why cannot other countries, no matter what their motives?[38] Unless Americans want a world where using force to revise power structures, alter borders, and change regimes is routine and acceptable, Washington should be careful about setting precedents for the use of force. US invasions, drone strikes, and the use of force to bring about regime change legitimize those behaviors. The same is true of uses of force that kill a great many civilians. While the United States certainly tries to avoid killing civilians, the fog of war means civilians still die. Much as American uses of force legitimize the use of force by others, US-caused civilian deaths give cover to others who are less careful or even desire civilian casualties.

Yet, a world where the use of force is regular and acceptable is contrary to US interests. It would make the world more dangerous and undermine the international security order. This is especially true for the unilateral use of force or even multilateral uses of force, such as NATO's 1999 intervention in Kosovo to halt Serbian attacks against ethnic Albanian rebels, that cannot obtain approval from the United Nations Security Council. Such actions further undermine the international legal and moral order. None of these outcomes advance long-term US interests.

## THE DISCONNECT BETWEEN FORCE AND ECONOMIC GOALS

Last, some policy goals are unrelated to the use of force. Economics goals, for instance, are not easily influenced through the use of force. America's impressive military preponderance does little good when negotiating trade treaties with Europe, Japan, China, or Latin America. Nor does it help prevent the spread of fiscal and currency crises.

In other words, military power is not very fungible.[39] Something is fungible if it can easily be turned into something else. The classic example of an item with high fungibility is money. Money is easily turned into food, clothing, movie tickets, and so forth through commonplace economic transactions. On the other hand, a house, especially in an economically depressed area, is far less fungible. Just because it is a good house doesn't mean it is easy to sell. Houses take a great deal of time and effort to sell, making them difficult to turn into whatever other good you want.

Force is similar to the hard-to-sell house. It is not very fungible. It is very difficult to turn military prowess into other sorts of power. The United States is not going to threaten its allies with military force to get better trade deals. Such threats would not be believable, and most Americans would find them repugnant. While the United States has struck mutually beneficial trade deals with its allies such as Canada, the European Union, and Japan, there is little reason to believe that the United States disproportionately benefits from these agreements compared to its allies. Analyses generally suggest the benefits of trade are largely balanced between the United States and its allies or, if anything, go disproportionately to US allies as a percentage of their economies rather than to the United States.[40] Thus, it does not appear that the US military protection of these countries has allowed Washington to extract better terms in trade agreements. Nor would any economic gains be worth the damage done to the alliance. Even threats against countries that are not friends are incredible. Would the United States really start a war with China just to improve trade agreements? Of course not. Such a war would be far more costly than any economic benefit it could possibly bring.

Likewise, conquest cannot improve the economy. The nature of modern economies makes it impossible for societies as a whole to profit economically from warfare.[41] The direct costs of war are far greater than the value of resources, such as oil, which could be seized. It is far cheaper to buy them instead. For example, the US invasion of Iraq so disrupted the country that oil production plummeted by nearly half despite the lifting of sanctions on

Iraqi oil exports.[42] Further, the costs of US military deployments to the Persian Gulf have greatly exceeded the value of the oil exports to the United States they ostensibly protect.[43] Likewise, prior to the Second Congo War (1998–2003), a considerable amount of Congolese gold, copper, and timber exports flowed through Uganda. Yet, Uganda's participation in that war—which resulted in the Ugandan military seizing the sources of some of those resources—actually disrupted their extraction, causing the level of exports of those materials through Uganda to fall significantly.[44] In other words, even without accounting for military expenditures and looking only narrowly at the gross value of easily lootable resources being exported through Uganda, the war made Ugandans worse off.[45]

Disruptions to manufacturing, high tech industries, banking, and various service sectors would be far more severe, meaning that advanced economies cannot be seized by war. Instead, war disrupts and destroys the economies of the countries involved. Even if foreign companies could be seized, what good would this do? If the United States invaded a country and seized its auto plants, how would this do Americans any good? It would simply turn a foreign competitor into a domestic one. Autoworkers in Michigan and Ohio, if anything, would be worse off. Further, the existence of complex global supply chains for things like automotive parts means that even the disruption of foreign auto industries would hurt US autoworkers.[46]

This is not to suggest that war must be stamped out everywhere for the US economy to thrive. While war does harm the economies of those countries involved in the war, there is little evidence that neutral countries' economies are significantly harmed by most wars.[47] The United States' economy is especially unlikely to be harmed by foreign conflicts. Given the size and diversity of the US economy, it would be able to weather war-caused disruptions better than most countries could. Certainly any negative effects would be smaller in monetary terms than the costs of imposing peace upon the warring countries.[48]

Norman Angell, an early twentieth-century British journalist and political writer, most clearly pointed out the folly of waging war for profit given the nature of modern economies. He did allow, however, that perhaps war was profitable in the distant past when wealth was mostly a function of arable land, animal herds, and easily looted items such as gold and gems. The same could hold in areas of limited economic development today. That said, the above Ugandan example makes even this questionable. Further, war seems not to have been profitable during medieval times, the Renaissance, or the Enlightenment.[49] Wars pushed kings and governments deeper into debt. For example, wars continuously drained the coffers of the English kings. Even highly successful campaigns rarely, if ever, turned a profit, and wars as a whole could prove ruinous even after accounting for loot and captured territories.[50] Instead, they were fought for the glory of the sovereign. As historian Garrett Mattingly said of wars launched by Renaissance kings and princes, "Whether such conquests would be worth to his people the blood and treasure they would cost was an irrelevant, absurd question. Nobody expected that they would."[51] Likewise, the wars of the 1500s and 1600s steadily drained and at times bankrupted the treasuries of Spain, France, England, and the Netherlands.[52] The net ledger is no better from the mid-1600s to mid-1700s either as an accounting of direct and indirect costs and benefits concludes that wars were net costs to European states.[53] Thus, even in earlier eras war did not pay.

Angell was not arguing that war is impossible or that it would never happen. He was arguing only that the notion that war could turn a profit was an illusion.[54] Thus, for war to be fought *for economic reasons* among modern, developed countries, one has to either assume foolish leaders—certainly a possibility—or that needed resources somehow cannot be acquired through normal economic intercourse. For example, Japan attacked Britain and the United States in December 1941 so as to be able to occupy the oil fields of the Dutch East Indies (now Indonesia). But this was because the British and Americans at that time controlled most of the world's oil and were attempting to cut Japan off to force it to halt its war against China. It was not that Japan believed it would profit economically from warfare, but rather the attack was an attempt to defeat the Anglo-American embargo. The war's roots were ultimately political—Britain and the United States disagreed with Japan over its invasion of China.

This is not to suggest that aggressors are unable to extract resources from conquered territories. At times, they can. Still, given the inevitable resistance from conquered populations, this is only true for especially ruthless conquerors that pose a "work or starve" dilemma to conquered peoples. Such policy can extract resources greater than the costs of occupation from modern, industrial societies—at least in the short run.[55] Of course, such tactics are ill-suited to democracies and countries that value human rights, such as the United States, as any lenience results in extraction costing more than it gains.[56] Even so, such brutal tactics cannot extract enough to offset the initial costs of conquest. In other words, even conquest backed by abhorrent brutality is a net economic loss once all costs are considered.[57] Thus, provided aggressors face opposition—something nationalism almost guarantees—conquest is still a net economic loss even for the most brutal of invaders. War then is poorly suited to achieve economic goals.

## HOW FORCE SEDUCES

So why, given the many challenges to the successful application of force does the United States keep trying to achieve its goals militarily? The answer in no small part lies in overconfidence. This overconfidence has roots in both basic human psychology and certain elements of American culture.

Mutual optimism is a major cause of war.[58] In other words, a major reason wars happen is both sides believe they can win or at least get a better deal through fighting than what the other side is willing to offer antebellum.[59] Such overoptimism has been widely noted by international relations scholars. Robert Jervis argues that "excessive military optimism is frequently associated with the outbreak of war."[60] Steven Van Evera goes even further, claiming that "at least some false optimism about relative power preceded every major war since 1740."[61] Obviously, much of this optimism must be false— there is a losing side for every winning side in war. Likewise, wars usually end up being more costly than expected.[62] That's not to say such mutual optimism is necessarily foolish. It is entirely possible to reach incorrect conclusions after carefully and reasonably considering all of the evidence at hand. Most clearly, mutual optimism can have rational sources. Each side could possess secrets that lead it to believe it will fare better than its opponent in the coming war.[63] While such private information likely plays an important role in causing many wars,[64] psychology also serves as a source of mutual optimism. In short, the way people perceive the world results in overconfidence.

### General Sources of Overconfidence

Leaders are faced with heavy information processing loads. They must deal with unreliable information, uncertainty, an indeterminate range of policy options, stress, time pressures, and conflicting policy preferences. Yet, leaders have inherently limited cognitive capacities and, therefore, cannot deal with all of these difficulties.[65] Instead, they, like all people, rely on cognitive shortcuts to make decisions. This reliance on heuristic shortcuts may be increased by the stresses inherent to high-level political leadership. Prolonged periods of stress, such as are common during diplomatic crises, reduce people's abilities to process information.[66] This leads to rapid, intuitive decision-making rather than reaching decisions through careful deliberation. While the use of such shortcuts to save time and keep cognitive demands manageable is often reasonable and even wise,[67] research has shown that many of these shortcuts skew decisions in a hawkish direction.[68]

For starters, continuous stress leads to perceiving danger even when a careful analysis of the situation would show that the fear is unwarranted.[69] Stress also creates a perception that options are narrowing, making war seem like the only choice.[70] Further, our inherent psychological makeup leads us to be unjustifiably confident in the efficacy of force. This overconfidence is an adaptive trait that helped our ancestors survive when human society was limited to small familial groups and clans.[71] When faced with physical dangers and an immediate need to act, optimism is useful. If you are charged by a bear, no matter how accurate your pessimism is, it's not clear that it is of any use, whereas action—spurred by optimism—might just get you out of the bind. Such optimism and rapid decision-making still prove useful in tactical battlefield situations and in a variety of civilian emergency situations. Given the complexity of modern human society, however, overoptimism no longer serves humanity well given sufficient time to deliberate.[72] Instead, such optimism leads to rash decisions and results in dangerous situations that could otherwise have been avoided.

One source of this overconfidence is the illusion of control.[73] We want to believe that our actions are responsible for much of what happens around us and that we largely control our own fate. Powerful individuals and countries are particularly susceptible to this illusion. Further, people assume others' actions are about them when in fact those actions frequently have other sources entirely.[74] Certainly individuals have a great deal of say in what happens to them and others' actions may indeed be in reaction to what that individual has done. Even so, much remains uncontrollable, and others' actions are often taken for reasons independent of the original individual's actions. This is especially true in international relations as the behaviors of other countries and groups are impossible to control.

Once a war has begun, this illusion of control is further enhanced by being on the offensive. Taking the offensive or initiating a war allows for the illusion that the campaign or war will go according to plan.[75] Reactive policies, such as deterrence or defensive campaigns in wars, do not allow for such self-delusion as by their very nature they are responses to actions taken by other countries. In other words, reactive policies explicitly require an element of improvisation. Thus, the illusion of total control is dismissed at the time the policy is formulated because the policy is designed to change in response to opponents' actions. But when countries seize the initiative, they are able to fool themselves into believing things will unfold as planned, as though somehow the enemy cannot upset the attacker's plans. This is pure hubris as no plan is perfect and opponents always have a say in the outcome of violent conflicts. Military combat always requires improvisation and never proceeds exactly as planned.

Second, people overestimate their own abilities.[76] For example, how many people think they are below average drivers? Very few,[77] yet by definition, roughly half of all drivers must be below average. Similarly, research has shown that students at elite business schools consistently overestimate their abilities.[78] These misperceptions of drivers and business students reflect a general human tendency to overestimate one's own abilities. This overconfidence is deepened by the all too human tendency to credit successes to our own actions, while dismissing failures as a product of circumstance.[79] When combined with the illusion of control, an overestimation of one's abilities is particularly dangerous. It leads to a belief that any preferred outcome can be obtained—all that is needed is to act.

Third, people engage in wishful thinking. This leads to overconfidence. It also results in an unwillingness to shift away from chosen policies even when faced with evidence of failure. Such problems are common in small group decision-making settings, especially when members of the group value their relations with others in the group.[80] Such a setup is common in foreign policy decision-making circles where small groups of elite advisors want to keep good relations with each other and the president so as to maintain their influence. This results in pressures toward conformity—even if such pressures are never stated or even intentional—creating an illusion of unanimity. This false sense of consensus in turn gives leaders undue confidence in the quality of the decision because there appears to be no dissent.[81] This "groupthink" can also result in the favoring of policies that are more extreme and riskier than any member of the group's initial preferences.[82] This, when combined with the appearance of unanimity, further increases the odds force will be used.

Fourth, people undervalue concessions, precisely because they were offered by an opponent. This is known as reactive devaluation. When the value of a concession is unclear, people often judge its value based on who is offering the concession.[83] So offers from opponents are often judged to be of less value than they really are. For example, if Iran made a concession to the United States, many Americans would be suspicious of its value, even if they had previously pushed for precisely that concession. They would do this based on the assumption that Iranians would never give the United States anything of value and would allow this assumption to trump evidence to the contrary. This dynamic makes it very difficult for countries to grant sufficient concessions to mollify their antagonists.

Fifth, people assume they are clearer in their words, actions, and intentions than they really are. Thus, when other countries' leaders misunderstand American actions or statements and react hostilely, it is tempting to take it as proof they were hostile all along when in fact they are simply misinterpreting Washington's muddled messages as more threatening than they really are.[84] Further, people assume others understand that their intentions are benign and fail to recognize that others are unable to perceive this. Thus, malign intent is unnecessary to provoke fearful reactions. Large aggregations of power—such as American military might—provoke fear in others simply because that power could be used to harm them.[85] For instance, people going home late at night may fear a muscularly built man walking toward them, even though he means them no harm. Finally, people do not see the constraints under which others are operating and neglect to consider others' viewpoints. Simultaneously, people fail to realize that others see them as threatening and falsely assume others understand the constraints under which they are operating.[86]

A nice example of the dynamic produced by these biases is the Able Archer exercise conducted by NATO in 1983. The idea of the training exercise was to prepare NATO's response to a potential military conflict with the Soviet Union that would culminate in a nuclear exchange. Such exercises are common and are vital for maintaining military readiness. NATO had engaged in similar military exercises in the past. The 1983 Able Archer exercise, however, was different as it contained a high level of realism including radio silences and the participation of heads of state. This realism prompted some in the Soviet Union to conclude that the exercise was in fact the preparation for an actual attack on the Soviet Union and its Warsaw Pact allies.

The Soviets responded by placing some of their nuclear forces on high alert. When the United States later learned of this through espionage, President Reagan was quite surprised. He knew the West did not intend to start

World War III and had always assumed the Soviets understood this. He had not considered that they genuinely feared the West just as the West feared the East.[87] To his credit, this revelation caused President Reagan to reassess his views. While he naturally continued to see the Soviet Union as a hostile and dangerous enemy, he accepted that they were genuinely fearful of the United States, and therefore, US government needed to be careful so as to avoid inadvertently pushing the Soviet Union into starting a war.

Last, military biases can make the use of force appear more attractive. Yet as will be seen below, unlike with the previously discussed biases, there are both theoretical and empirical reasons to discount the impact of military biases on US foreign policy. That said, internationally, the bias is quite real. Cross-national studies have found that military training increases individuals' willingness to use force.[88] This is important as military officers are always involved in deciding whether to use force or not—even if the ultimate decision is in the hands of civilian officials. This is because the military has the necessary expertise in the application of force. Officers must advise civilian decision-makers on technical military matters and the likelihood of whether a military operation could succeed or not. To exclude military officers is to invite disaster, yet including them means introducing the biases of military training into the decision-making process.

All people have biases that affect their perceptions of the world. Training and career paths—whether civil or military—introduce biases into leaders' thinking and decision-making. Military training favors the adoption of a decision-making style that values speed and decisiveness over deliberation. Such attributes are vital on the battlefield where there is little time to think and he who hesitates is not only lost but killed. In combat, suboptimal but decent, rapid decision-making is better than choosing the best option more slowly. Yet, away from the battlefield, rushing into a suboptimal decision is to court disaster. Also, officers are trained to see the world in military terms, and the solution they are most familiar with is the use of force. Furthermore, military leaders may insist combat operations are sufficient in and of themselves to exclude civilians from the decision-making process. This could be done out of professional or political rivalry or in an attempt to advance narrow organizational interests of the military. Such a breakdown in civil-military relations was especially common in European nations prior to World War I.[89] Finally, officers may argue that military necessity requires that certain actions be carried out even if politicians would prefer more peaceful options.[90] Thus, it is tempting to conclude that military officers would be more hawkish than civilians. Certainly, in some contexts such as in Russia, France, Germany, and Austria-Hungary prior to World War I, this was in fact the case.[91]

Yet, it is not clear this is true in the United States today. A survey of Cold War crises found US military officers were no more or less hawkish on average than their civilian counterparts.[92] Rather, significant variation existed in both groups and the officers' preferences often echoed those of the civilians. Only when it came to the escalation of ongoing military operations were officers consistently more hawkish than civilians. Further, US civilian officials were able to resist military demands and officers often backed down to preserve their access to the president. Last, military advice was most potent in advocating against, rather than for, the use of force.[93]

This fits with multi-country studies that have found that strong civilian oversight reduces hawkish tendencies in militaries.[94] Indeed, it is military juntas, as opposed to either democratic or authoritarian states with civilian control, that are most likely to initiate the use of force.[95] This implies that the American tradition of strong civilian oversight of the military—something that other mature democracies also possess—reduces the rate at which the United States employs force. Further, the same studies that found military training increases hawkishness also found that prior battlefield experience makes military officers more cautious.[96] Indeed, officers with combat experience are no more or less hawkish than civilians who have never served in the military. Given that most senior US military officers have combat experience, there is less reason to fear they would advocate for hawkish policies at a higher rate than civilian officials would. Thus, the United States' democratic institutions and, ironically, its history of frequent military action both insulate it against military biases and work to make the US military less hawkish.

Though these biases increase the odds of war, they do not make it inevitable. In fact, being aware of them can help walk back crises. This can be done by having both sides be especially careful in actions and statements and by understanding that an opponent's actions and statements may indicate not that they are irredeemably hostile but rather scared and constrained. This is neither to say that there are no real, serious differences between countries nor to claim that some countries don't wish each other ill. Rather, it is to point out that basic human biases lead to the unnecessary escalation of real disagreements. Thus, it is vital to be aware of them and consciously push back against them.

*American Sources of Overconfidence*

None of these hawkish biases are specific to Americans, and as just argued, the United States may be more insulated from military biases than is the average country. They are general human biases. They press all countries to adopt more hawkish positions. That said, the United States is especially prone to such overestimation of the efficacy of force. In no small part, this is because of the awesome disparity in military forces between the United States and any likely adversary.[97] Power fuels beliefs that it is possible to control events.[98] And there is no doubt about the United States' massive military power. To start, it is one of a very few countries capable of deploying large forces anywhere in the world.[99] Even US allies regularly rely on American logistical capabilities to deploy their forces abroad.[100] The United States outstrips the next ten countries combined in military expenditures[101] and many of those ten are US allies. The lead is even starker in researching new weapons. US military research and development expenditures account for 70 percent of the global total.[102] As British historian Paul Kennedy said,

> [N]othing has ever existed like this disparity of power; nothing. I have returned to all of the comparative defense spending and military personnel statistics over the past 500 years . . . and no other nation comes close.[103]

US policymakers have bought into this notion of American might.[104]

This huge disparity has also been achieved relatively cheaply. The United States spends only 3.5 percent of its gross domestic product (GDP) on the military. While this is high compared to other developed countries today, it is low compared to US spending during the Cold War. US military spending in 1960 was about 10 percent of GDP, and in 1985 it was about 6 percent of GDP. In other words, the United States can afford to spend what it does.[105] This is not to say the money could not be better used elsewhere,[106] but to achieve such a military preponderance without ruinous levels of spending only adds to the sense that the US military is invincible and assures that calls for reductions in military spending will be muted. Also, the United States does not have conscription so when conflicts do occur most families are not directly affected. Instead the burden falls on a small section of society— military families.[107] Only three-fourths of 1 percent of the US population has served in Iraq or Afghanistan.[108]

On top of this, the US military has embraced the use of advanced technology as part of what is called the revolution in military affairs. American commanders have access to real-time battlefield information and have precision munitions, which are far more likely to hit their target than traditional ordinance is. While this advanced technology gives the United States an important advantage on the battlefield and is a major part of why the United States is more powerful than its potential rivals, it also leads to an inflated sense of control.[109] Even with all of this real time intelligence, the United States still makes errors in targeting as discussed above and still has a hard time finding opponents or knowing what they are planning. Most importantly, this technology does not grant the United States control over its opponents and does little to shape how people perceive the United States and react to its policies. Thus, though it gives commanders a great edge on the battlefield, even advanced technology cannot control the complex process that is war. It can, however, fool people into thinking they are able to control events.

Equally important is that the US military is one of the most, if not the most, revered institutions in American society today. As Americans have lost faith in other institutions—Congress, churches, unions, colleges, and the police—they have remained steadfastly supportive and trusting of the US military.[110] Certainly, the military has done much to deserve its reputation in American society. It makes sense to respect those who have made sacrifices for the rest of us. But the reverence for the military *combined with a loss of confidence in other institutions* has perverse effects. This trust and adulation of the military leads Americans to turn to it to solve all sorts of problems— even ones it is poorly suited for, such as rebuilding political institutions in foreign countries. Seeing the military as the best of society and revering it for its members' sacrifices also makes questioning the military's performance feel unpatriotic and unseemly.[111] This is especially true when this reverence is combined with the fact that few Americans serve and are thus detached from military affairs.[112] It results in Americans being reluctant to critically examine the use of force.[113] This reverence ironically allows for the overuse of the military, which is deeply unfair to those servicemen and women who have sacrificed so much.

Further, Americans overestimate the threats the United States faces today.[114] Much as how power leads to a belief that one can control events, power also leads to perceiving more threats.[115] Yet, the threats the United States faces come from distant, less powerful countries such as Iran and North Korea or from international terrorist groups.[116] While such threats are real, they are less serious than the threats the Soviet Union or Nazi Germany posed in the past. They do not threaten to overturn the global international order because they are too weak to do so. These more limited threats are typical of the post-Cold War era.[117] Yet, many Americans, including foreign policy experts, judge current threats by the intentions and ideology of these opponents—which are indeed frightening—rather than by the means of these opponents, which are quite limited compared to the might of the United States.[118] Compared to many countries that use force far less frequently, the United States is remarkably safe. Yet, strikingly Americans perceive the world to be far more dangerous than Western Europeans do, despite the fact that Europe is geographically far closer to potential threats such as Russia, Iran, or ISIS.[119] By perceiving the world as more dangerous than it actually is, Americans overuse force and miss opportunities for gains using nonmilitary tools.[120]

Additionally, modern American foreign policy was established by and after the two world wars. This has caused Americans to see the world wars as templates for how the world, and especially force, works.[121] Americans think of wars as contests that are fought to the finish and that result in one side's unconditional surrender.[122] Yet, this is rarely how force is employed in practice. Many uses of force—such as raids against terrorist camps—fall short of war and most foreign policy issues never call for the employment of force. Even wars rarely end in unconditional surrender. Most wars end in negotiated settlements, and countries generally fight wars with that outcome in mind.[123] Very few foreign policy aims actually require that an opponent be totally defeated. Yet, this focus on unconditional surrender led the Bush administration to believe the removal of Saddam Hussein, rather than his containment, was necessary to secure US interests in the Middle East.

The failure to conceive of war in this manner also means Americans miss the continuous link between force and politics. Instead, Americans mistakenly see them as distinct.[124] Yet, without this link, force cannot deliver the desired policy outcomes.[125] For instance, the United States won most of the battles in Vietnam, but those battlefield successes did not translate to successful policy outcomes. A similar story has unfolded in the struggle against the Taliban in Afghanistan since 2001. In both cases, force could not work because there was no plausible strategy to link the battlefield successes to the desired political outcomes of stable, self-sufficient governments in South Vietnam and Afghanistan. Yes, battlefield victories would be necessary to bring about those outcomes but also insufficient. State-building and political reorganization were also necessary—and beyond America's ability to deliver. Yet, by narrowly focusing on the military requirements, it becomes possible to ignore the impossible side of the political equation and falsely believe that alone force is sufficient. In each case, the military element was only part of the equation.

Last, Americans have a strong inclination to do something.[126] When there is a problem in the world, Americans are strongly tempted to act and believe they can make a difference even if no good policy solutions exist.[127] They overestimate US capabilities and thus convince themselves that a solution is at hand.[128] Americans also doubt others will act and believe that if the United States does not act, nothing will be done.[129] While this is consistent with a general human bias toward action,[130] it has specifically American roots as well. Americans have a "can-do" attitude. This suggests that with a mix of hard work and cleverness, great things can be achieved.[131] While such a "can-do" attitude certainly has its virtues, it can also lead to wasting resources attempting to do the impossible and blind Americans to the limits of what they are able to do. This outlook and the nature of the American political system work to pressure presidents into taking action even if such actions are precipitous or unduly hasty.[132] Kennan argued that a prime example of Americans inability to see the limits of their powers was the belief that the United States "had lost" China to the Communists as though Americans had ever "had" China and it was theirs to keep or lose.[133] Rather, what happened to the government of China was beyond America's ability to significantly influence. More recent commentators, such as retired Colonel Andrew Bacevitch, agree that American hubris has repeatedly gotten the United States in trouble over the last hundred years.[134]

As argued in the previous chapter, Americans also want a moral foreign policy and see the United States as a force for good.[135] Most presidents also desire to export American values.[136] Indeed, it's hard to imagine a popular US foreign policy that was devoid of morality. This desire to do good and export American values is a positive. This desire for moral outcomes, however, has a significant downside. Given the intractable nature of much of the world's problems and how slowly nonviolent policies appear to work, it becomes tempting to resort to force to speed things up. An example of this is that surveys show that Americans favor the use of force—including in risky humanitarian interventions—at least before it goes wrong.[137] When combined with American military strength and an eagerness to act, this desire to spread American values can seduce presidents and the broader public into using force to pursue utopian notions.[138] In other words, these three factors work together to greatly increase the odds the United States would use force in response to a foreign policy problem. The desire to do something gives Washington the will to act. US military power gives Washington the ability to act using force. Overconfidence gives Washington an overly optimistic belief that a use of force would work. Thus, the effect is multiplicative. The totality of the factors pushing the United States to use force is greater than the sum of the individual parts.

In short, these American biases reinforce the more general psychological tendencies toward overreach and cause the United States to pursue overly risky military policies. These biases not only shift the terms of debate within an administration but the contours of public debate as well. As a result, doves struggle to get a fair airing of their views in government and in the media, meaning even superior dovish policies may be rejected.[139] This results in the frequent use of force despite its significant drawbacks.

## THE LIMITS OF PESSIMISM

Thus, there are many reasons to be skeptical about force. The great difficulty of controlling events within wars, the high direct costs in terms of lives and money, the disconnect between means and goals, and the negative precedents set by the frequent use of American force all conspire to undermine the effectiveness of force. Does such pessimism about the use of force mean that doves believe force should never be used and is always a mistake? No. Most doves realize that though force should rarely be used, force plays an important role in US foreign policy if used carefully and sparingly. The fact that force sometimes works is not an argument against dovishness. Eating, too, is useful, but one should not eat constantly and pointing out that food is necessary does not disprove arguments that one should take care to not overeat.

This means that pacifism is not possible. The United States must be able to protect itself and help protect US allies. Only countries under the security umbrella of another far more powerful state could afford to do away with their militaries. No such friendly superpower exists that could provide security for the United States. Nor would Americans accept relying on the benevolence of others for their safety. Thus, the United States must be prepared to defend itself from foreign military threats and terrorism—a topic that will be returned to in chapter 5. That said, this is achievable without resorting to the frequent, active use of force. As President Bush said at the 2002 West Point commencement address, "competition between great powers is inevitable, but armed conflict in our world is not."[140] In other words, it is possible to keep the United States and its allies safe while using force far less often than the United States has in recent decades. This positive side of the dovish argument—that many US foreign policy goals can be achieved through the use of nonmilitary tools—will be covered in the next chapter.

# CHAPTER 4

## *Doves as Optimists*

## How the United States Can Succeed
## without Waging War

But civilizations are not built by rapping people on the knuckles.

ALBERT CAMUS[1]

The previous chapter explained why doves are pessimistic about the effectiveness of force. It was the negative argument for a peaceful foreign policy: force fails to achieve US goals. This chapter will explore the positive case for a more peaceful foreign policy. Specifically, Americans can achieve their objectives without the active use of force for two reasons. First, as discussed in chapter 2, the United States has little need to use force offensively. Its goals are largely status quo in nature. The United States has no territorial ambitions and largely seeks to preserve the existing global order. It is blessed with a very favorable geographic position and possesses many loyal allies. This means, compared to most other countries, the United States is relatively secure.

Second, the United States possesses many highly effective nonmilitary foreign policy tools such as trade policy, aid, sanctions, international law, soft power, and diplomacy. These tools can both coerce and foster cooperation with other countries. It is vital to remember that even among self-interested countries, international cooperation not only is possible but in many issue areas it is common.[2] The wise use of these nonmilitary tools can encourage the emergence of such cooperation. They also can compel other countries to modify their actions when cooperation proves impossible. Yes, countries can always resort to force in the international arena, but civil wars teach us that force is also an option in the domestic arena. This means the possibility that force can be used does not eliminate the ability to use other tools. The key in any setting, foreign or domestic, to striking bargains that hold is constructing a set of incentives that make it so that no party to the agreement wants to renege.[3] Threats of force can play a role in this, but so can other inducements. Many countries in far less favorable security environments use nonmilitary tools to great effect, meaning the United States most certainly can use them as well. This means there is nothing inherent to the international arena preventing tools that work well domestically—economic levers, persuasion, and law—from working internationally, though of course their application must be modified. How and why these tools can work is the focus of this chapter.

Foreign policy tools come in three broad categories: guns, money, and words.[4] In recent decades, the United States has emphasized guns at the expense of the other two categories.[5] The utility of force is finite. It works well within a limited range of contingencies but is poorly suited for dealing with other problems.[6] Just as a hammer is not appropriate for all home improvement projects, force cannot fix all foreign policy problems. Yet, the United States' mighty military has led it to downplay or even ignore nonmilitary tools.[7]

This is particularly important as the vast majority of international interactions are not with enemies like North Korea but with allies or other friendly states. Even when dealing with an economic and diplomatic rival such as China, war or other active uses of force are very unlikely to be effective policies to address issues such as trade and cybersecurity. This is true even without considering China's considerable ability to retaliate. In other words, while security questions are an important part of international relations, they do not make up the bulk of those relations. On issues such as economic ties, the environment, health epidemics, and immigration, force is unlikely to be suitable. Other tools are more likely to be effective.[8]

Yet, Americans have acted as though force, and force alone, solves everything. In Iraq and Afghanistan, 95 percent of US expenditures have been military in nature even though, in order to bring stability to those countries, economic reconstruction and political development are vital.[9] Remarkably, when the US government has recognized the need for nonmilitary tools, it still has turned to the military to perform those tasks even though the military is not trained to do them. For instance, General Petraeus' FM 3-24 counterinsurgency manual—the guide the United States used to confront the Iraqi insurgency—emphasizes the need for nonmilitary missions such as rebuilding governance in countries beset by civil wars. Yet, the manual argues that the military should perform these tasks rather than letting the experts at the United States Agency for International Development (USAID), the US agency that focuses on economic development and democratization, or Foreign Service Officers perform them.[10] This narrow focus on the military is new. USAID sent 17,000 employees to Vietnam during that conflict yet has only 3,800 people on its payroll worldwide today, many of whom work in Washington.[11] In other words, the United States commits very few resources to diplomatic and economic efforts compared to what it devotes to the military, and when it does, it asks the military to perform them even though they are not tasks for which the military is best suited.

Even against enemies like North Korea, force has significant limitations. In the event of war, North Korea's small nuclear arsenal could easily cause massive damage to Japan and even hit US cities. Likewise, its conventional artillery would cause widespread damage to South Korea. South Korea's capital and most populous city, Seoul, is located very close to the border with North Korea and is highly vulnerable to bombardment. Yes, the American and South Korean militaries would eventually take out the artillery and defeat the North Koreans, but only after unacceptably high civilian casualties, including among the three-quarters of a million Americans that live in South Korea.[12] In other words, it would be a Pyrrhic victory with the costs far outweighing the benefits of removing the odious North Korean regime. Relying on deterrence to protect South Korea, Japan, and the United States itself from North Korean aggression is far wiser than resorting to the active use of force in an attempt to overthrow the North Korean regime.

Happily, there is no need to rely solely on the active use of force. Other tools exist. Even in relations dominated by security concerns, such as US-Iranian relations, such nonmilitary tools are still highly useful. Indeed, it was a combination of multilateral sanctions, an inspection regime led by an international institution, and diplomacy that compelled Iran to suspend its nuclear enrichment, not threats of force.[13] Of course, the United States has since unilaterally abandoned that deal.[14] Even given the serious imperfections in the deal, this abandonment of real gains is typical of a mindset that discounts gains achieved through peaceful means. Pulling out of the deal is particularly puzzling as the element of the deal most open to criticism—the releasing of frozen Iranian financial assets in the United States—had already been done. Those assets cannot be clawed back, and pulling out of the deal released Iran from the concessions it made in order to get those assets unfrozen in the first place. And of course, the reason the Trump administration pulled out of the deal was so that it could re-impose economic sanctions in hopes of weakening the Iranian regime—again a nonmilitary tool. In other words, the objection to the deal was not that sanctions don't work but that the Obama administration did not extract sufficient concessions to justify lifting those sanctions. Simply put, regardless if one believes the deal was wise or not, nonmilitary tools have dominated the US strategy toward Iran.

Thus, nonmilitary tools can play an important role in dealing with foreign countries including hostile adversaries. These tools include economics, international organizations, international law, soft power, and diplomacy. Each will be covered in turn.

## ECONOMIC STATECRAFT

Countries have used economic tools to achieve their foreign policy ends for millennia. Economic inducements and threats were used by ancient Greek city-states and were common tools of European trading empires. They remain common tools today.[15]

As the world's largest economy by nominal GDP and one that has many deeply embedded connections to other countries' economies,[16] the United States has potent economic tools at its disposal. These tools broadly fall under the categories of trade and investment, sanctions, and economic aid. Of these, foreign trade and foreign direct investment are probably the most powerful. Governments have long used trade and investment as inducements to encourage other countries to alter their foreign policies in favorable ways.[17] Strong economic ties bind the American alliance system together.[18] As countries' economies become enmeshed, political tensions become costly and maintaining the alliance grows in importance. Countries also develop a shared interest in each other's prosperity.[19] A great deal of scholarship has shown that countries with strong economic ties to each other, especially foreign direct investment, are less likely to go to war with each other or make military threats against each other.[20] This is because war severs these ties, making war less attractive. Also, free trade reduces the appeal of conquering territories as those territories' resources can be acquired far more cheaply through trade.[21] Further, regional trade organizations have been shown to promote security communities, those sets of countries discussed in chapter 2 where war between its members is unthinkable.[22]

Likewise, the promise of access to the US market can convince other countries to improve their relations with the United States. Such positive inducements often work better than threats.[23] There is no substitute for the American market in terms of the combination of size, wealth, and willingness of consumers to spend. This means countries seek to maintain good relations with the United States in order to maintain access. Of course, Americans also benefit from trade and foreign investment, so it's not as though the United States can dictate terms as others know Americans, too, desire these economic ties. Still, such inducements are powerful tools. Admittedly, given that the United States is a market economy, to a large extent these tools reside in private hands. That said, through trade agreements and by applying pressure on foreign governments to open up their economies to American investment, the government can encourage and partially direct these economic flows.

More directly manageable by the government are economic sanctions. Through sanctions, the US government can sever economic ties and pressure other countries into modifying their policies. For example, US-imposed sanctions played an important role in getting Libya to abandon its nascent nuclear program and hand over the Pan-Am 103 bombers.[24] Beyond this example, broader statistical analyses have found sanctions can be effective policy instruments.[25]

Generally, sanctions are thought of in terms of trade: banning another country's imports into the United States and also restricting American exports to that country. Economic sanctions, however, can also be the severing of financial ties. Such sanctions are often an attractive option for the United States because a great deal of international finance passes directly or indirectly through US banks, and the US dollar plays a central role in international economic exchange.[26] Thus, domestic laws that limit US banks' interactions with foreign powers have ripple effects throughout the international financial system. Also, the United States can pressure foreign banks to cut ties with America's enemies by threatening to deny banks engaged in such activities access to the US financial system. These financial levers allow the United States to pressure states by cutting off access to international capital and also have helped Washington limit the funds available to terrorist groups.[27]

Sanctions can even take noneconomic forms such as expelling foreign diplomats, pulling visas from foreign business personnel, or kicking countries out of international organizations.[28] Such noneconomic sanctions hamper other countries abilities to engage in diplomacy and economic exchange. They are often appropriate for early stages of a dispute or when Washington seeks to limit the conflict with another country while still applying some pressure. They can also be used as adjuncts to economic sanctions, much as economic sanctions themselves can be used in isolation or in conjunction with other policy tools.[29] If matters escalate, however, economic sanctions are a far more powerful tool and noneconomic sanctions are likely to play a side role.

US officials certainly recognize the power of these economic tools. Jack Lew, former Secretary of the Treasury, argued sanctions were "a new battlefield for the United States, one that enables us to go after those who would wish us harm without putting our troops in harm's way."[30] Likewise, Juan Zarate, a former senior US Treasury official, urged "the use of financial tools, pressure, and market forces to leverage the banking sector, private sector interests, and foreign partners in order to isolate rogue actors from the international financial and commercial systems and eliminate their funding sources."[31] Crucially, it is not just the belief of a few government officials that sanctions work. Large statistical studies, too, have found that sanctions achieve their ends much of the time.[32]

How well sanctions work—whether trade-based or financial—depends on several factors. First, countries with many economic ties to the United States are more vulnerable to American-imposed sanctions. This is one reason why the United States has difficulty pressuring North Korea with sanctions. Because of the closed nature of the North Korean economy, there just aren't many ties to cut. Second, if the target country expects further conflict with the United States, it may fear that concessions in the face of sanctions would result in new demands from Washington. This reduces the odds that sanctions would work.[33] Third, governments that are susceptible to public pressures or that have fragile, yet open, financial systems are more vulnerable to sanctions.[34] Fourth, sanctions are more effective when they are multilateral in nature. The more countries that cooperate in imposing sanctions, the better they work. This is why sanctions on Cuba fail—the United States is alone in the world in imposing them.[35] In contrast, the sanctions that helped bring Iran to the negotiating table were multilateral in nature.[36] Happily, American economic levers and diplomatic persuasion are often able to convince other countries to participate in US-backed sanctions meaning multilateral sanctions are an obtainable goal.[37] For example, recent sanctions on North Korea have imposed real costs on the regime because the sanctions are multilateral and include China, North Korea's closest economic partner, as a participant.[38] Last, sanctions work best when what it requested is proportional to the pain imposed by the sanctions. The pain imposed by sanctions must exceed the pain of giving into US demands for sanctions to work.[39] If too much is asked, sanctions won't work. For example, sanctions generally cannot achieve regime change—foreign governments would rather suffer economic pain than relegate themselves to the dustbin of history.

Critics of sanctions are right to point out they don't always work.[40] They are not a panacea, and their overuse can reduce the legitimacy of sanctions in general.[41] They must be part of a larger diplomatic strategy and must be well-designed to target an opponent's economic vulnerabilities.[42] Sanctions often fail because they are used when there are no other good options, and yet the government wants to signal that at least it did something. There is no easy way to bring about regime change in Cuba—force failed ignominiously at the Bay of Pigs—so sanctions get slapped on the communist regime. Likewise, the United States has imposed sanctions on North Korea in recent decades because all the other options, such as invasion, are worse. Such "we need to do something" sanctions may make Americans feel good but probably are foolish unless the main aim is to weaken an opponent's economy and military potential.[43] For example, sanctions on North Korea serve this purpose even though they are unlikely to convince the regime in Pyongyang to change its policies. Thus, they are effective in weakening the North Korean regime on the international stage, even if there are very unlikely to topple it. In practice, the sanctions on Cuba are ineffective because they ask too much (regime change) and are unilateral rather than bilateral in nature. They also harm US relations with the rest of Latin America, provide the Cuban regime with a ready-made excuse for its failed policies, and hurt US business interests. Any tool can be used wisely or foolishly. Cuban sanctions are an example of how not to use sanctions but should not be seen as an indictment against the use of sanctions in general. Fundamentally, how well sanctions work must be compared to how well other tools would work. As pointed out in the previous chapter, force often fails. Thus, the question is not "Do sanctions—or any other tool—work?" but instead is "Do sanctions work better than other tools and does their success rate justify the costs?" On this score, sanctions hold up well provided they are used in appropriate circumstances.

This means sanctions should not be imposed lightly or willy-nilly. They should be used when they have a fair chance of success. Also, economic sanctions cause real pain. They often harm the poor and individuals opposed to the targeted regime the most. True, well-designed sanctions aim to target the hostile regime and the elites that support it, but severe sanctions usually inflict harm on the broader population as well.[44] Sanctions also limit opportunities for US businesses and may encourage foreigners to avoid using American financial institutions.[45] US policy objectives have to be sufficiently important and sanctions should have a reasonable probability of success in order to justify these risks. This means they should be multilateral in nature and seek plausible, clear concessions from the targeted regime. Also, sanctions take time, meaning they should be used on issues where the United States can afford to be patient.[46] When these conditions are met, sanctions are useful policy tools and are more cost effective than the active use of force.

The last economic tool is foreign aid. This comes in two forms: economic aid and military aid. Economic aid has resulted in some of the most significant US foreign policy successes in past. The Marshall Plan—the huge US economic aid program to rebuild Western Europe after World War II—was probably the biggest US foreign policy success of the entire Cold War. It helped Western European countries avoid communist revolution. It also rebuilt their economies enabling them to make meaningful contributions to mutual defense through NATO. Last, it ensured they would be able to embrace the values of political openness, democracy, individual freedom, and market economics that have for decades tightly bound the West together.[47] In sum, the Marshall Plan resulted in the United States having as its willing allies some of the wealthiest and most powerful countries in the world, while the Soviets were stuck forcing the poorer and recalcitrant countries of East Central Europe into being their allies at gunpoint. These ultimately proved a net drain on the Soviet Union,[48] while the United States' position was greatly strengthened by its allies. In other words, the Marshall Plan was crucial to winning the Cold War.

More recently, US economic aid to Honduras has helped improve the situation in that country, though serious challenges remain. The United States sent roughly $100 million to Honduras through USAID in 2016. This aid helped build community outreach centers in Honduras for at-risk children and also supported nonprofit organizations that work to bring gangsters to justice. This aid has contributed to the reduction of violence in Honduras—it no longer has the highest murder rate in the world. The hope is that these programs will not only improve the lives of ordinary Hondurans but also reduce the number of unaccompanied minors coming to the United States from Honduras and break the power of gangs, like MS-13, which operate throughout much of Central America and in the United States as well.[49]

Thus, this money is not simply charity to Honduras but has real benefits for the United States. Given that a dollar goes further in Honduras than here in the United States, it is more cost effective to deal with the challenges of Honduran violence at the source of the problem rather than after gang members and fleeing children reach US borders.

Thus, successful economic aid has many potential benefits for the United States. Aid has been shown to contribute to countries' economic growth and economic development.[50] Promoting such growth abroad may open up new markets to American firms, leading to increased US economic growth. Further, such aid-fueled growth abroad helps stabilize countries politically, much as the Marshall Plan did for Europe, in turn reducing the incidence of political violence emanating from those countries.[51] Such economic growth and political stability also lowers the odds that people are forced to flee to the United States. Aid also helps combat and even eliminate diseases—reducing the chance those diseases will spread around the world. Last, smartly designed aid helps promote sound, environmentally sustainable development; address existing problems of environmental degradation; and even help fight climate change.[52]

Despite these potential benefits, this tool has barely been used in recent years. Total foreign aid composes about 1 percent of the federal budget with economic and development aid representing about six-tenths to two-thirds of that amount.[53] The United States also is well below the United Nations' goals for development aid and the average actually given by developed countries. The UN's goal is for countries to give 0.7 percent of their GDP to other countries as development aid, but the United States currently gives between 0.15 percent and 0.18 percent of its GDP out as development aid.[54] This is roughly half of what developed states give on average (0.3 percent GDP). Further, the United States used to give far more development aid. During the Marshall Plan, Washington spent 1 percent of GDP on development aid. This fell to 0.6 percent in the 1950s and 1960s and then to 0.2 percent to 0.3 percent during the 1980s.[55] In other words, the United States can significantly increase aid if it so chooses. Yet, President Trump and his allies in Congress have considered cutting US foreign aid still further.[56] The Trump administration has halted $450 million in aid to Guatemala, Honduras, and El Salvador aimed at curbing violence and corruption as well as improving local economic and agricultural conditions.[57] In other words, the cuts would end programs designed to reduce pressures that push Central Americans to flee their countries for the United States.

A partial shift in this thinking on aid, however, has recently occurred. The Trump administration and Congressional Republicans, led by Representative Ted Yoho, have embraced foreign aid as a tool to counteract growing Chinese influence. The idea is to use a new agency, the United States International Development Finance Corporation, to deliver $60 billion in loans to developing countries to directly compete with Beijing's aid programs and offset growing Chinese influence.[58] Thus, even leaders not initially favorably disposed to foreign aid are able to see its uses upon closer examination.

While the United States has turned away from economic tools of statecraft, other powerful countries have embraced them. The so-called BRICS (Brazil, Russia, India, China, and South Africa) have worked hard to increase their global influence through economic statecraft. They have set up alternative global and regional investment banks in hopes of rivalling those led by the West. In conjunction with this, Beijing has adopted a strategy of steering Chinese foreign direct investment to Africa in hopes of gaining influence in that region.[59] Likewise, while the United States has pulled out of the Comprehensive and Progressive Trans-Pacific Partnership, which was designed to tie Pacific Rim countries together and give them an alternative to being drawn more closely into China's economic orbit, China is investing vast sums of money into its "One Belt, One Road" initiative. China hopes to generate closer economic ties between China, Southeast Asia, and Central Asia through transportation infrastructure investments through this initiative.[60] Nor is Chinese investment limited to the "One Belt, One Road" initiative. The Chinese have invested significant sums of money throughout the developing world, creating both political and economic ties.[61] Thus, by not leveraging its economic might, the United States is ceding influence to other countries.

Further, roughly one-quarter of US economic and development aid goes to immediate disaster relief—something that, while useful and necessary, is unlikely to achieve long-term American goals or lead to long-term improvements in standards of living.[62] While disaster relief is important, the US focus on it helps reinforce the notion that American aid never fixes anything but rather is long-term charity for foreigners. That said, even short term humanitarian aid has benefits beyond relieving immediate suffering. Such aid has been shown to improve the United States' image in countries that receive American assistance. This is true both for countries where the United States generally has a positive image and those where historically the United States has been less popular. The number of Japanese holding favorable views of the United States increased from 66 percent to 85 percent after the United

States sent tsunami relief aid to Japan in 2011. Likewise in Indonesia, US humanitarian aid after the catastrophic 2004 tsunami improved favorable views of the United States from 15 percent to 35 percent and in the hardest hit region of Banda Aceh, 78 percent of respondents held favorable views of the United States after aid was delivered.[63] Most incredibly, US aid to Pakistan after the 2005 earthquake not only doubled the number of Pakistanis reporting they held favorable views of the United States (from 23 percent to 48 percent) but also actually reduced Pakistanis' support for al Qaeda. The number of Pakistanis disapproving of Osama bin Laden rose from 23 percent to 41 percent.[64] Of course, these effects are not permanent, and views of the United States in these countries respond to other events such as presidential elections and US military actions. (Indonesians' views of the United States in 2004 were especially low as a result of the 2003 invasion of Iraq. Historically, Indonesians hold reasonably favorable views of the United States).[65] Still, aid can help to improve US relations with a wide variety of countries.

Economic aid, of course, does not always work. Sometimes development projects are badly designed, and other times money gets siphoned off by corrupt officials. Also, American aid often ends up as profit for US contractors. In Iraq, 40 percent of the budget for civilian projects ended up as contractor profit.[66] While the private sector naturally won't participate in such projects without making a profit, this ratio of profit to aid is grossly inefficient. These are arguments for smarter aid, rather than arguments against using aid at all. The key is designing the best possible programs to reduce corruption and increase effectiveness.

In recent years, steps have been taken to move in this direction. For example, the Millennium Challenge Corporation, created by the Bush administration, requires countries to meet certain requirements for effectiveness and to reduce corruption before receiving US government aid through the Corporation.[67] Likewise, the US government has also worked to improve its own efficiency in delivering aid. The Global Food Security Act shifted the delivery of food aid from the Department of Agriculture to USAID because over many decades, USAID proved to be far more efficient. Similarly, a bipartisan bill, the Food for Peace Modernization Act, was introduced in the 115th Congress but failed to become law. It would have ended the requirements that food aid be purchased in the United States and shipped in American flagged vessels—both moves that would lower costs.[68]

In truth, the worst examples of corruption have often happened in times and places where Washington's main aim was buying a country's support for

US policy objectives. For instance, during the Cold War, the US government knew that the President of Zaire, Mobutu Sese Soko, was using American aid to line his own pockets and those of his supporters. Washington did not care. The idea was simply to prop up his regime and keep him aligned with the West during the Cold War.[69] That sort of corruption is easy to halt: simply stop sending economic aid that is designed to prop up corrupt regimes.

While perhaps not as natural for a dovish foreign policy as economic aid, military aid can also play an important role. Sending military aid can strengthen US allies, reducing the odds they will be attacked. This lowers the likelihood that the United States would be drawn into wars to defend them. Military aid can also serve as an inducement to other countries. The promise of US military aid to both Israel and Egypt was an important sweetener in convincing those countries to sign the Camp David Accords,[70] an agreement that has brought about lasting peace, if not friendship, between those two countries. Last, it is difficult and expensive to switch military suppliers,[71] so states that depend on US military aid would have a hard time turning to another supplier. This means that such aid may bind those countries to the United States and dissuade them from taking actions Washington finds objectionable.[72] Of course, as with economic aid, military aid can be used foolishly. For instance, in the past, aid was sent to rebel groups that engaged in brutal human rights violations and later turned on the United States. Again, the key is to use such aid wisely. Given sufficient care, military aid, like economic aid, can play a useful role and serve as a substitute for the active use of force.

## INTERNATIONAL INSTITUTIONS

International institutions are another effective nonmilitary tool. These institutions have countries as their members and come in a wide variety of forms. Some, such as the United Nations, are global in nature. Others, like the Organization of American States (OAS) are regional. Likewise, some, such as the aforementioned UN and OAS deal with a wide range of issues, while others such as the World Health Organization or World Trade Organization are issue-specific. (Alliances, especially highly institutionalized alliances like NATO, can also be seen as institutions).[73] Many of these institutions were created at the United States' behest or under significant American influence. This has resulted in the United States holding important leadership posts in many of these organizations.[74] For instance, the United States holds a permanent seat on the UN Security Council and possesses a veto in that body. Institutional rules also often reflect American preferences. One example of this is that the International Monetary Fund cannot make significant changes to its rules without 85 percent of the votes being in favor.[75] Votes are allocated by monetary contributions, which very roughly reflect the size of a country's economy. The United States has 16 percent of the votes, meaning Washington can veto any major changes to the organization.[76] Such favorable rules and positions of influence mean that these institutions should be especially useful for the United States.

Given that institutions are not free—though compared to militaries, they are quite cheap—the fact that countries are willing to fund them means countries believe institutions are effective policy instruments.[77] Another indication of institutions' usefulness is that countries that are members in a great many of the same institutions are less likely to go to war with each other, likely in part because of the effectiveness of those institutions in resolving disputes.[78] This is most clearly true for highly developed institutions with security mandates.[79] Specifically, international institutions can provide a number of useful functions. Institutions can solve collective action problems; prevent free-riding; mediate disputes; and help to create a stable, predictable international environment, which in turn lowers the costs of American leadership.[80] They can provide information to countries about the benefits and distribution of gains from agreements. Coming from a neutral party, this sort of information allays concerns about how benefits are shared, making agreements easier to reach. Institutions also create linkages between issues allowing for concessions on one issue to be offset by another country's concession on a different issue.[81] Likewise, they lend legitimacy to actions that otherwise would appear to be naked exercises of power. Such legitimization of power lowers the costs of getting others to comply with those actions.[82] Organizations can also mobilize private actors to pressure governments. For instance, the Financial Action Task Force has been able to leverage the international banking community to pressure countries into passing stronger laws to hinder the financing of terrorist groups.[83]

Another important function of international institutions is monitoring agreements to prevent cheating.[84] For example, one reason the agreement with Iran on its nuclear enrichment program was possible at all is that the International Atomic Energy Agency (IAEA) regularly monitors Iranian facilities to ensure Iran is fulfilling its end of the bargain.[85] The IAEA is an agency that both sides can trust. As an independent agency, it is above pressure to manipulate its findings. It reports what it finds honestly and won't engage in spying while going through Iranian facilities. It also has the technical expertise to do the job. It's impossible to imagine any Iranian inspections regime—even a more stringent one as preferred by the Trump administration—being agreed to by both sides without the IAEA playing a leading role. Further, monitoring can even play a role in bringing about multilateral actions in the first place. Sticking with the IAEA, the Bush administration skillfully used IAEA reports on Iran's program to build support for a multilateral sanctions regime against Iran[86]—support the Obama administration was able to capitalize on. The reason the IAEA reports were so crucial to building a multilateral sanctions regime targeting Iran is that other countries knew the reports were unbiased and truly showed that Iran was pursuing a nuclear weapon. Such reports from neutral agencies are crucial as American intelligence reports—no matter how accurate and truthful—might be discounted by other countries, especially countries that are not US allies.

A further example of institutional monitoring is peacekeeping. Research has shown that the deployment of peacekeepers to monitor cease-fires significantly lowers the odds that fighting resumes.[87] In certain instances, institutions can even act as guarantors to an agreement, thereby allowing countries to credibly commit to honor the agreement.[88] The key is that the United States should focus on traditional peacekeeping, which reduces the incidence of war, rather than military interventions, which reside under the name of "peacemaking," and are in fact simply acts of war endorsed by the United Nations or regional security institutions.[89]

Last, international institutions can help to lower transaction costs by providing forums for multilateral negotiations to take place. Transaction costs are essentially the costs of doing business. Examples of transaction costs in everyday life are the cost of a stamp to mail an electric bill; fees charged by realtors, inspectors, banks, and lawyers when buying a house; or the amount of gasoline burned and time lost when driving to buy used furniture in a neighboring county. In other words, they are not the cost of the electricity, house, or furniture itself but the additional costs you must pay to acquire those things. Multilateral negotiations involving dozens of countries would be incredibly time consuming if they were not conducted through international institutions. Agreements would have to be renegotiated bilaterally time and time again. In all likelihood, conditions would change before agreement was ever reached. Just as you wouldn't drive half-way across the country to buy a kitchen table no matter how low the price, at some point, the costs of negotiating an agreement become so high as to scuttle the negotiations. Thus, by lowering transaction costs, institutions widen the range of potential agreements.[90]

Taken together, these features make institutions a powerful tool for reaching and enforcing international agreements. Institutions created since 1945 have played key roles in shaping the existing Western-led international security, legal, and economic orders. The institutions help bind the West and Japan together and lower enforcement costs. They also help lock in American preferences, making US power less threatening to its allies.[91] True, these institutions constrain the United States to some extent short-term, but an unconstrained United States can appear imperial and threatening even to its friends.[92] Further, to the extent these constraints limit American uses of force, they may well benefit the United States and protect it from its own mistakes. Last, these constraints affect not only the United States but all other countries as well. Given that the international order to a large extent reflects US preferences and interests, constraining countries' actions brings long-term benefits to the United States even if specific constraints impose short-term costs.[93] Best of all, though such institutions are not free, they are remarkably affordable. For instance, the United States' share of the UN budget comes out to $1.80 per American per year.[94] One would be hard pressed to get a hot dog from a street vendor so cheaply. Thus, Washington can afford to invest in international institutions.

This is not to say that institutions are the solution to every problem. They are not. Like all tools, they have limitations. They work best when countries have some overlapping interests and a desire to cooperate. Even so, international institutions are a potent tool that the US government would be wise to embrace.

## INTERNATIONAL LAW

International law is another foreign policy tool available to the United States. Much as with international institutions, a great deal of existing international law reflects American values and preferences because it was created during the post-World War II era of US preeminence. International law has proven effective on a wide range of issues including improving and regularizing the treatment of prisoners of war,[95] peacefully resolving international border disputes,[96] preventing the recurrence of conflict,[97] dealing with international pirates,[98] and regulating economic activities at sea.[99] It can help countries coordinate their actions; regulate complex international interactions such as trade, investment, and the movement of people; and help countries reach agreement on contentious issues. Law clarifies what counts as a violation of an agreement and legitimizes retaliatory measures in response to those violations. This helps avoid escalatory spirals of reprisals.[100] It also often creates monitoring mechanisms so that violations can be detected even in situations where monitoring by other countries would be extremely difficult, such as the treatment of prisoners of war.[101] Acting in accordance with international law helps legitimize a country's actions and also aids in persuading other countries to accept those actions.[102] Finally, law allows countries to signal they are committed to a course of action as rhetoric without action can be dismissed as cheap talk.[103]

International law, much like domestic law, is an efficient, low cost means of resolving disputes in comparison to alternatives such as violent conflict or the breakdown of a mutually beneficial arrangement. Disputes are often resolved through nonjudicial means, such as negotiation or mediation, though when those methods fail, international courts can be asked to issue binding rulings. Thus, law often serves to guide negotiations and acts as a basis for reaching mutually agreed upon solutions to disagreements.[104]

Though many impugn the effectiveness of international law, countries usually follow international law and abide by rulings of international courts even when those rulings go against them.[105] While states are more likely to violate international law over issues of international security, studies have shown international law to be effective even in such tense situations.[106] Countries' adherence to international law often surprises people as there is no international equivalent to a police department to enforce these laws. Yet, countries would have little incentive to create international laws if they had no intention of following them and did not expect other countries comply. So how does international law work given the lack of international police?

Countries comply with international law for a number of reasons. First, international law is based on reciprocity.[107] Reciprocity is the notion that one side will return a good for a good or an ill for an ill. Two well-known statements of reciprocity are the notion of "an eye for eye, a tooth for a tooth" from the *Code of Hammurabi* and the *Old Testament*[108] and "if you scratch my back, I'll scratch yours." Both are examples of symmetrical reciprocity, with the former being an ill for an ill and the latter a good for a good.

Yet, reciprocity need not be symmetrical. Buying pizza and beer for a friend that helped you move would also be an example of reciprocity. Though the goods are quite different from each other, it is still a good for a good. Likewise, reciprocity may be quite general rather than the specific and explicit trade-offs mentioned above. Many friendships are buttressed by notions of general reciprocity in which a person will do a favor for a friend without any expectation of immediately receiving a return favor, knowing full well that the friend will help them out at some unspecified point in the future.

International law works in much the same way with countries following the law out of expectations of both specific and general reciprocity. In other words, countries comply with international law so that others will as well. If a country followed the law only when it benefitted from it or when courts ruled in its favor, then no other country would ever follow the law to its detriment when it favored the first country. Thus, countries comply with unfavorable international law so that they can use international law that benefits them in the future. To do otherwise would threaten to unravel an overarching beneficial set of agreements.[109] On the whole, countries realize they benefit from the use of law and are willing to pay some short-term costs to reap greater long-term benefits.

For instance, during the Bush administration the World Trade Organization found that the United States had violated international trade law by raising tariffs on foreign steel.[110] The United States complied with the ruling not only to avoid potential countervailing tariffs being imposed by the European Union but also because the United States benefits from international trade law. If the United States had ducked its legal obligations in this instance, others might have done the same in the future. Therefore, the United States complied because it benefits from the overarching legal structure that regulates international trade and wanted to maintain it. The long-term benefits outweighed the short-term costs.

Second, countries comply with international law because they care about their reputations and how others perceive them.[111] Violating international law hurts countries' reputations, making those illegal actions more costly and difficult to undertake.[112] A nice example of this is that countries that regularly interact with democracies are more likely to comply with international laws that prohibit the deliberate targeting of noncombatants during wars. They do this out of fears that democracies will punish them if they do not comply.[113] In other words, non-compliance would have real international costs.

Third, international institutions and domestic courts often play a role in enforcement.[114] International institutions can coordinate and legitimize countries' efforts to punish scofflaws. More importantly, in many countries, international law becomes part of domestic law. This allows domestic courts to rule on if their government is in violation and compel compliance. In the United States, per the Supremacy Clause of the US Constitution, this is true of international agreements ratified as treaties by the Senate, though is not true of other international agreements.[115] Even in countries where international law does not automatically become part of domestic law, legislation may incorporate some elements of international law into domestic law. International laws may also delegate enforcement and monitoring to domestic bodies. Taken together, this means enforcement of international law in many countries is often done domestically, and therefore, does not rely on the actions of other countries or international bodies. Further, when such domestic enforcement is combined with the incentives of reciprocity, cost-avoidance, and reputation covered above, international law is usually followed even though there are no international police to enforce it.

Despite international law's potential, the United States has turned away from it in recent years. Yes, the United States has generally continued to honor its existing legal obligations. What has changed is the United States no longer embraces new law. During much of the twentieth century, the United States was a leader in the crafting and adoption of new international laws to advance human rights, economic cooperation, and international security. Since the end of the Cold War, however, this has changed. The US Senate has become skeptical of new international legal commitments and has refused to ratify treaties that most other countries have ratified. Most clearly, the Senate has not ratified *any* United Nations treaties since 1993 and has been loath to ratify broad-based multilateral treaties in general.[116] For example, the United States has remained aloof from the International Criminal Court; the Ottawa Treaty, which bans the use of anti-personnel landmines; the Paris Climate Change Accord (the United States has announced it will withdraw from the accord in November 2020); the Convention on Biodiversity; and the Convention on the Rights of the Child. The United States is the only country in the world that is not party to the last three agreements and is frequently one of five or fewer countries that has not ratified treaties that the rest of the world has adopted.[117]

This reluctance to embrace new international law hinders the United States' ability to cooperate with other countries to curtail human rights violations, address environmental and economic challenges, deal with international criminals, and address weapons proliferation. While law is not necessary for such cooperation, it helps sustain and legitimize it. Without law, cooperation relies on ad hoc efforts with countries coordinating only when it suits their narrow, immediate interests. This means countries would not work with the United States if they have interests contrary to American interests in a given instance even if they agree with the United States on the general principal. Yet, if countries had signed an international legal agreement with the United States based on their agreement with the basic underlying principals, they would be compelled to follow that law even in instances contrary to their immediate interests. And they would do so because they would be confident others would follow the law in the future. Thus, sustained, broad-based efforts are more effective and are far easier to bring about through the use of law and institutions than without them.

It also reduces the United States' ability to shape new law. International law will continue to evolve regardless of American participation, yet these laws would reflect US interests and preferences only if the United States participates in the crafting of that new law. As a leading power, the United States would have significant influence over the content of any new laws[118]— provided the United States participates in the negotiations of and ratifies those laws. Further, when laws such as the International Criminal Court create new international courts, the judges that serve on those courts come from countries that have ratified the relevant agreement. As those judges' rulings shape how those laws are interpreted and enforced in the future,[119] by refusing to participate, the United States loses another avenue for shaping international law.

An example of the United States being hurt by not embracing new international law is the United Nations Convention on the Law of the Sea (UNCLOS). The United States played a key role in negotiating UNCLOS and the treaty embodies many long-cherished American principles such as Freedom of the Seas, which allows for unfettered navigation of international waters and generally free navigation even in countries' territorial waters.[120] The US Senate refused to ratify UNCLOS out of sovereignty concerns, but the United States has scrupulously observed the Convention despite this.[121] Yet by not joining the Convention, Washington cannot make appeals to its provisions when US interests or those of its allies are harmed by other countries.

Where this really hurts is in the South China Sea. Chinese attempts to establish a territorial claim over most of that body of water are based on debatable historical claims to a large number of reefs and other minor out-croppings. The Convention makes it clear that countries cannot use rocks, features that are submerged at high tide, or man-made islands to make terri-torial claims—the exact sort of features China bases its position on.[122] Yet, this is of no avail to the United States because it is not a party to the Conven-tion. In other words, by abstaining from joining the Convention, the United States has lost a means to pressure China.[123]

Similarly, in 1856, the United States declined to join the Paris Declara-tion, negotiated by the major European powers, which banned privateering. (Privateering is the practice of using private vessels to prey upon an enemy's sea-going commerce during a war. It is essentially legalized piracy. Privateers are distinct from government-owned naval vessels, such as the CSS Alabama, engaged in commerce raiding). The United States abstained from joining the treaty—one of only three maritime powers to not join—because it had used privateers in past wars, most notably in both the Quasi War and the War of 1812. When the American Civil War broke out, the Confederacy employed privateers against Union shipping. These Confederate privateers often took refuge in neutral ports to escape the US Navy, reprovision, and sell their prizes—something the United States was powerless to protest because it had never joined the anti-privateering treaty. This allowed Confederate priva-teers to have considerable success during the first year of the war. Ultimately, American acceptance of the principles of the treaty, which resulted in Euro-pean enforcement of its terms, contributed far more to the demise of Con-federate privateers than did the actions of the US Navy.[124]

None of this is to suggest that international law will always be useful or that violations will never occur. Domestic laws are also violated at times, but no one would argue this means domestic laws are useless. Naturally, there are limits to the uses of law—just as with any tool. Yet, international law is often an effective, low-cost way to achieve a country's aims. Given American diplo-matic clout, international laws are especially likely to reflect US interests and serve America well. The United States would be wise to embrace this tool.

## SOFT POWER

Another nonmilitary tool is soft power. "Soft power is the ability to affect others to obtain the outcomes one wants through attraction rather than coercion or payment."[125] In other words, it is the ability to draw others to you, get them to emulate you, and adopt your preferences simply because they find you appealing. It is a nonmaterial form of attractive power and, thus, is distinct from economic or institutional inducements. For countries, soft power emanates from their values, policies, successes, and broader culture.[126] Given the ideals of democracy and freedom that have historically been advanced by the US government, the openness and economic prosperity that have usually characterized American society, the country's excellent colleges and universities that attract foreign students and potentially inculcate them with American values,[127] and the global appeal of the American entertainment industry and other American cultural exports, the United States has a significant ability to attract others through the use of soft power.

Americans have long recognized the potential of soft power. In the 1920s, Charles Evan Hughes, US Secretary of State under Presidents Harding and Coolidge, argued that American domestic successes gave it "moral power" on the world stage and increased the odds others would support US policies.[128] More remembered perhaps is that in 1630, nearly a century and a half before the United States won its independence, John Winthrop, the future governor of the Massachusetts Bay Colony, told a group of immigrants he was leading that "wee must consider that wee shall be as a citty upon a hill, the eies of all people are uppon us" [sic].[129] Presidents Kennedy, Reagan, and Obama all later invoked this phrase in stating their beliefs that the world was watching the United States' actions and would judge America by its behavior and by its successes and failures.[130] President Jefferson, too, expressed similar sentiments about American democracy. All of these leaders believed that American successes and values would lead other countries to emulate the United States and draw them to America's side. While these efforts to act in ways others would want to emulate are not foreign policies strictly speaking and instead are more about good governance at home, US leaders recognized such actions would redound to our credit in the international arena as well as at home.

Soft power can be a significant advantage in foreign policy.[131] If publics around the world are favorably disposed toward the United States, this makes it easier for countries' leaders to work with the United States and support American foreign policies.[132] It can even lead publics to pressure leaders who might not otherwise be favorably disposed toward the United States to work with Washington or at least not actively oppose American initiatives. Nor is it only doves that recognize the importance of soft power. Even contemporary hawks such as Eliot Cohen, who served in the Bush administration, argue that American culture helps turn other countries into friends of the United States.[133]

Other countries understand the value of soft power. The Saudis actively promote Wahhabism, their version of Sunni Islam, throughout the Muslim world.[134] The Chinese tout their economic achievements, and the French have always worked to promote their culture abroad.[135] These countries understand that their ideals, domestic triumphs, and cultures are sources of influence on the international stage. The United States would be foolish to ignore a policy tool that others recognize is of great value.

Yet, the US government has invested little in promoting soft power in recent years. Former Secretary of Defense Robert Gates has called for an increase in funding for State Department programs aimed at enhancing American soft power and promoting the United States abroad. He has bemoaned how few resources are devoted to "America's ability to engage, assist, and communicate with other parts of the world—the 'soft power,' which had been so important throughout the Cold War."[136] An example of this tight-fisted approach to soft power is that the US government refused to pay for plane tickets for US economic delegations to go to the Middle East and promote American business methods, despite verbally encouraging members of the US business community to engage in these very actions.[137] Likewise, spending on cultural exchanges has fallen and the reach of US government media outlets such as the *Voice of America* have declined significantly from their Cold War peaks.[138] Finally, the number of foreign students studying in US universities fell 17 percent from 2016 to 2017, mostly because of a drop in the number of visas the US government issued to Chinese and Indian students, though also because other countries have begun to recruit foreign students more actively.[139]

Of course, not all elements of American culture will be appealing in other countries. While many may be drawn to American movies, others may be put off by their violence and nudity.[140] Further, many countries now enjoy the same liberties and economic prosperity that Americans do, and American domestic life is not without its challenges and ugly problems. As is to be expected of any human endeavor, the United States as a nation is not perfect. Likewise, American actions, such as torture and the abandonment of the Paris Climate Accord, undermine other countries' beliefs that Americans share their values and are able to engage in moral leadership.[141] The same is true when the United States enacts new tariffs that violate trade agreements as this behavior indicates the United States is unwilling to play by its own rules. Such actions open the door for countries like China to assume the mantle of global leadership on these issues.[142] In other words, a negative form of soft power is conceivable where actions and values repel rather than attract. This means that benefiting from soft power requires Washington to avoid taking actions that undermine America's moral standing and work toward solving US domestic problems. Obviously, in a free society, things will arise in the broader culture that many regret and that offend others. That is unavoidable. Still on balance, the United States' free society, values, prosperity, and democratic system of government draw others toward it. The sheer number of people that seek to immigrate to the United States is proof enough of this. Such soft power is an important element in American leadership and the success of US foreign policy.

That said, there are important limits to soft power. It is not controllable like economic and military tools as it is a byproduct of actions, not a direct product.[143] Unlike material power, it cannot be used in quid pro quo exchanges. Much of it is generated by the actions of private individuals— both attractive elements and unattractive ones. Of course, active public diplomacy can call the world's attention to American values and focus attention on the attractive elements of American culture by communicating directly with other peoples, not just with other governments.[144] Washington can also ease cultural and educational exchanges and ensure that its policies align with American values. By exploiting the United States' vast potential soft power, the US government can make others more willing to cooperate with American diplomatic efforts. Such soft power can make it easier for the United States to assume places of leadership in international organizations and direct the creation of new international law. Thus, soft power makes the exercise of hard power easier.

## DIPLOMACY

Diplomacy is a crucial foreign policy tool. As Winston Churchill put it, "The reason for having diplomatic relations is not to confer a compliment, but to secure a convenience."[145] In other words, diplomacy exists not to be polite but rather is a powerful tool for attaining foreign policy goals. Without it, no other tools work. Diplomacy is necessary to coordinate various foreign policy efforts and align them with those of US allies. Also, along with other more clandestine means of gathering intelligence, it's vital for determining the intentions and aims of other countries. In this broad sense, diplomacy is crucial no matter how warlike or peaceful one's foreign policy is. While that is important for anyone interested in foreign relations to remember and has been the focus of many classic works,[146] it doesn't have much to do with arguing how the United States can achieve its aims peacefully. Rather, the question is how and when can diplomacy be used as a substitute for force?

Often it is possible to find mutually acceptable solutions. This is especially true when dealing with friendly, or at least neutral, states but is possible even during confrontations with hostile foreign powers. The costs of failing to reach a compromise are often high—even without threats of force or sanctions. Thus, countries have strong incentives to find ways to craft mutually acceptable agreements. Where diplomacy comes in is that these agreements are often not obvious. Creativity and a deep knowledge of other countries' goals and limitations are vital.

Further, diplomacy is vital to persuade other countries to work with the United States and grant it concessions. As anyone in business, law, politics, or numerous other fields knows well, much of getting things done is convincing others that what you are suggesting would benefit them. Getting others to work with you because they believe your preferred policies are wise is far cheaper and easier than making them comply through the use of threats or bribing them with inducements. Obviously, verbal persuasion often is coupled with threats and promises, but it is a tool in and of itself.

Last, research has shown that diplomatic threats are effective at deterring other countries from attacking one's interests.[147] This is because bluffing is costly. Being caught in a bluff gives a country a reputation for lying, making future statements less credible. As both poker players and the boy who cried wolf know, having a reputation for bluffing has real costs as true statements will be ignored at a later date. Because of these reputational costs, verbal threats are able to convey intentions and thus carry weight.

Yet, resources have not been directed to the State Department in recent years.[148] The United States currently employs only 12,000 Foreign Service Officers while over 23,000 employees work in the Pentagon alone.[149] (The Defense Department has 1.3 million active duty personnel, 826,000 reservists, and 742,000 civilian employees, making it the largest single employer in the country).[150] This has resulted in the State Department struggling to fully staff its embassies. This long-term trend has been exacerbated since 2017 by the Trump administration's plan to reduce the overall diplomatic staff by 2,000 people and shift funding away from the State Department and to the

Defense Department.[151] It has also allowed senior vacancies to linger longer than usual.[152] A 2019 inspector general report found that the State Department's hiring freeze, which lasted from January 2017 until May 2018, significantly hurt the Department's ability to carry out its work. Specifically, the report found that a wide range of initiatives were harmed, including ones focused on counterterrorism, counternarcotics, diplomatic security, cybersecurity, global health, humanitarian relief, consular activities, and even departmental financial oversight.[153]

This personnel and budgetary stagnation, as compared to the substantial growth of the defense budget since 9/11, is commonplace across civilian agencies involved in US foreign policy.[154] Civilian pay, too, is generally lower than military pay given comparable levels of experience.[155] Commensurate with these budget cuts and low staffing levels, the United States' UN delegation has been halved, resulting in scores of meetings traditionally led by American diplomats during the UN General Assembly's annual session not occurring. Talks during the 2017 session with important countries like China, Brazil, Argentina, and Nigeria were all cancelled.[156] Likewise, US diplomats took a back seat in influencing what form the new regime in Sudan would take after Omar al-Bashir's April 2019 overthrow. While diplomats from the African Union, European Union, and Gulf monarchies all played active roles in the formation of the new government, US diplomats largely remained silent on the matter.[157] Likewise, the State Department has drastically curtailed its interaction with the media and public.[158] It's hard to influence the course of international diplomacy without actually being in the room or getting your message out. Decisions are still made, of course, just with no or limited American input.

While the Trump administration may be accelerating the trend of reducing the influence of the State Department, it is not new. Funding cuts to the State Department and understaffing began in the 1990s, and a greater share of the remaining budget has been shifted to embassy security and away from diplomacy.[159] By the Obama administration, this reached a point where there were more individuals in US military bands than professional American diplomats.[160] Similarly, while in the early days of the Cold War, the State Department had—including the Marshall Plan, which it oversaw—a budget about half the size of the Defense Department;[161] its budget is now less than one-tenth the size of the Defense Department—including foreign aid it oversees through USAID.[162] This longer term trend resulted in Robert Gates, Secretary of Defense under both Presidents Bush and Obama, suggesting it would be wise to reallocate some of his department's budget to the State Department.[163] Likewise in 2013, General James Mattis, then in charge of US military forces in the Middle East, told Congress,

> If you don't fund the State Department fully, then I need to buy more ammunition ultimately . . . I think it is a cost-benefit ratio. The more that we put into the State Department's diplomacy, hopefully, the less we have to put into a military budget.[164]

It's almost unheard of for bureaucracies to argue that their budgets should be reduced for the benefit of another department. Its occurrence starkly underlines the severity of the imbalance between diplomatic and military tools. Unsurprisingly, Republican and Democratic senators, as well as former senior staffers from the Obama, Bush, and Clinton administrations, have warned that hollowing out the country's diplomatic corps is harming American interests.[165] These concerns have been echoed by former Secretaries of State Schultz, Albright, Powell, Rice, Clinton, and Kerry.[166] Thus, the United States is underinvesting in diplomacy relative to force, meaning it is missing opportunities to influence international relations and advance its interests.

Taken together, these nonmilitary tools offer real and important ways to advance US interests around the world. A combination of rhetorical persuasion and economic inducements can go a long way toward achieving US goals, especially among America's friends and in the economic realm. Other countries use these tools, and the United States would be foolish to continue to deemphasize them. They work, are cost effective, and avoid needless killing. While these tools are especially appealing for doves, even a more hawkish foreign policy would benefit from them. Thus, doves are optimistic that nonmilitary tools work.

## THE LIMITS OF OPTIMISM

Naturally, there are limits to this optimism. No country, not even the United States, will always get what it wants in foreign affairs. Much as in the rest of life, perfection is unattainable. There will always be frustrations and failures. At times, the key to a good foreign policy is to select the least bad option. The goal is to maximize successes and to limit costs, not to achieve paradise on earth.

This means that the various tools mentioned above will, at times, fail. But they need not always work to be useful tools. They simply need to work well much of the time. Even were they not more effective than force, their costs, both when these tools work and when they fail, are so much lower as to make the net benefit they bring much higher than that of force. In other words, the question is not do these tools always work, but rather do they work better than force and are they more efficient given their much lower costs.

There will always be countries and international terrorist groups that threaten the United States. No US foreign policy can ever be so benign and unobjectionable that the United States would have no enemies. Threats will exist regardless of what policies are adopted. To think otherwise is to assume that everything that happens in the world is a reflection of American actions. To believe that the United States can eliminate evil through its own good behavior would be an act of extreme hubris and would be the mirror image of hawks' overoptimism when it comes to the use of force. Not everything is about the United States, and therefore, not all threats to the United States and its friends are a result of American policies. Countries always have divergent interests and the possibility of war remains.

Still, as has been shown, the best way to deal with the vast majority of foreign policy challenges that the United States faces is usually through a mix of nonmilitary tools. Active force is rarely the answer. The next chapter will show how this is true even when confronting hostile foreign countries and international terrorist groups. In particular, even when confronting military threats, deterrence—a passive use of force—is more effective than active uses of force such as waging preventive wars.

# CHAPTER 5

## Competing Strategies for Confronting Adversaries

Military glory—that attractive rainbow that rises in showers of blood.
ABRAHAM LINCOLN[1]

Foreign policies must be nonutopian. They must consider, anticipate, and react to the actions of other countries. Any foreign policy that does not do this—whether peaceful or war-prone, internationalist or isolationist—would flounder. For doves, the danger is dreaming of a world filled only with other peaceful or friendly states or believing that threats arise only in response to American uses of force. Yet, there clearly are countries that intend to harm the United States or US allies.[2] North Korea, for example, isn't simply misunderstood. It is hostile and dangerous. Yes, the North Korean leadership is scared of the United States, and this fear can help to explain some North Korean actions. But even if North Korea did not fear the United States, it would want to destroy South Korea. Pyongyang's malign intentions exist independently of any fear they have of the United States and its allies. Similarly, World War II didn't occur because Germany and Japan were afraid they were going to be attacked by other states.[3] Berlin and Tokyo had malign intent and started wars out of a desire to annex their neighbors' territories. Because of this, any foreign policy—including peaceful ones— must be prepared to face and confront hostile military threats. In other words, a dovish foreign policy cannot assume that if the United States plays nice with others they will play nice in return.

Likewise, no foreign policy, no matter how clever, can solve all of the problems posed by the world. Imagining that Washington can totally eliminate all dangers the United States faces is just as unrealistic as believing there are no dangers in the first place. It is equally impossible to impose one's will on the world as it is to escape from it. Rather, a good foreign policy must advance US interests and values at a reasonable cost while also recognizing the limits of what the United States can achieve. In other words, foreign policies must take the world as it is: an often dangerous place, filled with hostile countries and international terrorist groups that may want to harm the United States or its allies and also recognize the limits of what the United States can do in response to those threats.

Hawks and doves have responded to threats posed by hostile countries and international terrorist groups in very different ways. In confronting hostile countries, hawks have advocated preventive wars and the use of force to bring about regime change. Doves on the other hand have emphasized deterrence to protect the United States and its allies from foreign military threats. Likewise, in confronting international terrorism, hawks have emphasized military responses, while doves have focused on the use of intelligence gathering and law enforcement.[4] As will be seen below, beginning with preventive war, dovish solutions have worked far better than hawkish ones.

## PROBLEMS OF PREVENTIVE WAR

Hawks have strongly advocated the use of preventive war to remove foreign military threats faced by the United States. Preventive war is the idea that using force today would solve or avoid problems down the road. It also hinges on beliefs that deterrence is inadequate for dealing with hostile, foreign threats.[5] This logic motivated the 2003 invasion of Iraq, and preventive wars have been suggested as possible solutions to the threats posed by North Korea and Iran by hawks such as former National Security Advisor John Bolton and former Vice President Dick Cheney.[6] Given the United States' overwhelming military capabilities versus many of its potential enemies, such wars have been and will continue to be especially tempting for Americans. Yet, such wars are unwise. Why? Doesn't common sense say that prevention is smart? Certainly in much of life, such as health care, prevention makes sense. It is easier and cheaper to take steps to prevent or at least reduce the likelihood of maladies like heart disease and cancer than it is to treat them.

Preventive military force, however, is different in ways that make it deeply unwise. It requires waging a war now to avoid a problem that may *or may not* occur in the future. In other words, it requires incurring high, definite costs today to avoid speculative future costs. It also means deliberately provoking a war that could well be avoided. This requires assuming costs, risks, and moral culpability on the *belief* that the war is inevitable and necessary. Otto von Bismarck, the nineteenth-century German chancellor and certainly no dove, likened such logic to committing "suicide from fear of death."[7] Similarly, the Truman administration when formulating the United States' response to the Soviet Union rejected preventive warfare as disastrous.[8] Given that beliefs about the need for war are often mistaken due to changing conditions and the prevalence of other options, preventive wars are usually both unwise and morally dubious.[9] Further, as seen by the reaction to the 2003 invasion of Iraq, such wars are unpopular and hurt America's standing with its allies and other countries. Last, by waging such wars, the United States sets a precedent that such wars are acceptable.[10] This makes it easier for countries such as Russia, China, Iran, and North Korea to wage their own preventive wars. As argued in chapter 3, setting such precedents undermines the international security and legal orders that the United States created after World War II.

A closer look at the United States' 2003 preventive war against Iraq is instructive in grasping the dangers of preventive war.[11] The Americans and British sought to prevent Iraq from acquiring nuclear weapons by overthrowing Saddam Hussein's regime. While it is surely better to fight a nuclear-free Iraq than one armed with nuclear weapons, the preventive logic behind the decision to invade Iraq in 2003 made several assumptions.

One assumption was Iraq would get nuclear weapons if the United States didn't invade. As it turns out, Iraq's nuclear program was a shambles and decidedly not on a path to producing nuclear weapons.[12]

Two, the cost of confronting a nuclear-armed Iraq would have been higher than the cost of the war. This would be true only if nuclear war occurred—hardly a guarantee even given a nuclear-armed Iraq. For example, while a nuclear-armed North Korea is definitely uncomfortable and a negative for the United States and its allies, North Korea's possession of nuclear weapons has cost the United States far less than the Iraq War did. The United States has tolerated rivals possessing nuclear weapons since 1949. Nuclear deterrence—the threat to retaliate if a rival uses nuclear weapons against United States or its allies—has worked for decades. It worked against the Soviet Union, a far more formidable foe than either North Korea or Iraq. It is unlikely that it would fail now. Nor is it likely that countries would transfer nuclear weapons to other actors as this risks their own destruction if they are ever used.[13] Giving terrorists a nuclear weapon would require a great deal of faith that the terrorist group would use the weapons in the manner the country wished combined with a belief that the country would escape detection and, therefore, punishment. Few countries have such close ties to terrorists groups that they could trust them with such an ominous weapon. Further, the odds that the nuclear weapon used would be attributed to the state sponsor of the terrorist group is very high as the number of countries that sponsor terrorist groups is low and few of those possess nuclear capabilities.[14] Thus, countries are unlikely to give nuclear weapons to terrorists and are unlikely to use said weapons on their own unless their national survival is on the line. In other words, deterrence rather than preventive invasion is the wiser response to hostile countries' nuclear programs.[15]

Three, war against Iraq assumed that an invasion would solve the problem. While this would have been true at least in the short run if Iraq had possessed a functioning nuclear program given the large imbalance in military capabilities between the United States and Iraq, it would not solve the problem for all time. Nuclear programs can be rebuilt and restarted.

Wars, even successful ones, do not solve problems for all-time. There is no end of history or permanent political victory. If wars did solve problems permanently, World War I, instead of being followed by World War II, would not need a number at all. Furthermore, wars create the possibility that an even worse problem could emerge. The 2003 invasion of Iraq did remove Saddam, but it led to civil war and created an opening first for al Qaeda and then ISIS to set up shop. It also allowed for greater Iranian influence throughout the Middle East. Prior to the US invasion, Iran faced a hostile Iraq to its west. The war not only gravely weakened Iraq but also resulted in Shia militias and politicians favorable to Iran playing a major role in Iraq's governance. Thus, Iraq went from being a significant check on Iran to a country that not only could no longer rein in Tehran but even welcomed increased Iranian influence. In other words, American successes, such as they were, created new problems.

The rulers of the medieval Byzantine Empire understood this well. They realized that thoroughly defeating the various barbarian enemies they faced just cleared the path for new tribes to sweep down from the Russian steppes into the Balkans and threaten the Byzantines anew.[16] Therefore, they rarely sought to totally overthrow their enemies. As there would always be a new enemy, it did not make sense to expend more resources than necessary confronting current ones. Likewise, a survey of past empires found that, "the preventative pacification of one turbulent frontier usually led to the creation of another one, adjacent to the first."[17] In other words, conquest left empires no more secure than they were before the preventive war. Exhausting one's self unnecessarily to run up the score in the current contest just leaves you vulnerable and tired when the new foe emerges. In other words, it makes sense to limit one's effort in proportion to the danger faced and the goal being sought.[18] Preventive wars fail in this regard as they do in so many others.

So why are preventive wars waged if they are unwise? They are fought because leaders believe that it is better to fight a war now than to fight that same war later. Such wars are especially seductive for countries experiencing a decline in military power relative to their enemies. However, as mentioned above, they also require a belief that war will occur—something that is difficult to foresee with any certainty. Yet, leaders, especially military leaders, often come to see war as inevitable.[19] Why?

Containing enemies through the threat of retaliation—whether economic, conventional military, or nuclear—is effective but deeply uncomfortable.[20] Anyone old enough to remember the Cold War can attest to that. During the Cold War, the United States and its allies successfully deterred the Soviet Union from attacking the West by threatening nuclear retaliation. It remains one of the great foreign policy triumphs in American history. Yet, it led to many crises and sleepless nights. Of course, losing sleep is nothing compared to the alternative of nuclear holocaust, but some folks seem unable to bear the tension this sort of long-running, diplomatic confrontation requires. They would rather unleash war and "settle" the issue in one go.

For example, prior to World War I, Field Marshal Helmuth von Moltke the Younger, chief of the German general staff, had become convinced war with France and Russia would happen eventually and preferred to wage war sooner than later. When, during the crisis leading up to the war it briefly looked like war would be averted, Moltke became angry and distraught. He pushed unremittingly to get hostilities underway. Only actually launching the war relieved the tension he felt.[21] Similarly, US Secretary of War Henry L. Stimson's reaction to the attack on Pearl Harbor is telling. Even though the United States was the target of the preventive attack rather than the perpetrator, Stimson exhibited a similar relief to that of Moltke. He wrote in his diary on December 7, 1941 that,

> When the news first came that Japan had attacked us, my first feeling was one of relief that the indecision was over . . . This continued to be my dominant feeling in spite of the news of catastrophes which quickly developed.[22]

Similarly, most elite goalkeepers in soccer defending against a penalty kick jump left or right prior to knowing the direction of the kick. This behavior has been shown to result in a worse save percentage than waiting to observe the direction of the kick prior to reacting.[23] Yet, despite studies showing that such guessing is suboptimal, goalies continue to engage in this behavior. Perhaps it is more tolerable to be seen as having acted aggressively to save the kick if one fails, rather than failing after more passive behavior. In other words, much as stress can induce action to relieve the pressure, expectations of an event can push people to act even if the outcome is worse than waiting.[24] Thus, at times psychological pressures push leaders to wage unwise preventive wars.

## INTRACTABLE INSURGENCIES

Another hawkish attempt to deal with foreign military threats is regime change. The idea being that if a regime is incorrigible and is likely to always pose a threat to the United States, it's best to remove the regime and replace it with a new one—ideally a democracy—that is more amenable to American interests. Essentially, the belief is that revisionist, authoritarian regimes are inherent threats and that the threat can best or only be met through regime change rather than through deterrence or other more restrained policies.[25] Obviously, this is quite difficult as it requires, for starters, the military overthrow of the obnoxious regime. Yet, as seen in 2001 in Afghanistan and 2003 in Iraq, at least when the opposing country is relatively weak, this is often within the United States' power.[26] Those same examples, however, show that overthrowing the existing regime is in fact the easier task. Trying to replace it with a regime that is both stable and friendly is where the real problems begin. In both cases, groups opposed to the new US-backed regime resorted to guerilla warfare, dragging the United States into prolonged counterinsurgency campaigns. The enduring nature of those insurgencies, especially in Afghanistan, has made the limits on the effective use of force painfully clear.[27]

Why has the United States found itself facing guerrillas rather than conventional armies? It results from opponents doing their all to ensure the United States fails.[28] They know, just as Americans do, that at least tactically, the US military would easily win a conventional war. Yet, American military superiority does not extend to guerrilla conflicts.[29] So opponents of the United States avoid conventional wars and instead seek to turn any conflict into guerilla warfare. This allows the side with the weaker military to avoid defeat while imposing costs on its adversary.

By avoiding confronting the more powerful US military on equal terms, adversaries turn the conflict into one of political will. All they have to do is avoid defeat and wait for US willpower to crumble.[30] Research has shown that having superior resolve is more important than having superior capabilities in winning international conflicts.[31] This means the United States' greater military force only matters if Americans have the will to pay the costs of occupying a foreign country. And insurgents usually have the superior will. This is not because of some weakness of Americans. Rather it is because the conflict is happening in *the insurgents' country* and is about how *they* will be governed. Given the limited nature of US interests in places like Afghanistan when compared to *Afghans' interests in Afghanistan*, the United States won't have the needed will power to bear the necessary costs and thus will lose.[32]

For example, the United States never had nor could have had the same willingness to bear costs in Vietnam as North Vietnam and the Viet Cong had. Unsurprisingly, the Vietnamese cared more about their own country and were more willing to suffer to bring about a preferred political outcome than Americans cared about what happened in Vietnam. The remarkable thing about that conflict is not that the United States ultimately lost, but instead how much Americans were willing to suffer to influence the destiny of a distant country. In general, outside of defending the US homeland or close US allies like fellow NATO members or Japan, US willpower will be limited.

Even with the military's recent focus on how to win such wars, counterinsurgency remains exceedingly difficult.[33] There is no magic formula for winning such conflicts. Where countries have succeeded, such as the British in Malaysia in the 1950s, it was because of more favorable political circumstances rather than any particularly shrewd tactics the British employed. This is not to say the British did not use wise counterinsurgency tactics in Malaysia—they did—but many of those same tactics have been employed by the United States in Afghanistan, Iraq, and Vietnam and by the French in Algeria with far less success.[34]

Successful counterinsurgency operations always require effective cooperation from the local population.[35] Yet, foreign military forces are usually resented regardless of their behavior, let alone when they kill civilians as an unintentional but inevitable consequence of the military operations they are conducting.[36] Counterinsurgency operations also always require very large numbers of troops to occupy, control, and police the country in which the insurgency is occurring. Common estimates suggest that the counterinsurgency force must outnumber the guerrillas by ten to one or that twenty soldiers are required for 1,000 people living in the country.[37] Such large force requirements quickly drain political will and are hard to obtain with smaller, volunteer-based militaries such as the one the United States has today.

But can't the United States avoid being dragged into guerilla quagmires by limiting its actions to airstrikes? Alas, no. Bombing alone is rarely able to achieve policy aims.[38] While air power certainly makes important contributions to military campaigns, its utility is limited.[39] Populations rarely concede even when confronted with devastating air raids and instead rally around their own governments. The stoic resistance of the British, Germans, and Japanese in the face of massive aerial bombardments during World War II is well-known as is that of the North Vietnamese during the Vietnam War. More clearly, air power alone is never sufficient when waging counterinsurgency operations. Counterinsurgency theorists regularly emphasize the need for ground troops to protect and control the populace. Thus, relying on air power alone is not a panacea to the challenge of guerilla warfare. Nor can third parties entirely replace the need for American troops. While local allies and other proxies can be useful adjuncts to US forces, research has shown that proxies are difficult to control and are less likely to succeed.[40]

Thus, attempting to impose US-backed regimes on hostile foreign powers fails—and fails at great cost to the United States. Much as with preventive warfare, foreign-imposed regime change is a poor policy for dealing with foreign threats. In each case, the desire to be proactive and actively use force against foreign dangers leads the United States into unwise and costly policies. Happily, the frequent, *active* use of force is not needed to deal with these threats.

DETERRING FOREIGN MILITARY THREATS

Such threats can be dealt with through military deterrence, a passive use of force.[41] Deterrence is the threat of retaliation in response to some unwanted action. It can be military in nature but need not be. Parents and children are quite familiar with deterrence. Parents often threaten their children with some sort of punishment if they do not behave: grounding, no dessert, no electronic devices, and so forth. Countries can do the same thing by threatening various punishments such as economic sanctions or military actions in response to unwanted behaviors.[42] Deterrence can be used to dissuade attacks against the United States or its allies. It can be used after a threat or crisis has arisen or it can be an overarching sense that if a country militarily harms the United States or its allies at some point in the future, Washington would retaliate. This type of deterrence tends to be vague and unstated but can be highly effective.[43]

A simple example of military deterrence would be a threat that stated, "if you bomb our country, we will bomb your country." The key is the threatened punishment has to be severe enough to dissuade the target from taking the undesired action and yet small enough to be believable. For instance, threatening North Korea with economic sanctions in response to an invasion of South Korea would be grossly insufficient. North Korea would be willing to pay those costs and would not be deterred. Likewise, threatening a nuclear attack in response to a missile test would be overkill and, therefore, not believable. Only a monster would kill millions to punish a mere test.

Military deterrence has several advantages. First, it works. Deterrence was one of the keys to the West's victory in the Cold War. For forty-five long years, the United States and its allies stared down the Soviet Union in Europe and deterred the Soviets from invading Western Europe or using nuclear weapons. Deterrence worked even when the Soviet Union was led by a cold-hearted tyrant like Joseph Stalin or a true communist ideologue like Nikita Khrushchev. Yes, it was uncomfortable, but it was far cheaper than waging World War III and ultimately resulted in the West's triumph.

Deterrence works because it is far easier to persuade an opponent to not take some action than to defeat them militarily.[44] This is because it is only necessary to convince the opponent that their actions are not worth the cost. It is not necessary to actually fight battles. Also, provided the opponent hasn't started a crisis, there is no need for them to publically back down. Rather, they can just avoid taking the action that would result in a response. This involves no public humiliation, making it much more palatable than backing down publically. This in turn makes deterrence more likely to work.[45] In other words, deterrence, like war, can be used preventively. The United States can make it clear before threats emerge which countries it is willing to use force to protect and in which issue areas it would fight to uphold the status quo. By doing so, the United States can not only prevent threats from being actualized but can also reduce the odds they emerge in the first place.

Second, scholarship suggests that alliances are especially good at general deterrence.[46] In other words, by forming alliances with friendly countries around the world—something the United States has already done—Washington can deter potential foes from even threatening US allies. Given that the United States is far more likely to be drawn into conflicts defending its allies than defending its own territory—America has no significant territorial disputes—the fact that alliances are especially good at deterrence is reassuring. This strength of alliances results in part because they are a public declaration indicating the United States is committed to defending these other countries (and they likewise are committed to defending the United States).[47] As this puts the United States' reputation on the line, it serves as a costly signal making it more believable that Washington would come to the aid of its allies. Also, US forces are frequently based in these allied countries. This is another costly signal as it puts US troops directly in harm's way, further indicating America's commitment to its friends. By investing in these alliances and upholding America's commitment to deterrence, the United States stabilizes many regions and increases the odds that they will remain at peace. Such successful exercises of deterrence greatly reduce the odds of needing to fight a war to defend US allies.

Third, deterrence is much cheaper than active uses of force. If the deterrent threat works, there is no need to engage in combat. This doesn't make deterrence free. The risk of war and the costs of having the military establishment necessary to make a deterrent threat believable are real enough. Still, it is much cheaper and easier than trying to compel an opponent into taking an action through the active use of force. In such a circumstance, force must be used actively and continuously until the other side concedes, if ever. That is very costly.[48] This is what the United States attempted to do in Vietnam by bombing Hanoi and other vulnerable targets. The United States tried to compel North Vietnam to pull out of South Vietnam by inflicting pain. This strategy ultimately failed after both sides paid significant costs.

Fourth, deterrence can also work against nonmilitary threats such as cyberwarfare. Other countries using cyberattacks to disrupt US infrastructure such as causing dams or the electrical grid to fail; stealing business, political, or defense secrets; and casting doubt on election outcomes are all real concerns. Indeed, US government agencies, including the Defense Department, American businesses, states' voting systems, and US infrastructure facilities connected to the Internet have all already been targeted by hackers sponsored by foreign governments.[49] Such attacks usually are undertaken by agents working for other countries rather than terrorist groups.[50]

This is problematic as countries can shield individuals engaging in cyberwarfare from law enforcement. Thus, standard law enforcement remedies are unlikely to be effective, unlike when confronting cybercriminals or even cyberterrorists.

While governments (federal, state, and local) and private businesses should take steps to secure their networks, offense is often easier than defense when it comes to cyberwarfare. Yet, using our own formidable cyber capacities to strike first would do nothing to protect our own vulnerabilities and likely would prompt retaliation.[51] It would also normalize the use of cyberattacks, making such attacks against the United States more likely. Also, offensive use of cyber-weapons increases the odds they will fall into the hands of other countries. In recent years, the United States has lost control of various cyberwarfare software weapons it has developed, only to see them used by rivals such as China. This has happened when these tools were used offensively, discovered, and then repurposed by the intended targets.[52]

Rather, the United States should threaten proportional retaliation to deter such attacks from occurring. Such retaliation would not be military in nature unless the cyberattack caused many deaths but might instead be economic sanctions or even cyberattacks of our own. Threats of retaliation would be a credible deterrent because of the United States' own significant cyber capabilities, its aforementioned ability to impose costly sanctions (see chapter 4), and its much improved ability to determine the perpetrators of cyberattacks.[53] Of course, threats of retaliation must be made before attacks occur, and the US government must carry out the threats if cyberattacks happen. If this is done, however, serious cyberattacks by foreign governments can be deterred.[54] In other words, the logic of deterrence works exactly the same for nonmilitary threats as it does for military ones.

Despite these advantages, the United States has grown skeptical of deterrence in recent years.[55] The United States did not believe it could deter Iraq from using nuclear weapons if it were to obtain them and instead invaded that country in 2003.[56] Similarly, Washington at present lacks confidence that it can deter North Korea from using nuclear missiles from striking the continental United States. Instead, President Trump has alternated between attempts at reconciliation and threats of preventative war even though true reconciliation through North Korean nuclear disarmament is unlikely and a preventive war would be costly in the extreme. Such a war would risk considerable damage to Japan and South Korea, a war with China, and even the very North Korean missile strikes on US cities that are so feared.[57]

Perhaps this is because deterrence is a preventative measure, much like taking care of oneself. If one exercises regularly and eats well, it greatly reduces the odds of adverse outcomes like heart attacks. Nothing happening is a success. Likewise, when deterrence works, nothing happens. This is not to suggest the measures did not work. Healthy living reduces the likelihood of heart attacks. Deterrence reduces the odds of wars. But the success is largely invisible, especially to the inattentive. This causes people to forget just how effective those actions really are.

The United States also may have deemphasized deterrence because it hopes to do more than simply prevent attacks on itself and its allies. Continuing with the North Korean example, Washington would prefer regime change in North Korea. Barring that, the US government would opt for a North Korea that was incapable of inflicting serious harm on the United States or its allies. Yet, neither of these options can possibly be achieved anytime soon without a US attack on North Korea—an attack that would bring the very nuclear strikes Washington rightly fears. Even then, the likely result would be chaos and instability, not a reunified, peaceful, and democratic Korea. Hundreds of thousands or even millions would die for little gain.[58] Thus, there are no good options to achieve our ideal outcomes on the Korean Peninsula. This is frustrating, but foreign policy is often frustrating. A good foreign policy aims at obtaining the best outcome that is realistically possible. In the case of North Korea, this is deterring Pyongyang from attacking the United States, South Korea, and Japan. With apologies to the Rolling Stones, the North Korean case shows that we can't always get what we want—in this case, regime change—but the United States is powerful enough to get the outcome it needs—safety for itself and its allies—through the use of deterrence.

Thus, Washington should return to deterrence as the main tool of US military policy when dealing with hostile, foreign military threats. Deterrence has worked extremely well in the past. Relying on it today would save many American lives and dollars while better achieving US foreign policy goals than the recent overuse of active force has. The question then is how can America successfully deter its military foes?

The key to successful deterrence is that threats have to be credible. This in turn requires two things: capability and resolve. In other words, the United States must demonstrate that it could and would carry out its threats. Studies of what makes deterrence successful have found that possessing sufficient military capabilities is crucial.[59] Hence the Roman adage, "He who desires peace, let him prepare for war."[60] But this is an argument for being prepared to fight if necessary, not an argument for the active use of force. Given the United States' significant military capabilities, this requirement for successful deterrence is easily met.

While hawks often try to portray doves as naïve and argue that doves intend to dismantle the US security apparatus and radically defund the US military,[61] dovishness does not require disarmament or weakness. Far from it. It is entirely possible to believe that the active use of force generally fails to achieve US policy objectives and still be hardheaded enough to recognize serious threats for what they are. Doves can protect themselves and their allies. In fact, Norman Angell, the famous twentieth-century British dove, was far more ready to confront Nazi Germany in the 1930s than were so-called realists like E. H. Carr who favored the infamous policy of appeasement.[62] Thus, a well-armed but dovish United States would possess the needed capabilities for deterrence.

Of course, the need to maintain a strong military does not imply the United States must spend every penny it currently allocates to the military. A commitment to curtailing the active use of force should allow for lower military spending. Active deployments are especially expensive, and the size of the US Army could be trimmed as one of its major roles is to project force into other countries rather than to deter attacks against the United States. Reducing the size of the army could also spur continental European NATO members to spend more as land defense plays a more important role in their security than it does in US security given the countries' different geographic positions. Given the vast size and power of the US military—not to mention its nuclear arsenal—maintaining sufficient forces for successful deterrence is quite doable. Even with some reductions in size, the US military would remain the preeminent military force in the world. It would be quite capable of keeping America and its allies safe.

In fact, the savings achieved by avoiding frequent combat and overly large ground forces could even improve US security. If those savings were reinvested in the domestic economy (through investments in education and infrastructure or even well-targeted tax cuts), they could spur economic growth, which would result in the US government having a larger economic base to draw upon when future threats emerged. High military expenditures, especially in developed countries, have been found to be correlated with slower long-term economic growth.[63] This is one reason why President Eisenhower wanted to limit US military expenditures even at the height of the Cold War. He knew a robust economy meant a stronger America.[64]

Even if the savings were spent on the military, they could go to the research and development of new weapons systems, again with an eye toward future threats. Such investments in weapons research and force modernization are important. It is not impossible for the United States to fall behind on military technology—in fact, it could be argued that China and Russia both have better shore-to-ship missiles today than the United States does.[65] No matter how peaceful or hawkish US foreign policy is, modernizing and upgrading the technological capabilities of US armed forces is vital. Such a technological edge is important for a dovish foreign policy as it reduces the likelihood that America's enemies will attack it or US allies. Still, given American economic and scientific resources, this research and development challenge is quite manageable.

This ability to maintain US military preponderance means that, for the United States, successful deterrence would usually be a question of resolve. Resolve is the willingness to use force and pay costs in terms of lives and money in order to obtain an objective. Threats are credible only if opponents believe they will be carried out. This means that maintaining a reputation for carrying out threats is crucial. Hawks often argue that in order to demonstrate resolve, the United States must actively use force when and wherever potential enemies engage in bad acts. For instance, a number of hawkish foreign policy commentators have claimed that President Obama's refusal to use force after his "red-line" comment about chemical weapons in Syria led directly to Russian actions in Ukraine.[66]

This is absurd. While the Obama administration certainly warrants significant criticism for making a poorly thought-out bluff, there is no evidence that Russia's actions in Ukraine were motivated by anything other than events in Ukraine. Indeed, numerous leading Russian foreign policy experts and even a member of the Russian foreign ministry have said that the suggestion of a connection between Syria and Ukraine is dead wrong.[67] Even if President Obama had ordered a bombing run in Syria, it's not clear why Russia would have assumed the United States would have been willing to fight in Ukraine. Bombing a state that cannot resist says nothing about US willingness to risk a war with a major nuclear power (Russia) to defend a country (Ukraine) that is not an ally. Certainly, the extensive use of force by the Bush administration in the Middle East did not deter Russia from invading the country of Georgia in August 2008. Thus, there is no reason to think a firmer stand against Syrian chemical weapons use would have influenced Russian policy toward Ukraine.

Essentially, hawks are arguing that reputation is unsegmentable. An argument that backing down anywhere causes others to expect the United States would back down everywhere is silly. Teenagers don't think that because their parents relented and let them watch an extra hour of internet videos that their parents wouldn't be upset if they came home after curfew or got caught with illegal drugs. They know the two issues are distinct and not equivalent. Likewise, backing down in one area of international relations does not indicate that a country would back down everywhere.[68] Even when the United States withdrew from Vietnam, the Soviet Union never questioned the American commitment to NATO allies in Europe.[69] Leaving Vietnam did not increase the danger of a Soviet invasion. In fact, Western European countries had opposed US escalation in Vietnam and wanted Washington to pull out in part so that the United States could focus on Europe.[70]

Why doesn't restraint or inaction in one area harm one's overall reputation? It doesn't because reputation is segmentable and parsable.[71] Countries understand that not all issues and regions are created equal and that a willingness or lack of willingness to stand firm in one area says little about resolve in another.[72] Few countries believe that inaction in a remote region of the globe says anything about a country's resolve to act to defend its core interests.[73] When trying to anticipate America's reaction to a challenge, countries look at US capabilities and how much the United States cares about an issue,[74] not if the United States has repeatedly engaged in violent conflict in the recent past.[75] They also look at past US behavior regarding *that issue* or at other confrontations with that specific country.[76]

In other words, reputation matters, but it matters in specific ways rather than in the all-encompassing ways that some foreign policy theorists suggested early in the Cold War.[77] Reputation matters most in analogous situations. In particular, countries that back down in territorial disputes are more likely to be challenged in the future in other territorial disputes—especially if the hostile country is the same as in the last challenge.[78] The effects of reputation are far less clear when countries back down in non-territorial disputes and if the challenger is a different country than in the previous instance. In other words, as long the United States steadfastly upholds its commitments to defend its allies' territories and its own territories, reputational concerns should not be a major issue.

Crucially, initiating wars does not enhance countries' reputations to resist when challenged. While countries do take stock of when others back down from commitments they have made, starting wars does not increase others' belief in a country's resolve for self-defense.[79] Scholars have found no evidence that refraining from initiating wars invites attacks. Rather, such dovish policies have proved to be quite successful at securing countries from attack.[80] Furthermore, the more fragile credibility is perceived to be, the more careful the United States should be about undertaking military commitments abroad that may later have to be abandoned. Thus, hawks' arguments that the United States should frequently employ force abroad to uphold America's reputation is inherently paradoxical as such widespread commitments, if the hawkish view that credibility is universal rather than segmentable were correct, would in fact be deeply dangerous.[81] This is because the United States would often have to back down from military adventures abroad. The United States was ultimately compelled to leave Vietnam, Somalia, and Iraq. It is unlikely to remain in Afghanistan long enough to ensure the regime in Kabul faces no serious domestic threats. Thus, active, aggressive uses of force are more likely to weaken rather than to enhance credibility.

The key is to be clear about what is worth fighting for. On some issues, such as American territory, US willingness to fight is so obvious that it does not even need to be stated. On others, such as defending NATO or Asian allies, US resolve again should be fairly clear as long as Washington occasionally reiterates its commitment to defend allies from attack and does nothing to bring that commitment into question.[82] Maintaining credibility to defend these core interests is relatively straightforward. Given US military strength, this means deterrence in these areas will be successful. The United States may also, at times, wish to further extend its deterrent umbrella. Doing so successfully would be far more difficult but perhaps worthwhile on carefully chosen occasions. While a general reputation for responding resolutely has some influence on the credibility of deterrent threats in non-analogous situations,[83] by no means must aggression and bad behavior be resisted everywhere to uphold America's reputation or to make US deterrent threats credible. The United States can avoid taking on and can back down from ill-conceived commitments in peripheral areas without bringing into question its commitments to key allies and friends.

This means that US leaders can avoid taking on commitments they do not intend to honor. Half-committing to defend countries or values Washington doesn't want to fight for is usually a mistake as such behaviors needlessly harm the United States' reputation and risk drawing it into unnecessary and unwanted conflicts. This is not to claim it never makes sense to bluff. It may be logical on rare occasions. Just like poker players known for betting based on the cards they have, leaders with reputations for honesty may be able to score a cheap policy victory by claiming they would fight for some goal when in fact they would not. This, of course, risks having one's bluff called and accepting the resulting harm to one's reputation. This reduced reputation would decrease the effectiveness of future deterrent threats and the odds additional bluffs would work. So while bluffing on occasion may make sense, those occasions should be rare and carefully chosen.

The fact that deterrence works is crucial. If this was not true, a dovish foreign policy would be impossible. But because it is true, the United States can avoid wasting money and lives on issues and regions that are not vital to the United States. Indeed, to fritter away resources in such conflicts as hawks would have Washington do would leave the United States weaker—both materially and spiritually—and less able to act in areas that truly do matter. This is not to claim deterrence never fails.[84] No strategy works 100 percent of the time. This means the United States must be ready and able to actively use force to defend itself and its allies, thereby upholding its deterrent threats. In such cases, the United States would be in no worse shape than if it had actively employed force from the outset.

As long as doves do not renounce the use of force entirely, but instead reserve it to defend and protect core interests—US territory, the territories of allies, and the free navigation of the seas—it is entirely possible to demonstrate sufficient resolve to make deterrence credible and, therefore, effective. Likewise, it means force would be available if deterrent threats fail. Indeed, limiting military deterrence to core interests fits with Kennan's view of what containment of the Soviet Union should have been during the Cold War.[85] Such a narrower view of containment would have avoided US involvement in Vietnam and yet would have still resulted in winning the Cold War by defending Western Europe and Japan. Thus, a dovish foreign policy can meet the central international security challenge—stopping enemies from attacking vital US interests.

FIGHTING INTERNATIONAL TERRORISM

Despite its usefulness, deterrence cannot solve all US security challenges. Perhaps most clearly, deterrence isn't of much use in fighting international terrorism. While it may be theoretically possible to deter terrorist groups,[86] in practice it is very hard to threaten things those groups value. Washington cannot deter terrorists by threatening to kill them as the government already intends to capture or kill them if possible because of the attacks they have already carried out. It would be like the police telling criminals that as long as they committed no more crimes, they would not be arrested for the crimes they already committed. Such a stance is not believable, nor would it be acceptable to the American public. Another option would be to threaten the lives of terrorists' innocent loved ones, but that would be unconscionable. Punishing the innocent for the crimes of others is deeply immoral. Further, the clear injustice of it would fuel the recruitment of new terrorists, meaning such actions would be counterproductive as well as horrific.

Yet even in confronting international terrorism, dovish solutions work better than hawkish ones.[87] Specifically, the offensive use of force is of limited utility against terrorist groups. Why? For one, most recent terrorist attacks against the United States and American allies in Europe, even by groups with international reach, have been planned in those countries. Military force cannot stop terrorist cells located in Boston, San Bernardino, Paris, or Manchester. Americans are not going to bomb their own cities or those of their allies. Similarly, the United States is very limited in its ability to use force against terrorist cells in Pakistan, an ostensible US ally. Washington is not going to risk starting a war with a nuclear-armed state.

Furthermore, reprisal attacks against terrorist camps have not proven effective. The United States used such attacks against al Qaeda in the late 1990s with little success.[88] More broadly, the preventive use of force against terrorist groups has all of the same problems of preventive force covered earlier in the chapter.[89] Likewise, intervening in weak countries such as Afghanistan, Somalia, or Yemen out of a fear that those countries' poorly governed spaces would provide safe havens for terrorist groups has met with limited success. Al Qaeda still finds safe havens in Afghanistan and Yemen as does al-Shabaab in Somalia, despite years of military efforts by the United States and its allies in those nations.

Even drone strikes against terrorist leaders have proven to be of limited use. First, such attacks are feasible only against groups that are in the open, not hiding, amongst civilians.[90] Second, drone strikes are inferior to capturing terrorists because capturing terrorists aids US intelligence collection efforts. A great deal of information about terrorists' plans, methods, and contacts—including the identities and locations of other terrorists—is obtained from the analysis of materials such as phones and computers captured along with the terrorists. Also, much as the police are able to extract information from criminals, terrorists often reveal valuable information about their groups as a result of traditional interrogation methods.[91] Third, the use of force often results in the deaths of civilians and incites resentment in the broader population.[92] This resentment can fuel future terrorism. Law enforcement actions are far less likely to generate such high levels of animosity toward the United States. Fourth, repeatedly killing members of terrorist groups through drone strikes has not proven effective.[93] Al Qaeda in the Arabian Peninsula remains a robust threat despite years of US drone strikes.[94] This is not because the strikes have failed tactically. The strikes have often killed members of al Qaeda, including several high-ranking members. Rather, the group has been able to replace its losses, and in general decapitation strategies fail to destroy terrorist groups.[95] This is likely why President Obama, after ordering ten times as many drone strikes as President Bush, ultimately turned away from the widespread use of the tactic.[96] Drone strikes simply did not yield strategic success.

Even commando raids to capture or kill terrorist leaders have had a mixed record outside of the raid that killed Osama bin Laden. US soldiers were killed in an ambush in Niger during counterterrorism exercises, though some raids in Libya and Somalia have met with tactical success.[97] Most notably, a raid in Yemen in early 2017 failed badly,[98] and of course, one of the two helicopters used in the bin Laden raid broke down and had to be abandoned.[99] The margin between success and failure in that operation was exceedingly small. As President Obama said shortly after the bin Laden raid, such actions must remain rare:

> Our operation in Pakistan against Osama bin Laden cannot be the norm. The risks in that case were immense. The likelihood of capture, although that was our preference, was remote given the certainty that our folks would confront resistance. The fact that we did not find ourselves confronted with civilian casualties, or embroiled in an extended firefight, was a testament to the meticulous planning and professionalism of our Special Forces, but it also depended on some luck.

An exact accounting of the success rate of such actions is impossible to compile given the covert nature of many of the raids, though it seems likely that successes would be publicized, meaning it is unlikely that the record is substantially better than what is publically known.

Also, many of the foreign terrorist and guerilla groups against which it is tempting to use military force have local aims. Though repugnant in their goals and methods, crucially, such groups are not a direct threat to the United States. This is true even though they share al Qaeda's ideology. Boko Haram in Nigeria, al-Shabaab in Somalia, and Abu Sayyaf in the Philippines have limited their actions to the countries in which they are based and their immediate neighbors.[100] They lack the ability to act globally. Even some regional branches of al Qaeda, such as al Qaeda in the Islamic Maghreb have remained regional actors and have not planned attacks against the United States itself.[101] US military actions against those groups, therefore, do little, if anything, to protect Americans from terrorism.

Thus, the military is a quite limited tool in confronting terrorism. It may play an important role on occasion—such as the bin Laden raid—but on the whole can do little to secure America against the current international terrorist threat, which is largely characterized by small cells or lone wolves acting within the United States or US allied countries. More obviously, it does nothing to halt terrorism that is purely domestic in nature. Rather, counterterrorism efforts must rely on intelligence gathering and law enforcement.[102] Such efforts must be sustained and multilateral as other countries will often have access to intelligence Washington lacks, and their cooperation will be vital for arresting terrorists who are located abroad.[103] (Indeed, a strong intelligence network remains vital no matter how peaceful one's foreign policy. This is true not only for fighting terrorism but also so that the government knows what other countries are planning and what their military capabilities are. The need for intelligence is just as great for hawks as it is for doves).[104]

Such nonmilitary counterterrorism policies can work. Khalid Sheik Mohammed, the mastermind behind 9/11 and former number three in the al Qaeda command structure, was arrested in Karachi, Pakistan, as a result of a multinational intelligence and police operation. His capture was not an isolated incident. The same operation led to the arrest and conviction of dozens of al Qaeda members and disrupted at least three attacks.[105] Likewise, Ramzi Yousef, who led the 1993 attack on the World Trade Center, was arrested in Pakistan in 1995 as a result of an international investigation into another attack he was planning. Much as with the arrest of Khalid Sheik Mohammed, this operation resulted in the arrest and conviction of several coconspirators.[106] The foiling of plots resulting in multiple arrests and convictions has been repeated numerous times, both in the United States and abroad.[107]

Overall, police work has done more to disrupt terrorism than have military methods. Internationally, of terrorist groups vanquished between 1968 and 2006, 7 percent were defeated as a result of military measures while 40 percent were defeated through the use of law enforcement.[108] Nonmilitary methods can also be effective against state sponsors of terrorism. A mix of diplomatic pressure and sanctions coerced Sudan to extradite Carlos the Jackal and to expel bin Laden.[109] Likewise, the same mix of sanctions and diplomatic pressure convinced Muammar Gaddafi to end Libya's state sponsorship of terrorism. Compare that success to the 1986 US airstrikes in response to a bombing in West Berlin, which not only failed to end Libya's sponsorship of terrorism but instead preceded the Libyan-backed 1988 Pan Am bombing over Lockerbie.[110]

This is not to claim that nonmilitary measures will always work or that they can prevent all future terrorist attacks. Counterterrorism is a notoriously difficult endeavor and no counterterrorism policy—especially not one in a free society—can prevent all attacks. Rather, the point is that nonmilitary counterterrorism policies work better than do military counterterrorism policies. They also have far lower costs in terms of lives, money, and civil liberties. This means that an aggressive, forward military policy is not necessary to keep us safe from terrorism, and therefore, the threat of international terrorism, though very real, does not justify foreign military adventures.

## THE LIMITS OF EVIDENCE

Thus, even in the international security realm, dovish policies have better advanced US interests and protected Americans than have hawkish ones. This should not be surprising as a great many countries have more peaceful foreign policies than does the United States—even many that face serious threats from other countries or terrorist groups. Yes, many of these states are American allies and benefit from the security the United States provides. Most, however, are not. This is a strong indication that the United States, too, could use force less often while remaining safe. Through the use of deterrence when confronted by hostile countries and through a mix of intelligence and police work to address international terrorism, the United States can protect itself. In fact, such a restrained security posture may well make the United States safer than would a more forward policy as it would better shepherd US material and moral resources.

Yet despite this evidence in favor of dovish policies, hawkish strategies continue to be adopted. As Mill suggested over a century and half ago, facts alone do not win arguments. How they are presented matters. The concluding chapter, therefore, returns to the challenge laid out at the beginning of the book—how to win these debates. After briefly summarizing the book's main arguments, the conclusion offers advice on how doves can in fact win these policy debates by framing them in terms of debates about strategy and by speaking to American values, thereby bringing about a more peaceful US foreign policy.

# CHAPTER 6

# How Doves Win

*Their feet are swift to shed blood; ruin and misery lie in their wake; and the way of peace they have not known.*

ROMANS 3:15–17

Before laying out how doves can win debates with hawks, it's worth quickly reviewing the argument in favor of an internationalist, dovish US foreign policy. To start, the United States must remain engaged in the world. The current international security, legal, and economic orders depend upon American power. They were created by the United States and its allies after World War II. These orders, while imperfect, have reduced violent conflict and increased global economic prosperity compared to what came before. They benefit the United States and are unlikely to survive in anything resembling their current forms if the United States retreats into isolationism. Thus, the preservation and refinement of these three interlocking orders should form the core of any US grand strategy—hawkish or dovish.

Importantly, the active use of force rarely works to advance this overarching goal. This makes dovish US grand strategies superior to hawkish ones. This failure of force results from several things. One, tactical military victories often fail to produce political successes. In other words, it is all too common to win the battles but lose the war. This can be seen in Afghanistan, Iraq, and Libya, where quick conventional military victories brought disorder, and in the first two cases, led to grinding US counterinsurgency operations. While Iraq has recently stabilized after a long civil war,[1] as of 2020, disorder still reigns in Libya and Afghanistan meaning US political objectives are as far away as ever. Two, control of the battlefield is limited as a result of friction and the fog of war. This means plans will go awry, and the outcome of engagements are often not as expected. This makes the successful application of force—even for powerful militaries such as that possessed by the United States—challenging. Three, the frequent American use of force relaxes international restraints on the use of force by others. It legitimizes other countries, like Russia, using force against their neighbors, thereby undermining both the international security and legal orders. This in turn makes the world more dangerous. Four, many goals such as economic prosperity and stability are simply disconnected from military affairs. War does little to advance such goals. Yet, despite these failings, force remains seductive. A bias toward action, impatience, and the illusion of control all conspire to convince policymakers that force works. Leaders continue to mistakenly believe that preventive wars work and that force can remake the world.

Instead of the active use of force, the United States would better achieve its goals through peaceful means. In the security realm, deterrence—a passive use of force based on both the threat of retaliation and the existing US alliance structure—is better suited for preserving the security order than is active force. Deterrence played a central role in winning the Cold War. It effectively dissuades enemies from attacking the United States and its allies. As shown in chapter 5, it is unnecessary to initiate wars to make deterrence effective. While the United States must respond to attacks on its allies and its own territories to maintain a credible deterrent, initiating offensive wars is unnecessary. And when deterrence works, the United States and its allies are not attacked. The active use of force is only required if deterrence fails. Thus, successful deterrence provides safety without having to wage war. Likewise, international terrorism is better confronted through intelligence and law enforcement methods rather than through warfighting.

Further, nonmilitary tools such as sanctions, economic aid, international institutions, international law, soft power, and diplomacy are better at advancing US interests in all three orders—security, legal, and economic—than is the active use of force. These tools better align with US policy goals than does force, have worked well in the past, avoid setting negative precedents, and are cheaper than force. Many of America's rivals employ these nonmilitary tools, and the United States used them to good effect in the past. Washington would be wise to re-embrace them.

Yet, despite these advantages of a more peaceful foreign policy, doves have frequently lost policy debates. While some of this is explainable by the seductiveness of force itself, much of it is a result of how doves have advanced their position in the past. Too often, doves have waited for a crisis to occur to mobilize, and when they have done so, they have advanced arguments that cast aspersions on US motives or blamed the United States for creating the crisis in the first place. Such arguments alienate many Americans and win very few converts. In other words, the mistakes of doves themselves have allowed hawks to carry the day.

The question then becomes how to persuade Americans to consistently favor a more peaceful foreign policy. Two often suggested strategies—having Congress reassert its role in foreign policy decision-making and reinstituting the draft—are unlikely to work. The first of these ideas, having Congress take a more active role in US foreign policy decision-making, is a good idea though for reasons having little to do with dovishness. Congress has in recent decades abdicated a great deal of foreign policy decision-making to the presidency out of a fear of a public backlash at the polls were it to constrain the president.[2] The post-9/11 Authorization for Use of Military Force (AUMF) has been used by Presidents Bush, Obama, and Trump to justify a great many independent military missions around the world without Congress having to debate each individual campaign even if the enemy is only loosely connected to al Qaeda. Some have argued this Congressional acquiescence—both in general and the AUMF in particular—allows for more military adventurism.[3]

Certainly, greater Congressional involvement would better conform to the stipulations of the US Constitution than does the post-World War II and especially post-9/11 trend of presidential dominance in foreign policy. American uses of force should be authorized by Congress on a war by war basis to comply with US law, and constraints on the executive branch are good for democracy.[4] A repeal or significant curtailment of the AUMF would require Congress to once again debate the merits of individual military operations.

There are some signs many members of Congress agree with this line of thinking. The House of Representatives voted to repeal the AUMF in 2019, though the Senate rejected that initiative.[5] Likewise, that same year, both houses of Congress voted to force the Trump administration to end US military involvement in Yemen. Yet, because this was an attempt to undo authorization previous granted under the AUMF, President Trump was able to veto the bill and the Senate failed to override said veto.[6] Thus, while Congress has shown interest in reacquiring its authority over war and peace, it has proven difficult to retake what was previously ceded away by passing the expansive AUMF in the post-9/11 period.

Congressional involvement in US foreign policy can improve the quality of US decision-making.[7] Congressional involvement in foreign policy exposes the president to more perspectives.[8] It can also refine and improve existing presidential initiatives and increase public support for those policies.[9] This is important as policies with strong public backing are more effective internationally as other countries see that the United States has the will and resolve to carry them out.[10] It should also result in a more stable, consistent foreign policy as opposed to a policy that is dramatically altered when a new president is elected. Last, Congressional committees can oversee the implementation of foreign policy initiatives to ensure they are both effective and stay within the confines of US law.[11] Taken together, these factors mean Congress should play a more important role in US foreign policy.

That said, it's not clear that greater Congressional involvement would actually result in a more peaceful foreign policy. Some of those that have rightly called for Congress to play a larger role—such as former Senators John McCain, Arlen Specter, and Jim Webb—were hawks, not doves.[12] Further, historically, Congress has had great difficulty constraining presidential uses of force, especially minor uses of force.[13] The president, because of a higher public profile, is more able to shape public opinion than is Congress. This can be done in part by controlling the information national security institutions release to the media and public.[14] Also, in times of crisis, the public is more likely to look to the president for leadership than to Congress. For instance, after the 9/11 attacks, public and media opinion focused on what President Bush would do, not on what actions Congress would take. This again places the president in an advantageous position versus Congress when it comes to shaping public opinion. While there are real limits on the president's ability to shape public opinion,[15] it is nevertheless larger than Congress' ability. Likewise, while Congress can halt funding, it naturally has been reluctant to cut off resources to troops already in combat.[16] Even looking only at major uses of force, Congress has constrained the president primarily when the opposing party was in control. Major uses of force are 45 percent more likely during periods of one-party control.[17]

In other words, the constraint is partisan rather than institutional. Generally, support or opposition to foreign policies reflects domestic partisan divisions.[18] Indeed, presidents are often able to retain support for domestic reasons even when their foreign policies are unpopular. Members of the president's party—whether in Congress or members of the public at large—rarely openly challenge the president's foreign policy even when they oppose it.[19] Worse, given that voters usually select among candidates for public office because of reasons stemming from domestic politics rather than foreign policy, divided control cannot be relied upon, meaning a partisan check will often be weak or absent. In sum, greater Congressional involvement is no guarantee of a more peaceful foreign policy, though it should improve foreign policy in other ways.

A second commonly articulated strategy to move the United States to a more dovish foreign policy is to reinstate the draft. A number of commentators, including former Representative Charlie Rangel and retired General Stanley McChrystal, have suggested that if the burden of war was spread more evenly across American society, there would be less support for hawkish policies in the United States.[20] While a draft certainly would more evenly distribute the cost of war and would make the military more reflective of American society—useful outcomes to be sure—reinstating the draft is a long shot. This is because highly trained personnel are needed to fully take advantage of modern military technology. This in turn requires long-serving professionals rather than short-term conscripts.[21] The draft ironically would be a source of military weakness not strength.

Besides, the draft would not make war less likely. The United States became involved in both the Korean War and Vietnam War when the draft was already in existence. The United States also prosecuted both World Wars through the draft. And in the nineteenth century, the United States launched two foreign wars (the War of 1812 and the Mexican-American War) when the US Army was dependent on citizens volunteering to serve in those wars *after* war had been declared. In short, simply ensuring that many or most citizens feel the pain of war is insufficient to ensure a dovish foreign policy. Costs, even high personal costs, do not dissuade Americans from pursuing hawkish policies. This yet again shows why dovish arguments that focus on costs and that frame debates about war and peace as a trade-off between goods fail.

The exception to this skepticism about institutional solutions is when it comes to funding and staffing foreign policy agencies. By directing more resources to the State Department and USAID, there will be greater dovish means at the disposal of the US government. Currently, 60 percent of all federal discretionary spending, in other words money not going to pay interest on the debt or fund entitlement programs like Social Security, goes to the Defense Department.[22] No wonder that every problem would be seen through a military lens! Increasing funding for nonmilitary foreign policy agencies means that other options would be available and personnel invested in promoting those options would be on hand to argue their views. Devoting greater resources to diplomacy and aid would also increase the likelihood that dovish policies would succeed if chosen. These higher odds of success would further increase the chance that dovish options were selected. Obviously, such funding changes would be insufficient in and of themselves to insure a dovish foreign policy, but they would be a useful start.

If institutional solutions outside of altering the allocation of resources, such as a more active Congress or reinstituting the draft won't work, how can doves win? The answer is both simple and challenging: out argue hawks. Doves must advance their arguments in ways likely to sway public and elite opinion. The first step is to avoid the sort of counterproductive rhetoric covered in chapter 1. Blaming America or focusing on legalities is unlikely to sway hawks or fence-sitters. At a minimum, arguments should not repel those they are designed to persuade.

The second step, beyond avoiding such blunders, is that doves must make their arguments not just when crises emerge but in times of peace. People would be more receptive of such arguments when they can think coolly and are not inflamed by patriotic fervor and immediate dangers. Evidence suggests that crises are when publics are least receptive to dovish arguments.[23] Appeals to fear are effective tools in policy debates and are most potent in periods of crisis.[24] As George Kennan put it,

> The counsels of impatience and hatred can always be supported by the crudest and cheapest symbols; for the counsels of moderation, the reasons are often intricate, rather than emotional, and difficult to explain.[25]

Periods of calm also allow doves to point out the benefits of long-running, yet less visible, peaceful policies. For example, the Marshall Plan, US security guarantees in Europe and Northeast Asia, and investment in a rules-based international economic order have all helped create a more stable and prosperous world. Given that such successes are less dramatic than wars, doves must frequently remind the public of these successes. By doing so, doves can prime the public's thinking, thereby reducing the effectiveness of appeals to fear when crises inevitably emerge.

The third step is doves should also take care to point out that much is right with the world. Though it is dangerous, it is not as dangerous as Americans believe. There are fewer violent conflicts in the world today than during most of the twentieth century, and the average current conflict kills 90 percent fewer people than its 1950s counterpart.[26] More importantly, the United

States today faces no adversary that is nearly as dangerous as either Nazi Germany or the Soviet Union were. The public can easily be forgiven for not realizing the improved state of the world as the media focuses on the sensational in order to attract viewers and readers. This "if it bleeds, it leads" mentality can inadvertently make the world appear to be more dangerous than it actually is.[27] This is not to suggest there are not dangers—there are—but there is no need to panic. Emphasizing that the actual state of the world is better than one would expect based on the images that flood our television screens and Twitter feeds helps set the underlying tone and parameters of the debate. A public that is already thinking in dovish terms is less likely to be swayed by the emotion of the moment when crises arise.

Alas, this is made difficult by the fact that the attention of both the American public and many members of Congress to foreign affairs is episodic.[28] Typically, only when crises or major events occur does the public become engaged in foreign affairs. Prior to this, mass publics form their opinions by taking cues from trusted elites and media outlets.[29] In other words, public foreign policy views tend to reflect partisan divisions except in times of crisis. This means doves must work especially hard to gain the public's attention and sway them in times of peace. It also means doves must work to get elites and the media to voice dovish arguments. Though difficult, these efforts are vital.

The fourth and most important step is doves must frame their arguments in ways that appeal to non-doves. The goal is to persuade others, not to score fine points in a debate or feel good about one's self. This requires considering the target audience. Research shows that emotions play a major role in how people analyze arguments and weigh evidence. The key is to realize that policy debates are as much emotional as factual battlefields.[30] Arguments that are consistent with individuals' values are far more likely to be embraced by them than those that are not. Similarly, arguments that address the emotional source of individuals' concerns are more likely to resonate with those individuals when compared to arguments that focus narrowly on factual logic.[31]

This means that framing issues in relation to the target audience's values is the key to persuasion.[32] Values, not facts, drive what arguments the public finds acceptable.[33] Policy debates sort groups based on their values and divide the public into competing factions that seek truth based on their core values.[34] Those factions are not irrevocably set ahead of time. While beliefs and values influence foreign policy, they do not determine it.[35] In other words, multiple policies can be consistent with the same set of values. How positions are framed and which values each side appeals to help determine how large of a portion of the public backs a given position. This means arguments that do not resonate with the core values of the American public will fail to obtain sufficient support. If, however, doves are able to speak to values that potential hawks hold dear such as honor and glory, they can win many of them over to support a more peaceful foreign policy. Specifically, doves should argue that nonmilitary tools can serve as sufficient and effective responses to insults and slights and that the United States can exert clear and vigorous leadership without actively using force. Doves can employ tough rhetoric, take clear stands, and illustrate how the United States is at the forefront of responses to actions taken by hostile countries and human rights abusers. Doing so would align dovish policies with values like honor and glory. There is no need to appear weak. Doves should also strive to point out how their policies are far more consistent with other American values such as prudence, patience, and restraint than is the use of force.[36] Likewise, doves should argue that being reluctant to send troops into harm's way is in fact pro-military in many ways and thus is consistent with patriotism.[37]

Crafting rhetoric to persuade also requires returning to the four types of policy debates that were discussed in chapter 1: about strategy, about how to distribute a good, about how to trade-off between goods, and about what is a positive outcome. Recall that debates about what is a positive outcome end in deadlock, making them a poor choice and that few debates in the United States over the use of force are distributional in nature. This leaves debates over trade-offs and debates about strategy as potential frames. When debates are framed as trade-offs between goods—say money and security—they favor hawks. If the public is convinced the use of force would achieve the desired policy ends, it is willing to pay substantial costs.

Thus, doves should frame their arguments in terms of debates about strategy. Doves should argue that peaceful measures are better able to secure the country and achieve the foreign policy aims of Americans. This requires showing that force fails, not just that it is costly. When faced with questions of national security, people focus not on costs but on if a policy would work or not. This is especially true after crises arise. Doves must show how restraint and peaceful policies work as well as or better than the active use of force. They must show that it isn't just that force would cost lives and money, but that at the end of the day, it would not even produce the desired result. For instance, the most successful arguments against US military intervention against the Assad regime emphasized not only that such an intervention would be costly but it would likely fail to result in a stable, democratic Syria.[38] When doves frame their arguments in this manner, they can out argue hawks.

Doves should also encourage hawks to think through what failure would look like prior to engaging in military actions. Psychological studies have shown that carefully envisioning what defeat looks like reduces the appeal of the use of force.[39] Likewise, focusing the debate on required postwar commitments makes war less attractive as doing so shows that force is unlikely to achieve the government's desired policy outcomes.[40] Again, the focus should not just be on postwar costs but rather on that needed postwar tasks are likely to fail or be left undone. The refusal to do these sorts of calculations goes a long way toward explaining not only US failures in Iraq and Libya but also why the United States opted to go to war in the first place.

The culmination of a successful argument against the use of force would be to show how nonviolent solutions would produce a better result. The ability to offer positive arguments that are consistent with the values of ordinary Americans is crucial.[41] Criticisms alone fail. Doves should highlight the past successes of policies like containment, deterrence, and the Marshall Plan and show how current dovish initiatives are analogous to those past successes and, thus, are likely to work today. In short, doves can best win arguments in the same manner that any policy argument is won. Advance solutions that appeal to the interests, emotions, and values of ordinary Americans and show how competing policies are not just costly but, more importantly, are ineffective and contrary to American ideals. Obviously, this is not easy. It requires genuine political skill, and of course, hawks would be attempting to advance their preferred policies in the same way.

The fifth step is doves cannot reject or run away from the world. They must actively engage in politics, run for office, and serve in foreign policy bureaucracies such as the State Department and US intelligence agencies.[42] While participation in activist groups is beneficial, it is far better when doves have leverage within the government and even the ear of the president. Also, electing dovish politicians is crucial, so that when crises arise, dovish officials would already be in place. Having doves in the foreign policy decision-making elite would mean the idea that force fails would be heard and taken seriously in government circles and by the media.

Doves also need to engage with folks that are often not seen as allies: military officers. As discussed in chapter 3, US military officers are not necessarily more hawkish than US civilians.[43] Thus, they may be receptive to well-crafted dovish policy prescriptions. Certainly, military personnel would take dovish views more seriously if they are coming from individuals they have worked or studied with in the past. Just as with the general public, they would be easier to win over in times of peace rather than waiting for a crisis to present dovish arguments to them. Indeed, this is one of the reasons it was foolish for so many colleges and universities in the northeastern United States to ban Reserve Officers' Training Corps (ROTC) from their campuses. This was initially done in response to the Vietnam War and continued because of the "Don't Ask, Don't Tell" policy, which prevented homosexuals from serving openly in the US military.[44] With this latter policy repealed, the only thing banning ROTC from campuses accomplishes is deepening the rift between the officer corps and broader society[45] and preventing future military officers from absorbing the values and wisdom of those very universities that ban them. This isolation of the military from society is also bad for strategic thought as it cuts the military off from potential sources of new ideas.[46] Further, it weakens the bonds between the military and the society it serves. Happily, such policies have begun to be reversed in recent years, helping to bring future military personnel in contact with broader swaths of society.[47]

Last, doves must push back against the negative stereotypes associated with those who advocate for peace. Doing so is one of the major aims of this book. Doves are not naïve, nor are they unpatriotic. They want what is in the United States' best interest. It is this desire—matched with a realistic understanding of the world—that leads them to advocate for peaceful policies. Doves can do this by pointing out the serious limitations force has in achieving American goals. Doves should also avoid overly optimistic predictions. Dovish policies are not panaceas, and no matter what foreign policy the United States embraces, it will face setbacks. Doves must demonstrate that they are hardheaded, and it is hawks who are overly optimistic.

Winning the debate is vital. The American overuse of force strains US material and moral resources. It saps American willpower and feeds isolationist tendencies.[48] Isolationism is a policy with deep roots in US history and significant public support.[49] Thus, it poses a real danger as an American withdrawal from the world would undermine the international security, legal, and economic orders so carefully crafted by the United States and its allies over the last seventy-five years. By serving as a check on American overreach and preventing debacles, dovish policies can help maintain

American engagement with the world. Only a more peaceful foreign policy is able to maintain support across the US political spectrum. Without such broad support, US foreign policy is likely to be erratic and insufficiently internationalist.[50]

A dovish foreign policy would not only keep the United States engaged in international affairs, thereby allowing Washington to pursue a vigorous and honorable foreign policy, but it would result in a more successful foreign policy. A dovish grand strategy would result in policies better aligned with US goals, and its forbearance regarding the use of force would avoid making enemies out of countries that fear US power.[51] These successes would also be achieved at reduced costs.

A dovish foreign policy could also play a role in bringing about a more peaceful international order. The nature of the international order is not fixed. It varies by time and place with different types of order possible.[52] While the United States cannot dictate the nature of that order—as American failures of force have so clearly demonstrated—as the system's most powerful country, it can contribute significantly to shaping the international order. By focusing on peaceful methods including law, economic tools, and diplomacy, the United States can influence what tools other countries use and what behaviors are seen as legitimate. Of course, disputes would remain, but they could be resolved or at least be adjudicated without the use of force—much as is the norm in domestic politics. In short, it is possible to strengthen the global order and make the world safer by using force less often. The alternative is overusing force and creating enemies by seeing danger where it is not. As George Kennan said,

> It is the undeniable privilege of every man to prove himself right in the thesis that the world is his enemy; for if he reiterates it frequently enough and makes it the background of his conduct, he is bound to be eventually right.[53]

To avoid such a fate, American doves must advance the argument that peaceful means and passive uses of force best secure the nation's safety and interests. They must do this regularly and remember that their audience is not fellow doves but, rather, persuadable hawks and fence-sitters. Doves, whether elites or everyday Americans, must speak to the concerns of moderate hawks and the undecided in ways consistent with American traditions and values. The argument is eminently winnable, but it must be made repeatedly in both times of calm and crisis. Waiting for anti-war marches to do anything is a losing hand. In order to begin positively shaping events, the dovish argument must be made not only in dramatic demonstrations but in more mundane ways. It must be made in conversations with friends and family members, in letters and petitions to elected officials, and at the ballot box. The time to start is now.

# Notes

## Introduction

    1. Eisenhower (1958).

    2. Draper (2015).

    3. iCasualties.org (2019); US Department of Defense (2019). The fatalities include all US deaths in those countries because of US military operations, not just those killed in action, though the vast majority of the deaths are in fact from combat.

    4. The manpower strain was made more severe by the concurrent war in Afghanistan, but the Iraq War was responsible for the vast majority of the military manpower demands (Lind 2006, 163).

    5. Amadeo (2019b).

    6. Amadeo (2019a).

    7. Martinez and McLaughlin (2018).

    8. Calamur (2018); *CBS News* (2011).

    9. Brown (2003, 3 and 26–47); Lind (2006, 162).

    10. This is not to dismiss the moral argument. Moral arguments against the use of force are important but well-known.

    11. Dempsey (2019).

    12. Cohen (2016, 82).

    13. Bacevich (2008, 7); Brooks (2016, 20–21); Nexon (2018); Tierney (2015, 29 and 297).

    14. Cohen (2016, 59).

    15. Rothkopf (2014).

    16. Zenko (2017).

    17. Betts (2012, 280); Spaeth (2014).

    18. Brands (2018, 34–35); Wright (2016). This hawkishness no doubt stems from his worldview, which emphasizes coercion over persuasion.

    19. Cary (2017); Crowley, Hassan, and Schmitt (2020); Gaffey (2017); Heer (2017); Jaffe (2018); Landler and Gordon (2017); Liptak (2017); Schmitt (2017); Wright (2016).

    20. Atwood and Gaouette (2019); Baker and Haberman (2019); Edmondson

and Wong (2019); Lamothe and Dawsey (2019); Landler and Baker (2019); Landler, Haberman, and Schmitt (2019); Mashal (2019); Schmitt and Barnes (2019); Schmitt and Landler (2019); Shear, Cooper, and Schmitt (2019); Wong and Casey (2019).

21. Despite their shared hawkishness, Clinton and Trump obviously disagree about many aspects of foreign and domestic policy.

22. Landler (2016).

23. Sachs (2018, 77–79).

24. Kagan (2014). Kagan's data go through 2014, but as the United States has engaged in combat operations in every year since 2014, the numbers are updated to reflect that.

25. Kennan (1984, 174).

26. Posen (2014).

27. Johnson (2007, 234–35).

28. Political scientists often include being prepared to fight or deterring threats against oneself as a use of force (Art 1996; Baldwin 1999). That is not the sense in which I use the term in this book. By use of force, I mean the active deployment of military units in combat.

29. Allard (1995); Girard (2004).

30. Ross (2005).

31. Hawkish counterterrorism policies also rely heavily on intelligence gathering.

## Chapter 1

1. *"Parvi enim sunt foris arma, nisi est consilium domi."* (Cicero 1956|44 BC, 77: bk I, section 76).

2. Lorenzo (2016, 4–11).

3. Harrington (1935); Kinzer (2017b); Lorenzo (2016); McCartney (2004); McDougall (1997); Morgenthau (1952); Schmidt and Williams (2008); Schroeder (1973); Tompkins (1970).

4. For a full explanation of why people's expectations and beliefs should converge given sufficient information, see Slantchev (2003).

5. Given the inability to travel back in time and try all options, it is possible that the best strategy will never be known if certain strategies were time contingent.

6. Planck (1948, 22).

7. Krugman (2011); Mankiw (1997, 280–90); Wolfers (2014).

8. Wagner (2007).

9. Wagner (2007).

10. Wagner (2007).

11. Kecskemeti (1958).

12. Warfare in antiquity, at times, lacked this element. It wasn't unheard of for the entire population of a city to be slaughtered or sold into slavery after capit-

ulating, though even in those harsh times such behavior was the exception rather than the rule. See for instance the "Mytilenian Debate" (3.25–28 and 3.35–50) and the "Melian Dialogue" (5.84–116) in Thucydides (1993|c. 400 BC).

13. Fearon (1995).

14. 1 Kings 3:16–28.

15. Alexander (2018).

16. Bemis (1977, 317–40).

17. Thibodeau and Lynch (2017).

18. Such debates could also be about how much of a bad should be absorbed to achieve a good. In other words, is the end worth the cost?

19. In short, people will disagree about *where* to be on the Pareto frontier.

20. Decisions about military tactics and strategies can hinge on this question. For instance, should artillery be used in an area where enemy combatants and civilians are comingled, given such a tactic would likely save the lives of US military personnel but kill more civilians when compared to attacking without artillery support? For a thorough discussion of such difficult questions, see Walzer (1977).

21. Individuals that believe torture is justifiable in certain circumstances may then engage in debates about when it is wise to do so, but the fundamental debate usually comes down to if torture is ever justifiable. Opponents of torture generally argue not only is torture morally wrong but that it is also unwise and ineffective.

22. Fettweis (2013, 94–140); O'Neill (1999, 85).

23. Horowitz and Stam (2014); Sechser (2004).

24. Shoesmith and Kelly (2010).

25. In current US Air Force usage, both men and women in that service are referred to as airmen.

26. Beauchamp (2017); Steinhauer (2015).

27. Kroll (2017); Tyson (2016).

28. Schroeder (1973, 205–6).

29. Mandelbaum (2005, 170).

30. Public opinion was so heated surrounding the Jay Treaty, which Washington's administration had negotiated with Britain, that protestors hanged John Jay in effigy (McDougall 1997, 29).

31. Gordon (1997, 236).

32. Kaufmann (2004); Snyder and Ballentine (1996).

33. Kaufmann (2004, 37–43).

34. Thrall (2007, 456).

35. Gordon (1997, 239).

36. Krebs (2005, 197–98).

37. Jackson and Kaufmann (2007, 95).

38. Gordon (1997, 237).

39. Fettweis (2013, 1); Gordon (1997, 241).

40. Mill (1997|1859, 21 and 34–35); Gordon (1997, 238).

41. Mill (1997|1859, 21–24 and 63).

42. Gordon (1997, 238).

43. Mill (1997|1859, 40).

44. Gordon (1997, 239).

45. Mill (1997|1859, 63). Unfortunately, less partisan individuals also tend to be less informed and less inclined to follow the policy process, meaning that they may not be attentive to debates (Palfrey and Poole 1987).

46. Mill (1997|1859, 25).

47. Jagannathan (2017).

48. Newport (2003).

49. Walt (2013).

50. Jackson and Kaufman (2007, 96–99).

51. Scowcroft (2002).

52. Barkham (2013); Tharoor (2013).

53. Kaufmann (2004, 35).

54. Bullock (2007); Gilens (2001); Howell and West (2009); Nyhan et al. (2014); Thrall (2007, 461).

55. Nyhan and Reifler (2010).

56. Levy and Maaravi (2018). Dwelling on opponents' biases can also lead to defeatism. It may be psychologically comforting to think one's opponents are mistaken and not fully rational, but it does nothing to improve the odds that dovish policies are adopted. Besides, all people suffer from biases—doves as well as hawks.

57. Kuklinski et al. (2000); Nyhan and Reifler (2015).

58. Fettweis (2013, 230–31).

59. Nyhan and Reifler (2010, 308); Nyhan and Reifler (2015).

60. Nyhan and Reifler (2010, 315–23); Nyhan and Reifler (2015).

61. Lorenzo (2016).

62. Harrington (1935).

63. Fettweis (2013, 14).

64. Fettweis (2013, 21 and 94–140); Goldberg (2014).

65. Fettweis (2013, 97).

66. O'Neill (1999, 85–92).

67. O'Neill (1999, 103).

68. O'Neill (1999, 103).

69. O'Neill (1999, 85).

70. O'Neill (1999, 85).

71. Fettweis (2013, 94–140).

72. Fettweis (2013, 146).

73. Fettweis (2013, 164–65).

74. Osgood (1953, 6).

75. Fettweis (2013, 155–56).

76. Fettweis (2013, 6–8).

77. Fettweis (2013, 228-29).

78. Fettweis (2013, 228-32).

79. McCartney (2004); Schmidt and Williams (2008).

80. Lorenzo (2016, 69); Schroeder (1973, 203-7).

81. Lorenzo (2016, 52-53 and 204-5).

82. Harrington (1935); Lorenzo (2016); Schroeder (1973, 203).

83. Colaresi (2004).

84. Johnson and Tierney (2011).

85. Lorenzo (2016, 15-16); McCartney (2004); Schroeder (1973, 204); Schmidt and Williams (2008).

86. Lorenzo (2016, 41); Schroeder (1973, 163).

87. Baum and Potter (2015, 3-6 and 29).

88. Harrington (1935); Lorenzo (2016); Schroeder (1973, 208-9).

## *Chapter 2*

1. Betts (2012, xii).

2. Becker and Schmitt (2018); Zenko and Lissner (2017).

3. Haass (1997); Safire (2006). Clinton's foreign policy became more structured and coherent as he gained experience (Walt 2000).

4. Stares (2018, 17).

5. Shimko (2017, 26); Walt (2011).

6. Patrick (2015, 74).

7. Snow (2015, 104).

8. Preble (2009, 1).

9. International Monetary Fund (2017b); Posen (2014, 16-20); Stockholm International Peace Research Institute (SIPRI) (2017); United Nations (2017).

10. Bremmer (2015, 125-39); Cohen (2017, 2).

11. Legro (2015a, 26-27); Lind (2006, 173).

12. Roosevelt (1905).

13. Stares (2018, 1-16).

14. Brands (2018, 25-34 and 42-47); Walt (2006, 31); Wright (2017, 154 and 178-79).

15. Hoffman and Brinkbäumer (2018).

16. Legro (2015b|2000, 323).

17. Huntington (2015|1982, 307); Lind (2006, 81 and 171).

18. Osgood (1953, 429-32).

19. McDougall (1997, 153).

20. McDougall (1997, 147).

21. Whipple (1991).

22. Moore (2015).

23. Irwin (2005); Kaplan (1957).

24. Kennan (1984, 178).

25. Kennan (1947).

26. Snow (2000, 71–72).

27. Bemis (1977, 544 n. 46). Emphasis added.

28. Bemis (1977, 544).

29. *Treaty of Amity* (1794); *Treaty of Friendship* (1795).

30. Hamilton, Madison, and Jay (2003|1788). See especially numbers 3–6 and 11.

31. Betts (2012, 22); Nordlinger (1995, 6); Preble (2009, 90–91); Posen (2014, 16–20); Walt (2006, 39).

32. Casey (2019a; 2019b). This development in regards to civil wars is relatively recent. Much of Latin America was plagued by civil conflicts during the Cold War. Interstate peace has held far longer. The last interstate conflict in the hemisphere was a small border conflict between Ecuador and Peru in 1995. There were a number of small interstate conflicts in the 1980s (Falklands War and US invasions of Panama and Grenada). The last large-scale, multiyear interstate war in the hemisphere, not counting naval actions resulting from World War II, occurred in the 1930s between Paraguay and Bolivia.

33. The United States does have disagreements with both countries, especially with Mexico over immigration.

34. The United States has four minor maritime boundary disputes with Canada: two off Alaska, one off Washington, and one off Maine. The United States also disputes the Canadian claim that the Northwest Passage is an internal water of Canada rather than an international waterway (Gray 1997).

35. Pillar (2016, 7, and 46–48).

36. Kaplan (2017).

37. Cohen (2017, 94–95).

38. Bosworth (2012). The Rio Pact is less important today than it was during the Cold War, and several Latin American countries have withdrawn from the pact in the twenty-first century. Still, the Pact contains seventeen members pledged to mutual assistance.

39. Despite warm relations between the United States and New Zealand, the formal status of the relationship has been somewhat unclear since the mid-1980s when, because of New Zealand's decision to adopt a nuclear-free status, US naval vessels could no longer dock in New Zealand ports. This led the US government to label New Zealand as a "friend" rather than an "ally." Even so, New Zealand remained a member of "five-eyes," the multinational intelligence sharing group consisting of the United States, United Kingdom, Canada, Australia, and New Zealand. Likewise, New Zealand still considers itself as part of ANZUS, the trilateral defense pact between Australia, New Zealand, and the United States. Last, New Zealand and the United States resumed joint military exercises in 2013. Thus, it seems most accurate to label New Zealand as a US ally (Dougan 2013).

40. Mukherjee (2019).

41. Brands (2018, 16); Walt (2006, 34).

42. Jervis (2002).

43. Chaudoin, Milner, and Tingley (2018, 63); Nexon (2018).

44. Walt (2006, 32).

45. Betts (2012, 284); Gholz, Press, and Sapolsky (1997, 14).

46. Posen (2003; 2014, 136-44).

47. Brands (2018, 15); Walt (2006, 34).

48. Sachs (2018, 84).

49. Hartmann (1982); Jervis (2003, 382); Mueller (1994).

50. Kissinger (1994); Quester (1982, 19-20).

51. Cohen (2017, 92); Huntington (2015|1982, 308-11); Mandelbaum (2016, 9).

52. Drezner (2008, 56).

53. Sachs (2018, 1-2).

54. Legro (2015b|2000, 325).

55. Pillar (2016).

56. Fettweis (2013, 60); Tierney (2010, 23).

57. Pillar (2016, 84-90).

58. Huntington (2015|1982, 297); Lind (2006, 9-10); Patrick (2015, 6); Pillar (2016, 95).

59. Patrick (2015, 73); Tierney (2010, 22).

60. Huntington (2015|1982, 306-9); Tierney (2010, 22).

61. Fettweis (2013, 21); Sachs (2018, 21-37).

62. Huntington (2015|1982, 309); Pillar (2016, 84-90). For instance, leading up to the 1991 and 2003 wars with Iraq, many Americans favored retributive force to punish Iraq while others opposed the wars on humanitarian grounds. Obviously, debates on utilitarian grounds also swirled prior to both conflicts, but morality informed many Americans' preferences for and against the use of force (Liberman 2006).

63. Lind (2006, 25-34).

64. Cohen (2017, 13-14). This is one potential weakness of Trump's "America First" foreign policy, which focuses narrowly on US material benefits and burden-sharing. While Americans care about material costs and benefits, a foreign policy devoid of morality is unlikely to be able to maintain broad popular support from the American public. Nor is it clear that Trump's policies have succeeded even in narrow material terms.

65. Wright (2017, 169).

66. Kissinger (1994).

67. P. Miller (2016, 101-2); Schmidt and Williams (2008).

68. Huntington (2015|1982, 311).

69. Huntington (2015|1982, 309); Kissinger (1994).

70. Mead (2001, 10).

71. Ikenberry (2011, 2-4).

72. Cohen and Zenko (2019); Goldstein (2011); Holsti (2016); Lacina and Gleditsch (2005); Pinker (2011); Vayrynen (2013); Zenko and Cohen (2012). The number of both battlefield and civilian deaths due to warfare has dropped (Fettweis 2018, 15-38). Some of this drop is a result of better battlefield medical care, rather than a result of less conflict (Fazal 2014).

73. Fettweis (2013, 33-34).

74. Nexon (2018).

75. Council on Foreign Relations (2009, 1-2); LaFranchi (2018); *World Public Opinion* (2011).

76. Council on Foreign Relations (2009, 6); LaFranchi (2018); *World Public Opinion* (2011); Yale Program on Climate Change Communication (2016).

77. Council on Foreign Relations (2009, 5).

78. Betts (2014; 2012, 292-94). These alliance structures can and do vary significantly by region to reflect local realities and threats. Arrangements may be tighter or looser depending on the severity of threats and also the degree of overlapping interests. For instance, US alliances with Latin American countries are more about maintaining good relations than deterring military threats as there are few if any external military threats to that region. Alliances may also be multilateral or bilateral in nature depending on how well US allies get along with each other. Past rivalries between US allies in Asia have led to a series of bilateral alliances there, while the high level of interdependence and shared interests in Europe have allowed NATO to be both multilateral and highly integrated (Ikenberry 2011, 100).

79. George, Hall, and Simons (1971, 251-52); Posen (2014); Tierney (2015, 300-1).

80. Rosato and Schuessler (2015|2011, 120).

81. Bacevitch (2005, 211); Walt (2002, 142).

82. Tierney (2015, 300-1).

83. Bacevitch (2005, 214-15); Betts (2012, 274-75).

84. Lind (2006, 174); Mandelbaum (2005, 21-22 and 37-39); Stares (2018, 21).

85. Cohen (2017, 10); Lind (2006, 174); Mandelbaum (2005, 40).

86. Betts (2012, 292-94); Mandelbaum (2005, 41-52).

87. Ikenberry (2011, 37); Mandelbaum (2005, 33).

88. Stares (2018, 106-31).

89. Jervis (2002); Wright (2017, 178-79).

90. Holden (1995).

91. Goertz, Diehl, and Balas (2016, 69).

92. Mandelbaum (2005, 39). This is not to say that there are no issues around US military bases located on allies' territory. The US base in Okinawa, for instance, has been a major point of contention with locals on the island. The Japanese government has continued to support the US presence on the island but favors moving the base to a less contentious area on Okinawa (*Japan Today* 2018; Mason 2017).

93. Betts (2012, 292-94); Posen (2014).

94. Preble (2009, 10).

95. Beckley (2015); Cha (2010); Kim (2011).

96. The post-World War II legal order, of course, was not created out of whole cloth but built upon the already existing international legal order, which had

developed slowly over the preceding four centuries (Mattingly 1988; Watson 1992). While much of this order reflects Western legal notions, it also reflects input from the wider world (Acharya 2018).

97. Ikenberry (2011, 134).

98. Donnelly (2012); Stone (2004).

99. Ikenberry and Kupchan (2004); Lind (2006, 175–78).

100. Zakaria (2017).

101. P. Miller (2016, 24); Kissinger (2014); Organski (1968).

102. Ikenberry (2011, 122).

103. P. Miller (2016, 13); Ikenberry (2011, 159–219); Lind (2006, 24–25).

104. Ikenberry (2011, 135); Mandelbaum (2005).

105. Mandelbaum (2005, 7–9). The United States also benefits from these services and would likely provide them even if other countries did not benefit from them.

106. Ikenberry (2011, 134).

107. Lind (2006, 24–25).

108. Ikenberry (2011, xiii); Luce (2017); Roberts, Armijo, and Katada (2017); Stares (2018, 2–3).

109. Wright (2017, 31).

110. Mukherjee (2019); Wright (2017, 1–35).

111. Ikenberry (2011, 287–89).

112. Wright (2017, 35–66).

113. Brands (2018, 104–5); Hirsh (2016); MacKay and LaRoche (2018a; 2018b).

114. Luce (2017); Wright (2017, x and 162).

115. Ikenberry (2011, xiii).

116. Ikenberry (2011, xii and 6–8).

117. Armitage (2017).

118. Wright (2017, 192–95).

119. Ikenberry (2011, xiv).

120. Lind (2006, 34–35); Stares (2018, 69–71); Zacher (2001).

121. Lind (2006, 24–25).

122. Clark (2007); Kissinger (1994; 2014); Ruggie (1998); Watson (1992).

123. Clark (2007); Watson (1992).

124. Ikenberry (2011, 112).

125. Hurd (2017, 38–39).

126. Mandelbaum (2005, 144); Walt (2006, 226); Watson (1992).

127. Ikenberry (2011, 135).

128. Johnson (2007, 152).

129. For instance, see Nordlinger (1995, 7).

130. Bacevitch (2010, 234).

131. Human Rights Watch (2017); United Nations (1948); World Conference on Human Rights (1993). While the Universal Declaration of Human Rights is

sometimes criticized as reflecting a Western view of human rights, the Vienna Declaration was adopted by 171 countries meaning it reflects a broad view of human rights, not just a Western one.

132. Gholz, Press, and Sapolsky (1997, 10); Posen (2014, 56–57).

133. Brands (2018, 94).

134. Nexon (2018).

135. Mandelbaum (2005, 18–19 and 90–91).

136. Hartz (1955); Patrick (2015, 82–83).

137. Patrick (2015, 81).

138. Ikenberry (2011, 271–72).

139. Ikenberry (2011, 177).

140. Angell (1933); Gartzke (2007); Keohane and Nye (1987); Russett and Oneal (2000); Stares (2018, 69–76).

141. Krugman (2018); Nexon (2018). This allows these corporations to extract rents—profits that are in excess of those corporations' economic contributions to the economy.

142. Grenville (1998); Mansori (2011).

143. Kaminsky and Schmukler (2008); Korinek (2011); Ostry et al. (2011); Ostry et al. (2012); Rey (2018).

144. McGregor (2018).

145. McGregor (2018).

146. Kennedy (1987); Mandelbaum (2005, 28).

147. Walt (2006).

148. Mandelbaum (2005, 147–52).

149. Adams (1821, 29).

150. Kissinger (2014, 3–7).

151. Watson (1992). An international system is a set of countries that regularly interact with each other and whose actions can influence each other. An international order is a set of rules that governs or regulates the behaviors of countries within an international system or subsystem.

152. Ikenberry (2011, 299).

153. Betts (2012, 278–79); Stares (2018, xvi–xvii).

154. Mandelbaum (2016, 10–11).

155. Mandelbaum (2016, 372).

156. Betts (2012, 285–88).

157. Luard (1989, 14–16).

158. Luard (1989, 81–85 and 92–104).

159. Betts (2012, 50–80); Shirkey (2012); Snow (2000, 121; 2016, 115).

160. Betts (2012, 62).

161. Bacevitch (2016). Elsewhere I have predicted, though certainly not prescribed, that the United States would remain militarily involved in the Middle East despite its growing self-sufficiency in oil (Shirkey 2013). I would love to be wrong, but unfortunately the prediction so far has been borne out.

162. Bacevitch (2013, 109). The deliberate limiting of actions one would undertake is just as much of a strategy as any other (Nordlinger 1995, 8–9).

163. Engel (2016).

164. Snow (2000, 71–72).

165. Bacevitch (2010, 20).

166. Sachs (2018, 172).

167. Eisenhower (1954).

168. Morello and DeYoung (2015).

169. The George H. W. Bush administration's foreign policy was largely realist in character but contained significant elements of liberal internationalism such as the embrace of multilateralism and international institutions.

170. For instance, see Kennan (1947).

171. Gholz, Press, Sapolsky (1997); Mearsheimer (2018, 3 and 222–27); Nordlinger (1995); Preble (2009, 12); Walt (2018, 13, 16, 32–37, and 62–66).

172. Mearsheimer (2018); Nordlinger (1995); Preble (2009, 97–102); Posen (2014, 33–44); Sullivan (2019, 170); Walt (2018, 72–73).

173. Gholz, Press, Sapolsky (1997, 5–25); Mearsheimer (2018). Walt (2018, 269–70) would maintain US alliances in Asia but pull back from Europe.

174. Walt (2018, 264).

175. Sullivan (2019, 174).

176. Some offshore balancing strategies want the United States to shift resources to Asia to prevent China from becoming a regional hegemon (Mearsheimer 2018, 222–27; Sullivan 2019, 172; Walt 2018, 269). Such strategies run the risk of simultaneously undermining the European security order while increasing the odds of the military conflict with China.

177. Sullivan (2019, 171); Walt (2018, 260–63).

178. P. Miller (2016, 11).

179. P. Miller (2016, 9); Sullivan (2019, 168–69). See Walt (2018, 14 and 259) and especially Mearsheimer (2018, 1, 120–22, and 222) for examples of this sort of false dichotomy.

180. P. Miller (2016, 14).

181. There are exceptions to this. For instance, see Posen (2014) and Walt (2018) for examples of advocates of strategic restraint or offshore balancing that also leave a place for or even insist on a moral element in US foreign policy.

182. Mearsheimer (2018, 2 and 20–24).

183. For instance, see Kaufmann and Pape (1999).

184. Osgood (1953, 1 and 20–21); Sullivan (2019, 171). Of course, aligning interests with values can be quite challenging at times.

185. Kissinger (1994).

186. Osgood (1953, 442).

187. P. Miller (2016, 12).

188. Osgood (1953, 445–46).

## Chapter 3

1. Churchill (1987, 232).

2. Bacevich (2008, 159–60); Betts (2012, 4).

3. *ABC News* (2013).

4. Snow (2000, 69).

5. Bacevitch (2016).

6. Fallows (2015).

7. Bacevich (2008, 166–67); Snow (2015, 67).

8. Specia and Sanger (2018).

9. Boot (2014); Brennan (2014).

10. Boot (2014); Fallows (2015).

11. Freedman (2017).

12. Some goals are directly connected to battlefield success such as defense of allies and one's homeland. Yet, the United States rarely has needed to engage in such uses of force because it is so clear that it will prevail in those contests.

13. George, Hall, and Simons (1971, 14–15).

14. Abrahms and Mireau (2017).

15. Abbas (2013); Ludvigsen (2018).

16. Posen (2014, 57); Snow (2015).

17. Dempsey (2019).

18. Freedman (2017).

19. Bacevich (2008, 159–60); Betts (2012, 4); Brown (2003, 5–7).

20. Betts (2012, 290–91).

21. Betts (2012, 232–42).

22. Betts (2012, 250).

23. Freedman (2017).

24. Clausewitz (1976, 75–99, 113–21 and 603–10).

25. Myers (2000).

26. Mashal and Rahim (2016).

27. Benac (2014).

28. The use of drones to collect intelligence is a separate issue and is something drones are particularly adept at compared to other forms of battlefield surveillance.

29. Shane (2015; 2016).

30. Bacevich (2005, 21–22).

31. Bowden (2006).

32. Mazzetti (2011).

33. Mathews (1990). Whether he did this because he knew the D-Day landings would occur the following day and his capture of Rome would receive far less attention if it was delayed or because he doubted his force was strong enough to cut the Germans off is debated.

34. Burns (1786).

35. Brown (2003, 155); Shimko (2017, 101–4).

36. Bacevich (2013, xiii).

37. Brooks (2016, 279–81).

38. Brown (2003, 151); Luard (1989, 88–89).

39. Baldwin (1999).

40. Congressional Budget Office (2003); Gowa and Kim (2005); Mellnik and Williams (2018); Petri and Plummer (2016). In absolute terms, the United States often gains the most, but this results from the large size of the US economy, which turns small percentage gains into large absolute numbers.

41. Angell (1933). Angell's argument developed out of a long, liberal tradition arguing war was not profitable. See, for instance, Cobden (1870), Constant (1988|1819), and Smith (1937|1776). Individuals, as opposed to whole societies, however, can profit from looting. See note 45 in this chapter.

42. Collier (2005).

43. Betts (2012, 289); Stern (2010). Whether a US presence in the Middle East is necessary to ensure the flow of oil from the Persian Gulf is unclear (Preble 2009, 108).

44. Clark (2001, 275–78; 2002, 152–230).

45. It did, however, allow a number of Ugandan elites to *personally* enrich themselves. Similarly, specific individuals or companies could conceivably profit from wars waged by the United States or other countries with modern economies even while the country as a whole would be made worse off. Narrow individual profit at the expense of broad costs to society as a whole, however, is hardly a good reason to wage war—especially in a democracy.

46. This is one reason why foreign governments did not object to the 2009 US auto industry bailout. German and Japanese auto companies would have been harmed by the collapse of US auto parts manufacturers, which would have certainly occurred had General Motor or Chrysler—two of the biggest purchasers of US auto parts—gone under.

47. Gholz and Press (2001).

48. Gholz and Press (2001).

49. Mattingly (1988, 116–18); McEvedy (1961; 1986); Smith (1937|1776, 653–69).

50. Jones (2012, especially 384–90 and 430–33); Postan (1964).

51. Mattingly (1955, 162–63).

52. Howard (1976, 22, 48–49, and 62–63).

53. Anderson (1998, 135–56).

54. Opponents of Angell argued that World War I discredited his hypothesis because they either misunderstood what he was arguing or deliberately misconstrued his position to make it seem that he was arguing that war was impossible (Weiss 2013).

55. Liberman (1996).

56. Liberman (1996). It does mean, however, that countries must confront aggressors as the holding of conquered territories by aggressors would not necessarily be a net drain short run. Thus, while force does not result in net economic gains, the use of force by others is still dangerous. As will be shown in chapter 5, doves can successfully deal with such foreign military threats.

57. Liberman (1996). Nationalism makes this true for the occupation of poorer states as well. While it is debated whether colonialism was profitable prior

to World War II, there is little reason to believe it would pay today given the modern mix of nationalism, complex economies, and guerilla warfare.

58. Blainey (1973); Hafner-Burton et al. (2017). Fey and Ramsay (2007) attempt to show that mutual optimism is not a cause of war, however, Slantchev and Tarar (2011) demonstrate that their results depend on one side being able to unilaterally impose peace. This is not a realistic assumption as one side can always launch a war whether the other side wants to fight or not.

59. Wagner (2000).

60. Jervis (1988, 676).

61. Van Evera (1999, 16).

62. Betts (2014).

63. Fearon (1995).

64. Reiter (2009); Weisiger (2013).

65. Tetlock and McGuire (2015|1985, 490).

66. Stanley (2018).

67. Lupia (1994).

68. Kahneman and Renshon (2007; 2009).

69. Stanley (2018).

70. Levy (1986).

71. Johnson (2004). Individuals suffering from depression have somewhat more realistic assessments of their own abilities (Moore and Fresco 2012).

72. Johnson (2004).

73. Jervis (1976, 343–48); Johnson (2004). Such "perceived control" has been shown to reduce stress and, provided that the illusion does not lead to poor decision-making, can be seen as beneficial on an individual level (Glass et al. 1973).

74. Fettweis (2013, 187; 2018, 38–41); Jervis (1976, 349).

75. Snyder (1984).

76. Johnson (2004).

77. Svenson (1981).

78. Alpert and Raiffa (1982).

79. Jervis (1976, 344). This is known as self-serving bias.

80. Kahneman and Renshon (2009, 79).

81. Badie (2015|2010, 475–76).

82. O'Connor (2002). This latter phenomenon is known in social psychology as polarization.

83. Malhotra and Ginges (2010); Maoz et al. (2002); Ross (1995); Ross and Stillinger (1991).

84. This is known as the fundamental attribution error. This is where others' actions are perceived to be a result of who they fundamentally are as opposed to a result of the circumstances they find themselves in. Thus, hostile actions by others are perceived to reflect not a logical response to a given situation but an innate desire to inflict harm (Tetlock 1985).

85. Jervis (1976, 71).

86. Jervis (1976, 61); Mintz and Wayne (2015, 3).

87. Fischer (2000). Actions that increase the security of one country but reduce the security of another are common in international relations. The difficulty of determining whether another country's actions are being done to make them more secure or to harm another country is known as the security dilemma (Herz 1950; Jervis 1978).

88. Horowitz, McDermott, and Stam (2005); Horowitz and Stam (2014).

89. Levy (1986); Snyder (1984); Van Evera (1984).

90. Betts (1977, 88-90).

91. Snyder (1984); Van Evera (1984).

92. Betts (1977).

93. Betts (1977, 210).

94. Sechser (2004).

95. Lai and Slater (2006).

96. Horowitz, McDermott, and Stam (2005); Horowitz and Stam (2014).

97. Ikenberry (2011, 127).

98. Fettweis (2018, 80).

99. Shimko (2017, 95).

100. For example, the relatively small French deployment to Mali in 2013 to fight a mix of Islamist groups and Tuareg secessionists would have been impossible without US airlift capabilities (Callon 2013). Even after the French troops arrived, they remained partially dependent on US airpower for resupply (Everstine 2015).

101. Fettweis (2018, 5); Shimko (2017, 95).

102. Fettweis (2018, 5).

103. Kennedy (2002, 12). This superiority won't last forever—at least not in relation to great power rivals. Presumably, as China's economy continues to grow, its military spending will grow apace, thereby closing the gap between its military capabilities and those of the United States.

104. Bacevitch (2016).

105. Betts (2012, 281); Brands (2018, 34-35); Johnson (2007, 123); Mathews (2019).

106. Betts (2012, 281); Lind (2006, 160); Mandelbaum (2016, 378); Mathews (2019).

107. Bacevich (2005, 29; 2013, 124).

108. Fallows (2015).

109. Brown (2003, 78-104).

110. Brooks (2016, 20); Fallows (2015); *Gallup* (2016).

111. Bacevich (2005, 23-24)

112. Brooks (2016, 14-18).

113. Fallows (2015).

114. Betts (2012, 7-8); Pillar (2016, 21 and 147). Both those on the far left and libertarians tend to be isolationists rather than internationalists (though libertarians do favor free trade), meaning that Americans who favor an active, inter-

nationalist foreign policy are especially prone to inflating the amount of threat the United States faces.

115. Fettweis (2018, 75–76).

116. The United States also faces homegrown terrorism, but that is a domestic, rather than foreign, policy problem.

117. Luard (1989, 57–68).

118. Bacevitch (2008); Fettweis (2018, 124–29).

119. Fettweis (2018, 150–53).

120. Sachs (2018, 9–10).

121. Snow (2015, 62–63).

122. Kennan (1984, 175); Mead (2001, 254); Pillar (2016, 122–26).

123. Wagner (2000).

124. George, Hall, and Simons (1971, 1).

125. Clausewitz (1976, 87).

126. Smeltz, Daalder, Friedhoff, and Kafura (2017).

127. Cooper (2014); Snow (2015, 104–13); Spaeth (2014).

128. Fettweis (2013, 189–93).

129. Bacevich (2005, 2).

130. Ashford (2018).

131. Pillar (2016, 50).

132. Ashford (2018).

133. Kennan (1984, 165–67).

134. Bacevitch (2013, 124).

135. Fettweis (2018, 41–43).

136. McDougall (1997).

137. Kreps and Maxey (2018a; 2018b).

138. McDougall (1997).

139. Cooper (2014).

140. Lind (2006, 128).

## Chapter 4

1. Camus (1960, 58).

2. Axelrod (1984); Axelrod and Keohane (1985); Keohane (1989); Ostrom (1990); Oye (1986); Snidal (1991); Stein (1982).

3. Wagner (2007).

4. Mandelbaum (2016, 11).

5. Bacevitch (2016); Johnson (2007, 138–40); Rohde (2013, xv); Shimko (2017, 93). Osgood (1953, 447–48) argued in the 1950s that Americans focused too narrowly on the use of force at the expense of other policy tools so this narrow conception of national power is not a new phenomenon.

6. Bacevitch (2008, 160).

7. Preble (2009, 2).

8. Tierney (2015, 272–74).

9. Rohde (2013, xvi).

10. Bacevitch (2010, 199–200). See Gibbons-Neff (2019) for an example of this from US counterterrorism development projects in the Philippines.

11. Rohde (2013, 12); USAID (2016, 3). USAID is the main American agency in charge of the distribution of economic and development aid to foreign countries. The employment numbers are from 2016.

12. Gordon and Schmitt (2017).

13. Broad and Peçanha (2015).

14. Landler (2018).

15. Drezner (1999, 6).

16. Johnson (2007, 186).

17. Baldwin (1985); Hirschman (1980).

18. Bremmer (2015, 112–17).

19. McDonald (2009, 39).

20. Gartzke (2007); Gartzke and Li (2001); Ikenberry (2011, 62); McDonald (2004; 2009, 18); Nye (2002); Russett and Oneal (2000). In particular, the freeness of economic exchange appears to be at least as important as the volume of the trade (McDonald 2009, 288–92). These modern findings in political science build on a long line of argumentation developed by economic and political thinkers such as Bastiat, Bentham, Cobden, Mill, Montesquieu, Paine, and Schumpeter. See McDonald (2009, 36–38) for a brief survey of this line of classical liberal thought.

21. McDonald (2009, 38); Nye (2002).

22. Goertz, Diehl, and Balas (2016, 61).

23. Davis (2000); George, Hall, and Simons (1971, 25).

24. Hufbauer, Schott, and Oegg (2001); Leverett (2004). Other factors were at play as well. Rarely do events in international relations have a single cause.

25. Bapat et al. (2013); Marinov (2005).

26. Nephew (2018, 47); Mandelbaum (2005, 119–20); Wright (2017, 131).

27. Putnam (2014).

28. Nephew (2018, 44).

29. Baldwin (1999/2000, 83).

30. Wright (2017, 132).

31. Wright (2017, 132).

32. Drezner (1999); Hufbauer, Schott, and Elliott (1990a; 1990b).

33. Drezner (1999).

34. Nephew (2018, 54–55).

35. Griswold (2000).

36. Maloney (2014). The reimposed sanctions are unilateral, suggesting they are less likely to be effective.

37. Nephew (2018, 78–79).

38. Choe (2019).

39. Baldwin (1999/2000, 91); Nephew (2018, 1–16).

40. Cohen (2017, 16–17); Pape (1997); Shimko (2017, 105).

41. Wright (2017, 132).

42. Nephew (2018, 4–5).

43. Bremmer (2015, 110–11); Shimko (2017, 106). Signaling displeasure and

harming a target country are often major goals of sanctions regimes (Baldwin 1999/2000, 87–90 and 102–3).

44. Nephew (2018, 11). Poorly designed sanctions that don't impose costs on the ruling elite are likely to fail (Drezner 1999, 13).

45. Baldwin (1999/2000, 84); Drezner (1999, 7); Griswold (2000); Roberts (2019).

46. Nephew (2018, 126–40).

47. Baldwin (1985, 320–22); Bremmer (2015, 118); Ikenberry (2011, 198–200); Kennan (1984, 168).

48. Bunce (1985).

49. Nazario (2016).

50. Kosack and Tobin (2006); McGillivray et al. (2006).

51. Fearon and Laitin (2003).

52. Roberts et al. (2009).

53. Bearak and Gamio (2016); McBride (2018).

54. McBride (2018); Sachs (2018, 172–73).

55. Sachs (2018, 172–73).

56. Taylor (2017).

57. Wroughton and Zengerle (2019).

58. Thrush (2018).

59. Pilling (2017); Roberts, Armijo, and Katada (2017).

60. Dollar (2015); Mui (2017).

61. Dollar (2017).

62. McBride (2018).

63. Wike (2012).

64. Haqqani and Ballen (2005).

65. Wike (2012).

66. Rohde (2013, 10–11).

67. Rieffel and Fox (2008).

68. Corker and Coons (2017); Schaefer (2018).

69. Shirkey (2012, 106).

70. Yemma (1981).

71. Hirschman (1980); Savic and Shirkey (2017, 98 n33).

72. Another benefit of military aid is it provides additional markets for US arms manufacturers—though, of course, at US taxpayer expense. This may keep additional arms manufacturers in business, thereby making the bidding process for weapons systems more competitive. The dwindling number of independent arms manufactures has, in recent decades, made the bidding process less competitive and has pushed up the costs of US arms procurement.

73. Gelpi (1999); Richardson (1999); Tams (1999); Tuschhoff (1999).

74. Chaudoin, Milner, and Tingley (2018, 61–62).

75. Lipscy (2015).

76. International Monetary Fund (2017a).

77. Keohane and Martin (1999).

78. Russett and Oneal (2000).
79. Boehmer, Gartzke, and Nordstrom (2004).
80. Ikenberry (2011, 91–92); Luard (1989, 160–61).
81. Keohane and Martin (1999); Mitchell and Hensel (2007).
82. Clark (2007); Watson (1992).
83. Morse (2019).
84. Keohane and Martin (1999).
85. International Atomic Energy Agency Director General (2017). This monitoring continued even after the United States pulled out of the agreement.
86. Nephew (2018, 36–42 and 67–69).
87. Fortna (2008).
88. Mitchell and Hensel (2007).
89. Tierney (2015, 300–1).
90. Similarly, people often find ways in everyday life to lower transaction costs such as online bill-paying services.
91. Ikenberry (2011).
92. Ikenberry (2011, 269–70).
93. Ikenberry (2011, 94).
94. Sachs (2018, 180–81).
95. Morrow (2001).
96. Huth, Croco, and Appel (2011).
97. Fortna (2004).
98. Roach (2010).
99. Oxman (2006).
100. Abbott and Snidal (2000).
101. Morrow (2001).
102. Hurd (2017, 3–5, 48, and 51).
103. Goldsmith and Posner (2005).
104. This is not unique to international law. In the domestic sphere, individuals and companies will often prefer to resolve their legal disputes with each other through negotiation, mediation, or arbitration to avoid the costs associated with going to court.
105. Brooks (2016, 283); Koh (1997).
106. Huth, Croco, and Appel (2011); Morrow (2001).
107. Keohane (1986).
108. Prince (1904, 607). The "eye for an eye" formula was conceived as a way to limit the scale of punishment sought by aggrieved parties, not as a way to increase sanctions on perpetrators. In that sense, it worked to prevent escalatory spirals of reprisals much like international law does today.
109. Abbott and Snidal (2000).
110. Ackman (2003).
111. Simmons (2000).
112. Hurd (2017, 131).
113. Prorok and Appel (2014). Such punishments need not be military in nature.

158                                    NOTES TO PAGES 95–99

114. Abbott and Snidal (2000); Goldsmith and Posner (2005).

115. The term "treaty" in US law refers to a specific form of international agreement ratified by the Senate and is distinct from what the term means in international law where it refers to a wider range of written agreements between countries. US law dictates what types of agreements must go through the Senate treaty ratification process and what types can go through other ratification processes. See Congressional Research Service (2001).

116. Kaye (2013); Sachs (2018, 177).

117. Friedman (2017); Mehta (2015); Sachs (2018, 178–79). Widely adopted multilateral treaties that the Senate has not ratified include: the Convention on the Elimination of All Forms of Discrimination against Women, the Convention on the Rights of the Child, the Basel Convention on Transboundary Hazardous Wastes, the United Nations Convention on the Law of the Sea (unsigned), the Convention on Biological Diversity, the Comprehensive Test Ban Treaty, the Ottawa Treaty (unsigned), the Rome Statute of the International Criminal Court (unsigned), the Criminal Law Convention on Corruption, the Civil Law Convention on Corruption (unsigned), the Optional Protocol to the Convention against Torture (unsigned), the International Convention for the Protection of All Persons from Enforced Disappearance (unsigned), the Convention on the Rights of Persons with Disabilities, and the Paris Climate Agreement (ratification not required, but the Trump Administration has announced its intention to withdraw from the agreement in 2020).

118. Hurd (2017, 50).

119. Lupu and Voeten (2012); Verdier and Voeten (2014); Voeten (2010).

120. Almond (2017).

121. Gallo (2016).

122. Savic and Shirkey (2017, 116–17).

123. Almond (2017); Cardin (2016).

124. Lemnitzer (2014). Commerce raiders, which were not covered by the treaty, continued to wreak havoc on Union shipping throughout the war.

125. Nye (2008, 94).

126. Nye (2008).

127. Walt (2006, 38).

128. Costigliola (1983, 65). Hughes was also the Governor of New York (1907–1910), a US Supreme Court Associate Justice (1910–1916), the US Supreme Court Chief Justice (1930–1941), and the Republican nominee for president (1916).

129. Winthrop (1838|1630, 47). Of course, the ideals of the seventeenth-century Puritans differ from those of modern Americans in a number of important respects.

130. Fournier (2016); Kennedy (1961); Reagan (1984).

131. Bremmer (2015, 149–52).

132. Osgood (1953, 449); Shimko (2017, 112).

133. Cohen (2017, 16).

134. Kinzer (2017a).
135. Albert (2017); Masters (2017).
136. Shimko (2017, 113–14).
137. Shimko (2017, 113).
138. Nye (2008, 98).
139. Kight (2018).
140. Nye (2008, 95).
141. Lord (2014); Masters (2017).
142. Sanger and Perlez (2017).
143. Fettweis (2013, 205); Mandelbaum (2016, 375).
144. Betts (2012, 8–12); Nye (2008, 95); Walt (2006, 229–31).
145. Langworth (2008, 16).
146. For example, see Mattingly (1988) or Schelling (1966).
147. Sartori (2005).
148. Bacevitch (2005, 216).
149. Rohde (2013, 171).
150. US Department of Defense (2017).
151. Farrow (2018, 270–73); Harris (2017a); Rappeport and Thrush (2017).
152. *Economist* (2017).
153. Gramer (2019).
154. Brooks (2016, 19).
155. Brooks (2016, 319).
156. Harris (2017b).
157. Walsh (2019).
158. Quealy (2017).
159. Barton (2018, 212); Farrow (2018, xxii–xxiii). Obviously, embassy security is important, but it's a cost of doing business rather than activity that helps achieve American policy goals.
160. Broder (2016); Mathews (2019).
161. Broder (2016).
162. Taylor and Karklis (2016); US Department of State (2015).
163. Betts (2012, 282).
164. Farrow (2018, 273).
165. Burns and Crocker (2017); Harris (2017a).
166. Farrow (2018, 274–77).

## Chapter 5

1. Lincoln (1848).
2. Cohen (2017, 63–78).
3. Lind (2006, 156). This is not to claim that Germany and Japan had no security concerns. They did (Reiter 2009; Weisiger 2013).
4. Hawks, too, emphasize the importance of intelligence in confronting terrorism.

5. Jervis (2003).

6. Fuchs (2018); MacAskill and Borger (2007); Walsh (2008).

7. Germany (1875, 1329-30).

8. National Security Council (1950, 52-54).

9. Bacevich (2008, 163); Betts (2012, 131-36); Walt (2006, 224-25).

10. Walt (2006, 224-25).

11. The war was sold as being preemptive rather than preventive in nature as preemption is legal under international law while preventive wars are not. However, preemption under the *Caroline* test requires that the danger be "instant, overwhelming, and leaving no choice of means, and no moment for deliberation." (Webster 1983, 62). Given that the concern was Iraq's possession of nuclear weapons at some point in future, the case fails this test and thus was preventive rather than preemptive in nature (Beinart 2017).

12. Borger (2004).

13. Walt (2006, 224-25).

14. Lieber and Press (2013, 92-95).

15. Betts (2012, 277). Certainly, if a country could be convinced to abandon its nuclear program without the United States employing force that would be preferable and a great triumph.

16. Luttwak (2009).

17. Snyder (2009, 41).

18. Clausewitz (1976, 75-99, 566-73, and 603-10).

19. Levy (1986); Snyder (1984); Van Evera (1984).

20. Betts (2012, 142).

21. Tuchman (1962).

22. Stimson diary entry, December 7, 1941. Quoted in Prange (1981, 554-55).

23. Bar-Eli et al. (2007).

24. Bar-Eli et al. (2007); Ritov and Baron (1994).

25. Jervis (2003).

26. When the initial overthrow of a regime is clearly beyond the United States' power, the danger of waging war for regime change is low as US leaders know such policies cannot work.

27. Gentile (2013).

28. Betts (2012, 260).

29. Bacevich (2008, 130). Terrorist groups, unlike countries, can risk attacking the United States as they rarely hold significant territory and individual members can hide. This means both the members of groups and the things they value are less vulnerable to retaliation than are countries.

30. Snow (2015, 63-66).

31. Maoz (1983).

32. Betts (2012, 16); George, Hall, and Simons (1971, 216 and 251); Mack (1975).

33. Snow (2015, 74-76 and 118).

34. Gentile (2013).

35. Betts (2012, 159–60). This is true even when governments employ extremely brutal tactics—tactics that hopefully will never be acceptable to the American public. For example, despite using brutal tactics against the Chechens, Russia was only able to secure control of Chechnya through collaboration with local Chechen elites (Yaffa 2016).

36. Bacevitch (2010, 203–4; 2016); Gentile (2013); Snow (2015, 7, 34, and 119–21).

37. Betts (2012, 154–55).

38. Betts (2014); Byman and Waxman (2000); Clodfelter (1989); Mandelbaum (1999); Pape (1996).

39. Byman and Waxman (2000); Mandelbaum (1999); Pape (1996; 2004).

40. Salehyan (2010).

41. Art (1996).

42. Often the threatened punishment will be in the same issue area as the unwanted action: economic punishments for economic misdeeds, military actions in response to military aggression, and no cake in response to bad table manners. This is not necessary but fits with common sense notions of proportionality and reciprocity.

43. Deterring attacks against oneself is direct deterrence. Deterring attacks against one's allies is extended deterrence. Deterring attacks after a crisis has arisen is immediate deterrence and deterring threats from arising in the first place is general deterrence. Thus, there are four broad types of deterrence: immediate-direct, immediate-extended, general-direct, and general-extended. See Huth (1999).

44. Johnson (2007, 137); Mandelbaum (2005, 31–32); Schelling (1966).

45. Schelling (1966).

46. Fang, Johnson, and Leeds (2014); Huth (1999, 39); Leeds (2003).

47. Huth (1999, 30–31); Leeds (2003).

48. Schelling (1966).

49. Associated Press (2017); Barrett and Zapotosky (2018); Berger (2016); Denning (2017); Jansen and Weise (2018); Martin (2016).

50. Lillington (2016). Cybercrime, however, is of course quite common, but it is a law enforcement rather than foreign policy challenge.

51. Craig (2019, 40).

52. Perlroth, Sanger, and Shane (2019).

53. Craig (2019, 39–40). Other than attacks that focus purely on espionage, countries would have to make their identities known in order to tie any demands to the attacks, making identification and successful deterrence even more likely (Gartzke 2013, 47).

54. Burton (2018); Paul and Waltzman (2018).

55. Johnson (2007, 137).

56. Iraq was not close to developing a functioning nuclear program, meaning the entire rationale for invasion was based on false premises.

57. Pickrell (2017).

58. Daniels (2017). The Pentagon estimates that 20,000 people would die each day in South Korea during a conventional Korean conflict. Obviously, the death rate would be much higher if the conflict became nuclear. Twenty-five million people live in the Seoul metropolitan area, which is within artillery range of the North Korean border.

59. Huth (1999, 30 and 35-37); Nye, Allison and Carnesale (1985, 209). Similarly, Savic and Shirkey (2017) show that when deciding whether or not to oppose potential aggressors, countries tend to focus on the distribution of military capabilities between them and the potential aggressor.

60. Vegetius Renatus (2001|c.383, 63).

61. Cohen (2017).

62. Weiss (2013). After the war, Carr managed to obscure the historical record by distorting both his and the so-called idealists' positions to make it appear that he had understood the German danger and that his opponents had not.

63. D'Agostino, Dunne, and Pieroni (2017).

64. Huntington (1961, 67-80); Kinnard (1977).

65. Cohen (2017, 63-79). Whether the Chinese have sufficient real-time battlefield information gathering and dissemination capabilities to make their missiles truly effective is unclear (Erickson 2017).

66. Cohen (2017, 196); B. Friedman (2014).

67. Ioffe (2016).

68. Huth (1999, 32-34).

69. Fettweis (2013, 117-18).

70. Blang (2011); B. Friedman (2014); Goscha and Vaïsse (2003).

71. Walter (2006); Weisiger and Yahri-Milo (2015).

72. Hopf (1994); Huth (1999, 41); Huth and Russett (1984); Mercer (1996).

73. Fettweis (2013, 103).

74. Huth (1999, 34).

75. Press (2005).

76. Huth (1988); Huth, Bennett, and Gelpi (1992); Huth, Gelpi, and Bennett (1993); Huth and Russett (1988); Sartori (2002).

77. Weisiger and Yahri-Milo (2015).

78. Weisiger and Yahri-Milo (2015).

79. Countries can have other sorts of reputations such as for honesty, abiding by agreements and international law, and respecting human rights. These types of reputations also matter.

80. MacDonald and Parent (2011).

81. B. Friedman (2014).

82. This is why so many commentators were disturbed by President Trump's disinclination to steadfastly commit to Article 5 of the NATO treaty, which states an attack on one member is an attack on all members (Gray 2017). That said, it is perfectly reasonable to affirm the United States' commitment to NATO while simultaneously trying to get US allies to pick up a larger share of the military

burden. Such calls should be structured so that Washington reaffirms its belief and commitment to NATO while at the same time arguing that European members of the alliance must do their share to make the alliance effective. If, instead, calls for more spending by European members of NATO are paired with rhetorical attacks on NATO itself or questioning of the alliance's usefulness, they can open up serious rifts within the alliance (Barnes 2019; Sanger 2019).

83. Weisiger and Yahri-Milo (2015).

84. Similarly, people who eat well and exercise do occasionally have heart attacks.

85. Gaddis (2011, 309–36).

86. Trager and Zagorcheva (2005/2006).

87. Obviously, some of the terrorism that targets the United States is purely domestic in nature. While confronting such terrorism is vital, that is a challenge for domestic policy, not foreign policy.

88. Sahay (2013).

89. Nacos (2016, 262–64).

90. Nacos (2014, 220).

91. Weiser (2014).

92. Plaw and Fricker (2012, 358); Zenko (2013, 11).

93. Plaw and Fricker (2012, 360–62).

94. Schmitt and al-Batati (2017).

95. Cronin (2006).

96. G. Miller (2016); Purkiss and Serle (2017).

97. *Associated Press* (2013); Callimachi et al. (2018); Cloud and De Leon (2015); Miklaszewski et al. (2013).

98. McFadden, Arkin, and Uehlinger (2017).

99. Shalal-Esa (2011).

100. Hart (2017); Matfess (2015); Young and Beehner (2015).

101. Bencherif (2017). Al Qaeda in the Islamic Maghreb is also known as Jama'at Nasr al-Islam wal Muslimin.

102. Lizza (2013); Nacos (2016); Shirkey (2014b); Sunstein (2016).

103. Cronin (2014); Ikenberry (2011, 272); Shirkey (2014a; 2014b). States often share intelligence through informal country-to-country networks, known as transgovernmental networks (Slaughter 2005).

104. This is not to call for unregulated intelligence gathering. The United States should be circumspect about spying on friends and allies—the information obtained is often not worth the fallout from being caught. Likewise, intelligence gathering to counter terrorist groups should be mindful of individuals' civil liberties.

105. Van Natta and Butler (2004).

106. Fried (1995); Jenkins (1996).

107. Anderson and DeYoung (2006); Johnson (2012); *New York Daily News* (2017); Rashbaum and Johnston (2009); Watts (2017).

108. Nacos (2014, 221).

109. Nacos (2014, 217).
110. Nacos (2014, 214-15).

### Chapter 6

1. Iraq is not entirely free of political violence. As of late 2019, ISIS continues to launch attacks against Iraqi security forces and civilians (Schmitt, Rubin, and Gibbons-Neff 2019).

2. Ornstein and Mann (2006); Owens (2009).

3. Bacevitch (2005, 210); Brooks (2016, 291-95); Preble (2009, 91); Sachs (2018, 90-91).

4. Johnson (2007); Tierney (2015, 303-4).

5. Edmondson and Fandos (2019); Golshan (2019).

6. Demirjian and Ryan (2019).

7. Hamilton (2003, 50); Johnson (2007); Tierney (2015, 303-4).

8. Hamilton (2003, 53 and 73).

9. Hamilton (2003, 47, 53, and 55).

10. Debs and Weiss (2016); Hamilton (2003).

11. Hamilton (2003, 63).

12. McCain (2017); Specter (2009); Webb (2013).

13. Auerswald and Cowhey (1997); Howell and Pevehouse (2015|2005, 244); Kaufmann (2004, 93-8); Kupchan and Trubowitz (2015|2007, 252).

14. Kaufmann (2004, 37-43).

15. Krebs (2005, 198-99).

16. Hamilton (2003, 11); Howell and Pevehouse (2015|2005, 243).

17. Kupchan and Trubowitz (2015|2007, 251).

18. Baum and Potter (2015, 3-6).

19. Baum and Potter (2015, 23). They also find that this inclination of partisans to back their party leaders' foreign policies regardless of the content of those foreign policies means that publics in democracies with multi-party, proportional representation systems are more likely to constrain the use of force than are publics in two-party majoritarian systems such as the one in the United States.

20. Bacevitch (2013, 124); Fisher (2013); Matishak (2015); Snow (2009, 154).

21. Cohen (2004); Preble (2009, 72).

22. Mathews (2019).

23. Colaresi (2004).

24. Fettweis (2013, 82-84); Wolfers (1962, 151).

25. Fettweis (2013, 80).

26. Cohen and Zenko (2019); Zenko and Cohen (2012, 83).

27. Fettweis (2013, 76-77).

28. Cillizza (2014); G. Friedman (2014); Friedman (2012); Hamilton (2003, 63); Holsti (1996, 24-45); Lawton (2015).

29. Baum and Potter (2015, 20).

30. Fettweis (2013, 2-4).

31. Mercer (2010).

32. Thrall (2007, 467).

33. Thrall (2007, 457).

34. Thrall (2007, 454).

35. Fettweis (2013, 9).

36. Fettweis (2013, 242).

37. Walt (2018, 289-90).

38. The United States intervened militarily in Syria in limited ways.

39. Tierney (2015, 302).

40. Brown (2003, 170-71).

41. Lorenzo (2016, 204); Schmidt and Williams (2008); Tompkins (1970).

42. Walt (2018, 285).

43. As discussed in chapter 3, this is because combat experience and strong civilian oversight tend to cancel out the hawkish tendencies that military service can inculcate. Given the many recent US wars, even if no new wars are fought in the foreseeable future, senior American military personnel, for decades to come, are likely to have had combat experience.

44. Lewin and Hartocollis (2010).

45. Bacevitch (2005, 221).

46. Cohen (2017, 82).

47. Michaels (2016).

48. Bacevitch (2005, 215); Kissinger (1994).

49. Brands (2018, 91-94); Johnson (2007, 185-200); Osgood (1953, 433).

50. Kupchan and Trubowitz (2015|2007).

51. Walt (2002).

52. Kissinger (2014); P. Miller (2016, 12); Osiander (1994; 2001); Watson (1992).

53. Kennan (1947, 569).

# References

Abbas, Hassan. 2013. "How Drones Create More Terrorists." *The Atlantic*, August 23.

Abbott, Kenneth and Duncan Snidal. 2000. "Hard and Soft Law in International Governance." *International Organization* 54, no. 3: 421–56.

*ABC News*. 2013. "'This Week's Transcript: Gen. Martin Dempsey, Reps. Rupperberger and King, and Glenn Greenwald." August 4.

Abrahms, Max and Jochen Mierau. 2017. "Leadership Matters: The Effects of Targeted Killings on Militant Group Tactics." *Terrorism and Political Violence* 29, no. 5: 830–51.

Acharya, Amitav. 2018. *Constructing Global Order: Agency and Change in World Politics*. Cambridge: Cambridge University Press.

Ackman, Dan. 2003. "Bush Cuts Steel Tariffs, Declares Victory." *Forbes*, December 5.

Adams, John Quincy. 1821. *An Address Delivered at the Request of a Committee of Citizens of Washington: On the Occasion of Reading the Declaration of Independence, on the Fourth of July 1821*. Washington: Davis and Force.

Albert, Eleanor. 2017. "China's Big Bet on Soft Power." *Council on Foreign Relations*, May 11.

Alexander, Ryan. 2018. "The Farm Bill and Federal Food Stamp Program Romance Is Dead. Time for a Clean Divorce." *USA Today*, October 14.

Allard, Kenneth. 1995. *Somalia Operations: Lessons Learned*. Washington: National Defense University Press.

Almond, Roncevert Ganan. 2017. "US Ratification of the Law of the Sea Convention." *The Diplomat*, May 24.

Alpert, Marc and Howard Raiffa. 1982. "A Progress Report on the Training of Probability Assessors." In *Judgement under Uncertainty*, edited by D. Kahneman, A. Tversky, and P. Slovic, 294–305. Cambridge: Cambridge University Press.

Amadeo, Kimberly. 2019. "Afghanistan War Cost, Timeline, and Economic Impact: The Ongoing Costs of the Afghanistan War." *The Balance*, June 15.

Amadeo, Kimberly. 2019. "Cost of Iraq War: Its Timeline, and the Economic Impact." *The Balance*, January 2.

Anderson, John Ward and Karen DeYoung. 2006. "Plot to Bomb US-Bound Jets Is Foiled." *Washington Post Foreign Service*, August 11.

Anderson, M. S. 1998. *War and Society in Europe of the Old Regime, 1618–1789.* Montreal: McGill-Queen's University Press.

Angell, Norman. 1933. *The Great Illusion, 1933.* London: William Heinemann.

Armitage, David. 2017. *Civil Wars: A History in Ideas.* New York: Alfred A. Knopf.

Art, Robert. 1996. "American Foreign Policy and the Fungibility of Force." *Security Studies* 5, no. 4: 7–42.

Ashford, Emma. 2018. "Trump's Syria Strikes Show What's Wrong with US Foreign Policy." *New York Times*, April 13.

*Associated Press.* 2013. "US Commando Twin Raids Hit 'High Value' Terrorism Targets in Somalia, Libya." October 5.

*Associated Press.* 2017. "US Tells 21 States That Hackers Targeted Their Voting Systems." September 22.

Atwood, Kylie and Nicole Gaouette. 2019. "Amid Confusion Trump Admin Signals Syria Pullout Won't Be Rapid." *CNN*, January 9.

Auerswald, David and Peter Cowhey. 1997. "Ballotbox Diplomacy: The War Powers Resolution and the Use of Force." *International Studies Quarterly* 41, no. 3: 505–28.

Axelrod, Robert. 1984. *The Evolution of Cooperation.* New York: Basic Books.

Axelrod, Robert and Robert O. Keohane. 1985. "Achieving Cooperation under Anarchy: Strategies and Institutions." *World Politics* 38, no. 1: 226–54.

Bacevich, Andrew J. 2005. *The New American Militarism: How Americans Are Seduced by War.* Oxford: Oxford University Press.

Bacevich, Andrew J. 2008. *The Limits of Power: The End of American Exceptionalism.* New York: Macmillan.

Bacevich, Andrew J. 2010. *Washington Rules: America's Path to Permanent War.* New York: Macmillan.

Bacevich, Andrew J. 2013. *Breach of Trust: How Americans Failed Their Soldiers and Their Country.* New York: Henry Holt.

Bacevich, Andrew J. 2016. *America's War for the Greater Middle East: A Military History.* New York: Random House.

Badie, Dina. 2015|2010. "Groupthink, Iraq, and the War on Terror: Explaining US Policy Shift toward Iraq." In *American Foreign Policy*, edited by G. J. Ikenberry and P. L. Trubowitz, 469–86. Oxford: Oxford University Press.

Baker, Peter and Maggie Haberman. 2019. "Trump Undercuts Bolton on North Korea and Iran." *New York Times*, May 28.

Baldwin, David. 1985. *Economic Statecraft.* Princeton: Princeton University Press.

Baldwin, David. 1999. "Force, Fungibility, and Influence." *Security Studies* 8, no. 4: 173–83.

Baldwin, David. 1999/2000. "The Sanctions Debate and the Logic of Choice." *International Security* 24, no. 3: 80–107.

Bapat, Navin A., Tobias Heinrich, Yoshiharu Kobayashi, and T. Clifton Morgan. 2013. "Determinants of Sanctions Effectiveness: Sensitivity Analysis Using New Data." *International Interactions* 39, no. 1: 79–98.

Bar-Eli, Michael, Ofer H. Azer, Illana Ritov, Yael Keidar-Levin, and Galit Schein.

2007. "Action Bias among Elite Soccer Goalkeepers: The Case of Penalty Kicks." *Journal of Economic Psychology* 28, no. 5: 606–21.

Barkham, Patrick. 2013. "Iraq War 10 Years On: Mass Protest that Defined a Generation." *The Guardian,* February 15.

Barnes, Julian E. 2019. "With Trump, NATO Chief Tries to Navigate Spending Minefields." *New York Times,* April 2.

Barrett, Devlin and Matt Zapotosky. 2018. "12 Russian Intelligence Officers Charged by Mueller in Hack of DNC, Clinton Emails." *Chicago Tribune,* July 13.

Barton, Rick. 2018. *Peace Works: America's Unifying Role in a Turbulent World.* Lanham: Rowman and Littlefield.

Baum, Matthew A. and Philip B. K. Potter. 2015. *War and Democratic Constraint: How the Public Influences Foreign Policy.* Princeton: Princeton University Press.

Bearak, Max and Lazaro Gamio. 2016. "The US Foreign Aid Budget, Visualized." *Washington Post,* October 18.

Beauchamp, Zack. 2017. "Trump's Case against the Iran Nuclear Deal Has Very Little to Do with Nuclear Weapons." *Vox,* September 13.

Becker, Jo and Eric Schmitt. 2018. "As Trump Wavers on Libya, an ISIS Haven, Russia Presses On." *New York Times,* February 7.

Beckley, Michael. 2015. "The Myth of Entangling Alliances: Reassessing the Security Risks of US Defense Pacts." *International Security* 39, no. 4: 7–48.

Beinart, Peter. 2017. "How America Shed the Taboo against Preventive War." *The Atlantic,* April 21.

Bemis, Samuel Flagg. 1977. *John Quincy Adams and the Foundations of American Foreign Policy.* Norwalk: The Easton Press.

Benac, Nancy. 2014. "The Long, Unfortunate History of Friendly Fire Accidents in US Conflicts." *PBS Newshour,* June 11.

Bencherif, Adib. 2017. "Al-Qaeda in the Islamic Maghreb: A Meta-Strategy of Survival." *Sustainable Security,* December 29.

Berger, Joseph. 2016. "A Dam, Small and Unsung, Is Caught Up in an Iranian Hacking Case." *New York Times,* March 25.

Betts, Richard K. 1977. *Soldiers, Statesmen, and Cold War Crises.* Cambridge: Harvard University Press.

Betts, Richard K. 2012. *American Force: Dangers, Delusions, and Dilemmas in National Security.* New York: Columbia University Press.

Betts, Richard K. 2014. "Pick Your Battles." *Foreign Affairs* 93, no. 6: 15–24.

Blainey, Geoffrey. 1973. *The Causes of War.* New York: Free Press.

Blang, Eugenie M. 2011. *Allies at Odds: America, Europe, and Vietnam, 1961–1968.* Lanham: Rowman & Littlefield.

Boehmer, Charles, Erik Gartzke, and Timothy Nordstrom. 2004. "Do Intergovernmental Organizations Promote Peace?" *World Politics* 57, no. 1: 1–38.

Boot, Max. 2014. "More Small Wars." *Foreign Affairs* 93, no. 6: 5–14.

Borger, Julian. 2004. "There Were No Weapons of Mass Destruction in Iraq." *The Guardian,* October 7.

Bosworth, James. 2012. "Cold War Defense Treaty Under Fire in Latin America." *Christian Science Monitor,* June 8.

Bowden, Mark. 2006. "The Desert One Debacle." *The Atlantic* 297, no. 4: 62–77.

Brands, Hal. 2018. *American Grand Strategy in the Age of Trump.* Washington: Brookings.

Bremmer, Ian. 2015. *Superpower: Three Choices for America's Role in the World.* New York: Penguin.

Brennan, Rick. 2014. "Withdrawal Symptoms." *Foreign Affairs* 93, no. 6: 25–36.

Broad, William J. and Sergio Peçanha. 2015. "The Iran Nuclear Deal—A Simple Guide." *New York Times,* January 15.

Broder, Jonathan. 2016. "Why the US Spends More on War than It Does on Diplomacy." *Newsweek,* June 29.

Brooks, Rosa. 2016. *How Everything Became War and the Military Became Everything: Tales from the Pentagon.* New York: Simon & Schuster.

Brown, Seyom. 2003. *The Illusion of Control: Force and Foreign Policy in the 21st Century.* Washington: Brookings.

Bullock, John G. 2007. "Experiments on Partisanship and Public Opinion: Party Cues, False Beliefs, and Bayesian Updating." PhD diss., Stanford University.

Bunce, Valerie. 1985. "The Empire Strikes Back: The Evolution of the Eastern Bloc from a Soviet Asset to a Soviet Liability." *International Organization* 39, no. 1: 1–46.

Burns, Nicholas and Ryan C. Crocker. 2017. "Dismantling the Foreign Service." *New York Times,* November 27.

Burns, Robert. 1786. "To a Mouse." *Burns Poems.* Kilmarnock: John Wilson.

Burton, Joe. 2018. "Deterring Cyber Attacks: Old Problems, New Solutions." *The Conversation,* June 6.

Byman, Daniel L. and Matthew C. Waxman. 2000. "Kosovo and the Great Air Power Debate." *International Security* 24, no. 4: 5–38.

Calamur, Krishnadev. 2018. "The US Will Spend Billions in Syria—Just Not on Rebuilding It." *The Atlantic,* August 20.

Callimachi, Rukmini, Helene Cooper, Eric Schmitt, Alan Blinder, and Thomas Gibbons-Neff. 2018. "'An Endless War:' Why 4 US Soldiers Died in a Remote African Desert." *New York Times,* February 20.

Callon, Nathanael. 2013. "US Planes Deliver French Troops to Mali." *United States Air Forces in Europe/Air Forces Africa Public Affairs,* January 29.

Camus, Albert. 1960. *Resistance, Rebellion, and Death.* Translated by J. O'Brien. New York: Vintage Books.

Cardin, Ben. 2016. "The South China Sea Is the Reason the United States Must Ratify UNCLOS." *Foreign Policy,* July 13.

Cary, Nathaniel. 2017. "Graham Supports Trump's Hard Line Stance on North Korea." *USA Today,* May 1.

Casey, Nicholas. 2019. "Colombia Army's New Kill Orders Send Chills Down Ranks." *New York Times,* May 18.

Casey, Nicholas. 2019. "Colombia's Peace Deal Promised a New Era. So Why Are These Rebels Rearming?" *New York Times,* May 17.

*CBS News.* 2011. "Libya Mission Cost US More than \$1 Billion." October 21.

Cha, Victor D. 2010. "Powerplay: Origins of the US Alliance System in Asia." *International Security* 34, no. 3: 158–96.

Chaudoin, Stephen, Helen V. Milner, and Dustin Tingley. 2018. "Down but Not Out: A Liberal International American Foreign Policy." In *Chaos in the Liberal Order*, edited by R. Jervis, F. J. Gavin, J. Rovner, D. N. Labrosse, and G. Fujii, 61–97. New York: Columbia University Press.

Choe, Sang-Hung. 2019. "North Korea's State-Run Economy Falters under Sanctions, Testing Elite Loyalty." *New York Times*, April 18.

Churchill, Winston. 1987. *My Early Life: A Roving Commission.* New York: Charles Scribner's Sons.

Cicero, Marcus Tullius. 1956|44 BC. *De Officiis.* Translated by W. Miller. Cambridge: Harvard University Press.

Cillizza, Chris. 2014. "Voters (Still) Don't Care about Foreign Policy." *Washington Post,* September 10.

Clark, Ian. 2007. *Legitimacy in International Society.* Oxford: Oxford University Press.

Clark, John F. 2001. "Explaining Ugandan Intervention in Congo: Evidence and Interpretations." *Journal of Modern African Studies* 39, no. 2: 261–81.

Clark, John F. 2002. "Museveni's Adventure in the Congo War: Uganda's Vietnam?" In *The African Stakes of the Congo War*, edited by J. F. Clark, 145–65. New York: Palgrave Macmillan.

Clausewitz, Carl von. 1976. *On War.* Translated by M. E. Howard and P. Paret. Princeton: Princeton University Press.

Clodfelter, Mark. 1989. *The Limits of Air Power: The American Bombing of North Vietnam.* New York: Free Press.

Cloud, David S. and Sunshine De Leon. 2015. "A Heavy Price Paid for Botched Terrorist Raid by Philippines and US." *Los Angeles Times*, September 10.

Cobden, Richard. 1870. *Speeches on Questions of Public Policy.* Edited by J. Bright and J. Rogers. London: Macmillan.

Cohen, Eliot. 2004. "Change and Transformation in Military Affairs." *Journal of Strategic Studies* 27, no. 3: 395–407.

Cohen, Eliot. 2017. *The Big Stick: The Limits of Soft Power and the Necessity of Military Force.* New York: Basic Books.

Cohen, Michael A. and Micah Zenko. 2019. *Clear and Present Safety: The World Has Never Been Better and Why That Matters to Americans.* New Haven: Yale University Press.

Cohen, Roger. 2016. "The Limits of American Realism." *New York Times,* January 11.

Colaresi, Michael. 2004. "When Doves Cry: International Rivalry, Unreciprocated Cooperation, and Leadership Turnover." *American Journal of Political Science* 48, no. 3: 555–70.

Collier, Robert. 2005. "Iraq Invasion May Be Remembered as State of the Age of Oil Scarcity." *San Francisco Chronicle*, March 20.

Congressional Budget Office. 2003. *The Effects of NAFTA on US-Mexican Trade and GDP.* Washington: Congressional Budget Office.

Congressional Research Service. 2001. *Treaties and Other International Agreements: The Role of the United States Senate. A Study Prepared for the Committee on Foreign Relations, United States Senate.* Washington: Library of Congress.

Constant, Benjamin. 1988|1819. "The Liberty of the Ancients Compared with that of the Moderns." In *The Political Writings of Benjamin Constant,* edited by B. Fontana, 309–28. Cambridge: Cambridge University Press.

Cooper, Ryan. 2014. "Stop Listening to Dick Cheney on Iraq." *The Week,* June 20.

Corker, Bob and Chris Coons. 2017. "A Better Way to Help the World." *New York Times,* May 10.

Costigliola, Frank. 1983. "John B. Stetson, Jr. and Poland: The Diplomacy of a Prophet Scorned." In *US Diplomats in Europe, 1919–1941,* edited by K. P. Jones, 63–74. Santa Barbara: ABC-Clio.

Council on Foreign Relations. 2009. *Public Opinion on Global Issues: Chapter 9: US Opinion on General Principles of World Order.* New York: Council on Foreign Relations.

Craig, David J. 2019. "The Age of Cyberwarfare." *Columbia Magazine,* Summer: 38–41.

Cronin, Audrey Kurth. 2006. "How al-Qaida Ends: The Decline and Demise of Terrorist Groups." *International Security* 31, no. 1: 7–48.

Cronin, Bruce. 2014. "International Organizations Are Necessary for Fighting Terrorism." In *Debating Terrorism and Counterterrorism,* 2nd ed., edited by S. Gottlieb, 291–311. Washington: CQPress.

Crowley, Michael, Falih Hassan, and Eric Schmitt. 2020. "US Strike in Iraq Kills Qassim Suleimani, Commander of Iranian Forces." *New York Times,* January 2.

D'Agostino, Giorgio, J. Paul Dunne, and Luca Pieroni. 2017. "Does Military Spending Matter for Long-Run Growth?" *Defense and Peace Economics* 28, no. 4: 429–36.

Daniels, Jeff. 2017. "Pentagon Scenario of a New Korean War Estimates 20,000 Deaths Daily in South Korea Retired US General Says." *CNBC,* September 25.

Davis, James W., Jr. 2000. *Threats and Promises: The Pursuit of International Influence.* Baltimore: Johns Hopkins Press.

Debs, Alexandre and Jessica Chen Weiss. 2016. "Circumstances, Domestic Audiences, and Reputational Incentives in International Crisis Bargaining." *Journal of Conflict Resolution* 60, no. 3: 403–33.

Demirjian, Karoun and Missy Ryan. 2019. "Senate Fails to Override Trump's Veto of Resolution Demanding End to US Involvement in Yemen War." *Washington Post,* May 2.

Dempsey, Jason. 2019. "Coming to Terms with America's Undeniable Failure in Afghanistan." *War on the Rocks,* February 11.

Denning, Dorothy. 2017. "Cyberwar: How Chinese Hackers Became a Major Threat to the US." *Newsweek,* October 5.

Dollar, David. 2015. "The AIIB and the 'One Belt, One Road.'" *Horizons* 4: 162–72.

Dollar, David. 2017. "Yes, China Is Investing Globally—But Not So Much in Its Belt and Road Initiative." *Brookings*, May 8.

Donnelly, Jack. 2012. "The Differentiation of International Societies." *European Journal of International Relations* 18, no. 1: 151–76.

Dougan, Patrice. 2013. "NZ, US Resume Bilateral Military Ties after Nearly 30 Years." *New Zealand Herald*, October 29.

Draper, Robert. 2015. "Between Iraq and a Hard Place." *New York Times Magazine*, September 1.

Drezner, Daniel. 1999. *The Sanctions Paradox: Economic Statecraft in International Relations*. Cambridge: Cambridge University Press.

Drezner, Daniel. 2008. "The Realist Tradition in American Public Opinion." *Perspectives on Politics* 6, no. 1: 51–70.

*Economist*. 2017. "Neglecting the State Department Does Real Damage." April 29.

Edmondson, Catie and Nicholas Fandos. 2019. "Senate Rejects Curb on Trump's Authority to Strike Iran." *New York Times*, June 28.

Edmondson, Catie and Edward Wong. 2019. "Pompeo Is Warned against Side-stepping Congress for Conflict with Iran." *New York Times*, April 10.

Eisenhower, Dwight D. 1954. "Remarks at the Annual Conference of the Society for Personnel Administration, May 12, 1954."

Eisenhower, Dwight D. 1958. "State of the Union Address, January 9, 1958."

Engel, Pamela. 2016. "Obama Reportedly Declined to Enforce Red Line in Syria after Iran Threatened to Back Out of Nuclear Deal." *Business Insider*, August 23.

Erickson, Andrew S. 2017. "Chinese Anti-Ship Ballistic Development and Counter-Intervention Efforts." *Testimony before Hearing on China's Advanced Weapons Panel I: China's Hypersonic and Maneuverable Re-Entry Vehicle Programs US-China Economic and Security Review Commission*, February 23. Washington: US Congress.

Everstine, Brian. 2015. "US Pledges Continued Support for French Operations in Africa." *Air Force Times*, July 8.

Fallows, James. 2015. "The Tragedy of the American Military." *The Atlantic* 315, no. 1: 72–90.

Fang, Songying, Jesse C. Johnson, and Brett Ashley Leeds. 2014. "To Concede or to Resist? The Restraining Effect of Military Alliances." *International Organization* 68, no. 4: 775–809.

Farrow, Ronan. 2018. *War on Peace: The End of Diplomacy and the Decline of American Influence*. New York: W. W. Norton.

Fazal, Tanisha. 2014. "Dead Wrong? Battle Deaths, Military Medicine, and the Exaggerated Reports of War's Demise." *International Security* 39, no. 1: 95–125.

Fearon, James D. 1995. "Rationalist Explanations for War." *International Organization* 49, no. 3: 379–414.

Fearon, James D. and David D. Laitin. 2003. "Ethnicity, Insurgency, and Civil War." *American Political Science Review* 97, no. 1: 75–90.

Fettweis, Christopher J. 2013. *The Pathologies of Power: Fear, Honor, Glory, and Hubris in US Foreign Policy*. Cambridge: Cambridge University Press.

Fettweis, Christopher J. 2018. *Psychology of a Superpower: Security and Dominance in US Foreign Policy*. New York: Columbia University Press.

Fey, Mark and Kristopher W. Ramsay. 2007. "Mutual Optimism and War." *American Journal of Political Science* 51, no. 4: 738–54.

Fischer, Beth A. 2000. *The Reagan Reversal: Foreign Policy and the End of the Cold War*. Columbia: University of Missouri Press.

Fisher, Max. 2013. "Stanley McChrystal Says the US Should Reinstitute the Draft." *Washington Post,* February 19.

Fortna, Virginia Page. 2004. *Peace Time: Cease-Fire Agreements and the Durability of Peace*. Princeton: Princeton University Press.

Fortna, Virginia Page. 2008. *Does Peacekeeping Work? Shaping Belligerents' Choices after Civil War*. Princeton: Princeton University Press.

Fournier, Ron. 2016. "Obama's New American Exceptionalism." *The Atlantic,* July 28.

Freedman, Lawrence. 2017. *The Future of War: A History*. New York: PublicAffairs.

Fried, Joseph P. 1995. "Sheik and 9 Followers Guilty of a Conspiracy of Terrorism," *New York Times,* October 2.

Friedman, Benjamin A. 2014. "The Credibility Debate in US Foreign Policy." *The National Interest,* August 11.

Friedman, George. 2014. "The American Public's Indifference to Foreign Affairs." *Forbes,* February 19.

Friedman, Lisa. 2017. "Syria Joins Paris Climate Accord, Leaving Only US Opposed." *New York Times,* November 7.

Friedman, Uri. 2012. "8 Crazy Things Americans Believe about Foreign Policy." *Foreign Policy,* October 16.

Fuchs, Michael H. 2018. "John Bolton Has North Korea and Iran in His Sights. He Must Be Stopped." *The Guardian,* March 23.

Gaddis, John Lewis. 2011. *George F. Kennan: An American Life*. New York: Penguin.

Gaffey, Conor. 2017. "Why Is Trump Sending More US Troops to Somalia?" *Newsweek,* April 19.

Gallo, William. 2016. "Why Hasn't the US Signed the Law of the Sea Treaty?" *Voice of America News,* June 6.

*Gallup*. 2016. "Confidence in Institutions." June 1–5.

Gartzke, Erik. 2007. "The Capitalist Peace." *American Journal of Political Science* 51, no. 1: 166–91.

Gartzke, Erik. 2013. "The Myth of Cyberwar: Bringing War in Cyberspace Back Down to Earth." *International Security* 38, no. 2: 41–73.

Gartzke, Erik and Quan Li. 2001. "Investing in the Peace: Economic Interdependence and International Conflict." *International Organization* 55, no. 2: 391–438.

Gelpi, Christopher. 1999. "Alliances and Instruments of Intra-Allied Control." In *Imperfect Unions*, edited by H. Haftendorn, R. O. Keohane, and C. A. Wallander, 107–39. Oxford: Oxford University Press.

Gentile, Gian. 2013. *Wrong Turn: America's Deadly Embrace of Counter-Insurgency*. New York: The New Press.

George, Alexander L., David Kent Hall, and William E. Simons. 1971. *The Limits of Coercive Diplomacy: Laos, Cuba, Vietnam*. Boston: Little, Brown.

Germany. 1875. *Reichstag Protocols*. Vol. 76.2. Munich: Münchener DigitalisierungsZentrum.

Gholz, Eugene and Daryl G. Press. 2001. "The Effect of Wars on Neutral Countries: Why It Doesn't Pay to Preserve the Peace." *Security Studies* 10, no. 4: 1–57.

Gholz, Eugene, Daryl G. Press, and Harvey M. Sapolsky. 1997. "Come Home, America." *International Security* 21, no. 4: 5–48.

Gibbons-Neff, Thomas. 2019. "For US Commandos in the Philippines, a Water Pump Is a New Weapon against ISIS." *New York Times*, April 27.

Gilens, Martin. 2001. "Political Ignorance and Collective Policy Preferences." *American Political Science Review* 95, no. 2: 379–96.

Girard, Philippe R. 2004. *Clinton in Haiti: The 1994 US Invasion of Haiti*. New York: Palgrave MacMillan.

Glass, David. C., Jerome E. Singer, H. Skipton Leonard, David Kranz, Sheldon Cohen, and Halleck Cummings. 1973. "Perceived Control of Adverse Stimulation and the Reduction of Stress Responses 1." *Journal of Personality* 41, no. 4: 577–95.

Goertz, Gary, Paul F. Diehl, and Alexandru Balas. 2016. *The Puzzle of Peace: The Evolution of Peace in the International System*. Oxford: Oxford University Press.

Goldberg, Jonah. 2014. "National Honor Matters." *National Review*, September 10.

Goldsmith, Jack L. and Eric A. Posner. 2005. *The Limits of International Law*. Oxford: Oxford University Press.

Goldstein, Joshua S. 2011. *Winning the War on War: The Decline of Armed Conflict Worldwide*. New York: Penguin.

Golshan, Tara. 2019. "House Democrats Vote to Repeal 9/11-Era Law Used to Authorize Perpetual War." *Vox*, June 19.

Gordon, Jill. 1997. "John Stuart Mill and the 'Marketplace of Ideas.'" *Social Theory and Practice* 23, no. 2: 235–49.

Gordon, Michael R. and Eric Schmitt. 2017. "Even the Most Precise Strike Could Prompt Retaliation." *New York Times*, August 11.

Goscha, Christopher and Maurice Vaïsse, eds. 2003. *La guerre du Vietnam et l'Europe 1963–1973*. Brussels: Bruylant.

Gowa, Joanne and Soo Yeon Kim. 2005. "An Exclusive Country Club: The Effects of the GATT on Trade, 1950–94." *World Politics* 57, no. 4: 453–78.

Gramer, Robbie. 2019. "Hiring Freeze Put US Diplomats under Threat Worldwide, Report Says." *Foreign Policy*, August 9.

Gray, David H. 1997. "Canada's Unresolved Maritime Boundaries." *IRBU Boundary and Security Bulletin* 5, no. 3: 61–66.

Gray, Rosie. 2017. "Trump Declines to Affirm NATO's Article 5." *The Atlantic*, May 25.

Grenville, Stephen. 1998. "The Asia Crisis, Capital Flows and the International Financial Architecture." *Monash University Law School Foundation*, May 21.

Griswold, Daniel. 2000. "Going Alone on Economic Sanctions Hurts US More than Foes." *Cato Institute*, November 27.

Haass, Richard N. 1997. "Fatal Distraction: Bill Clinton's Foreign Policy." *Foreign Policy* 108: 112–23.

Hafner-Burton, Emilie M., Stephan Haggard, David A. Lake, and David G. Victor. 2017. "The Behavioral Revolution and International Relations." *International Organization* 71, no. S1: S1–S31.

Hamilton, Alexander, James Madison, and John Jay. 2003|1788. *The Federalist Papers*. New York: Signet.

Hamilton, Lee H. 2003. *A Creative Tension: The Foreign Policy Roles of the President and Congress*, with J. Tama. Washington: Woodrow Wilson Center Press.

Haqqani, Husain and Kenneth Ballen. 2005. "Revisiting US-Pakistan Relations in Light of Earthquake Relief." *Wall Street Journal*, December 28.

Harrington, Fred H. 1935. "The Anti-Imperialist Movement in the United States, 1898–1900." *The Mississippi Valley Historical Review* 22, no. 2: 211–30.

Harris, Gardiner. 2017. "Diplomats Sound the Alarm as They Are Pushed Out in Droves." *New York Times*, November 24.

Harris, Gardiner. 2017. "With Cost-Cutting Zeal, Tillerson Whittles UN Delegation, Too." *New York Times*, September 15.

Hart, Michael. 2017. "Is Abu Sayyaf Really Defeated?" *The Diplomat*, November 23.

Hartmann, Frederick. 1982. *The Conservation of Enemies: A Study in Enmity*. Westport: Greenwood Press.

Hartz, Louis. 1955. *The Liberal Tradition in America: An Interpretation of American Political Thought Since the Revolution*. New York: Harcourt Brace and World.

Heer, Jeet. 2017. "Does Trump's Syria Policy Remind You of Someone?" *New Republic*, June 20.

Herz, John. 1950. "Idealist Internationalism and the Security Dilemma." *World Politics* 2, no. 2: 171–201.

Hirschman, Albert O. 1980. *National Power and the Structure of Foreign Trade*. Berkeley: University of California Press.

Hirsh, Michael. 2016. "Why the New Nationalists Are Taking Over." *Politico*, June 27.

Hoffman, Christiane and Klaus Brinkbäumer. 2018. "We Are Seeing What Happens When the US Pulls Back." *Der Spiegel*, January 8.

Holden, Stephen. 1995. "Film Review: America's Cold War with Canada. Just Kidding!" *New York Times*, September 22.

Holsti, Kalevi. 2016. "The Decline of Interstate War: Pondering Systemic Explanations." In *Kalevi Holsti: Major Texts on War, the State, Peace, and International Order*, edited by K. Holsti, 43–64. New York: Springer.

Holsti, Ole R. 1996. *Public Opinion and American Foreign Policy*. Ann Arbor: University of Michigan Press.

Holy Bible. 1971. Grand Rapids: Zondervan Publishing House.

Hopf, Ted. 1994. *Peripheral Visions*. Ann Arbor: University of Michigan Press.

Horowitz, Michael C., Rose McDermott, and Allan C. Stam. 2005. "Leader Age, Regime Type, and Violent International Relations." *Journal of Conflict Resolution* 49, no. 5: 661–85.

Horowitz, Michael C. and Allan C. Stam. 2014. "How Prior Military Experience Influences the Future Militarized Behavior of Leaders." *International Organization* 68, no. 3: 527–59.

Howard, Michael. 1976. *War in European History*. Oxford: Oxford University Press.

Howell, William G. and Jon C. Pevehouse. 2015|2005. "Presidents, Congress, and the Use of Force." In *American Foreign Policy*, edited by G. J. Ikenberry and P. L. Trubowitz, 243–62. Oxford: Oxford University Press.

Howell, William G. and Martin R. West. 2009. "Educating the Public." *Education Next* 9, no. 3: 41–47.

Hufbauer, Gary Clyde, Jeffrey Schott, and Kimberly Elliott. 1990. *Economic Sanctions Reconsidered: History and Current Policy*, 2nd ed. Washington: Institute for International Economics.

Hufbauer, Gary Clyde, Jeffrey Schott, and Kimberly Elliott. 1990. *Economic Sanctions Reconsidered: Supplemental Case Histories*, 2nd ed. Washington: Institute for International Economics.

Hufbauer, Gary Clyde, Jeffrey J. Schott, and Barbara Oegg. 2001. "Using Sanctions to Fight Terrorism." *Peterson Institute for International Economics*, November 1.

Human Rights Watch. 2017. *World Report, 2017*. New York: Human Rights Watch.

Huntington, Samuel P. 1961. *The Common Defense*. New York: Columbia University Press.

Huntington, Samuel P. 2015|1982. "American Ideals versus American Institutions." In *American Foreign Policy*, edited by G. J. Ikenberry and P. L. Trubowitz, 297–322. Oxford: Oxford University Press.

Hurd, Ian. 2017. *How to Do Things with International Law*. Princeton: Princeton University Press.

Huth, Paul K. 1988. "Extended Deterrence and the Outbreak of War." *American Political Science Review* 82, no. 2: 423–43.

Huth, Paul K. 1999. "Deterrence and International Conflict: Empirical Findings and Theoretical Debates." *Annual Review of Political Science* 2: 25–48.

Huth, Paul K., D. Scott Bennett, and Christopher Gelpi. 1992. "System Uncertainty, Risk Propensity, and International Conflict among the Great Powers." *Journal of Conflict Resolution* 36, no. 3: 478–517.

Huth, Paul K., Sarah E. Croco, and Benjamin J. Appel. 2011. "Does International Law Promote the Peaceful Settlement of International Disputes? Evidence from the Study of Territorial Conflicts since 1945." *American Political Science Review* 105, no. 2: 415–36.

Huth, Paul K., Christopher Gelpi, and D. Scott Bennett. 1993. "The Escalation of Great Power Militarized Disputes: Testing Rational Deterrence Theory and Structural Realism." *American Political Science Review* 87, no. 3: 609–23.

Huth, Paul K. and Bruce Russett. 1984. "What Makes Deterrence Work? Cases from 1900 to 1980." *World Politics* 36, no. 4: 496–526.

Huth, Paul K. and Bruce Russett. 1988. "Deterrence Failure and Crisis Escalation." *International Studies Quarterly* 32, no. 1: 29–45.

*iCasualties.* 2019. "Iraq Coalition Casualty Count." January 9.

Ikenberry, G. John. 2011. *Liberal Leviathan: The Origins, Crisis, and Transformation of the American World Order.* Princeton: Princeton University Press.

Ikenberry, G. John and Charles Kupchan. 2004. "Liberal Realism: The Foundations of a Democratic Foreign Policy." *The National Interest* 77: 38–49.

International Atomic Energy Agency Director General. 2017. *Verification and Monitoring in the Islamic Republic of Iran in Light of United Nations Security Resolution 2231 (2015).* Vienna: IAEA Board of Governors.

International Monetary Fund. 2017. "IMF Members' Quotas and Voting Power, and IMF Board of Governors." Washington: International Monetary Fund.

International Monetary Fund. 2017. "World Economic Outlook." Washington: International Monetary Fund.

Ioffe, Julia. 2016. "How Russia Saw the 'Red Line' Crisis." *The Atlantic,* March 11.

Irwin, Douglas A. 2005. "The Welfare Cost of Autarky: Evidence from the Jeffersonian Trade Embargo, 1807–09." *Review of International Economics* 13, no. 4: 631–45.

Jackson, Patrick Thaddeus and Stuart J. Kaufman. 2007. "Security Scholars for a Sensible Foreign Policy: A Study in Weberian Activism." *Perspectives on Politics* 5, no. 1: 95–103.

Jaffe, Greg. 2018. "White House Ignores Executive Order Requiring Count of Civilian Casualties in Counterterrorism Strikes." *Washington Post,* May 1.

Jagannathan, Meera. 2017. "Majority of Americans Approve of President Trump's Syria Missile Strike: Poll." *New York Daily News,* April 10.

Jansen, Bart and Elizabeth Weise. 2018. "Russia Is Sponsoring Cyberattacks in US Homes and Businesses, US and UK Officials Warn." *USA Today,* April 16.

*Japan Today.* 2018. "Abe Vows to Proceed with US Base Relocation in Okinawa after Mayoral Election." February 6.

Jenkins, Brian. 1996. "Plane Terror Suspects Convicted on All Counts." *CNN,* September 5.

Jervis, Robert. 1976. *Perception and Misperception in International Politics.* Princeton: Princeton University Press.

Jervis, Robert. 1978. "Cooperation under the Security Dilemma." *World Politics* 30, no. 2: 167–214.

Jervis, Robert. 1988. "War and Misperception." *The Journal of Interdisciplinary History* 18, no. 4: 675–700.

Jervis, Robert. 2002. "Theories of War in an Era of Leading-Power Peace." *American Political Science Review* 96, no. 1: 1–14.

Jervis, Robert. 2003. "Understanding the Bush Doctrine." *Political Science Quarterly* 118, no. 3: 365–88.

Johnson, Dominic D. P. 2004. *Overconfidence and War: The Havoc and Glory of Positive Illusions.* Cambridge: Harvard University Press.

Johnson, Dominic D. P. and Dominic Tierney. 2011. "The Rubicon Theory of War:

How the Path to Conflict Reaches the Point of No Return." *International Security* 36, no. 1: 7–40.

Johnson, Kirk. 2012. "New Sentence Is Imposed in Bomb Plot from 1999." *New York Times*, October 24.

Johnson, Loch K. 2007. *Seven Sins of American Foreign Policy*. New York: Pearson Longman.

Jones, Dan. 2012. *The Plantagenets: The Warrior Kings and Queens Who Made England*. New York: Penguin.

Kagan, Robert. 2014. "US Needs a Discussion on When, Not Whether, to Use Force." *Washington Post*, July 15.

Kahneman, Daniel and Jonathan Renshon. 2007. "Why Hawks Win." *Foreign Policy* 158: 34–8.

Kahneman, Daniel and Jonathan Renshon. 2009. "Hawkish Biases." In *American Foreign Policy and the Politics of Fear*, edited by A. T. Thrall and J. A. Cramer, 79–96. New York: Routledge.

Kaminsky, Graciela Laura and Sergio L. Schmukler. 2008. "Short-Run Pain, Long-Run Gain: Financial Liberalization and Stock Market Cycles." *Review of Finance* 12, no. 2: 253–92.

Kaplan, Lawrence S. 1957. "Jefferson, the Napoleonic Wars, and the Balance of Power." *The William and Mary Quarterly* 14, no. 2: 196–217.

Kaplan, Robert D. 2017. *Earning the Rockies: How Geography Shapes America's Role in the World*. New York: Random House.

Kaufmann, Chaim D. 2004. "Threat Inflation and the Failure of the Marketplace of Ideas: The Selling of the Iraq War." *International Security* 29, no. 1: 5–48.

Kaufmann, Chaim D. and Robert A. Pape. 1999. "Explaining Costly International Moral Action: Britain's Sixty-Year Campaign against the Atlantic Slave Trade." *International Organization* 53, no. 4: 631–68.

Kaye, David. 2013. "Stealth Multilateralism: US Foreign Policy without Treaties—Or the Senate." *Foreign Affairs* 92, no. 5: 113–24.

Kecskemeti, Paul. 1958. *Strategic Surrender: The Politics of Victory and Defeat*. Palo Alto: Stanford University Press.

Kennan, George Frost. 1947. "The Sources of Soviet Conduct." *Foreign Affairs* 25, no. 4: 566–82.

Kennan, George Frost. 1984. *American Diplomacy*. Chicago: University of Chicago Press.

Kennedy, John F. 1961. "Address of President-Elect John F. Kennedy Delivered to a Joint Convention of the General Court of the Commonwealth of Massachusetts," January 9.

Kennedy, Paul. 1987. *The Rise and Fall of Great Powers*. New York: Random House.

Kennedy, Paul. 2002. "The Greatest Superpower Ever." *New Perspectives Quarterly* 19, no. 2: 8–18.

Keohane, Robert O. 1986. "Reciprocity in International Relations." *International Organization* 40, no. 1: 1–27.

Keohane, Robert O. 1989. *After Hegemony: Cooperation and Discord in the World Political Economy*. Princeton: Princeton University Press.

Keohane, Robert O. and Lisa L. Martin. 1999. "The Promise of Institutionalist Theory." *International Security* 20, no. 1: 39–51.

Keohane, Robert O. and Joseph S. Nye. 1987. "Power and Interdependence Revisited." *International Organization* 41, no. 4: 725–53.

Kight, Stef W. 2018. "The Disappearing Chinese Student Visa." *Axios*, May 6.

Kim, Tongfi. 2011. "Why Alliances Entangle But Seldom Entrap States." *Security Studies* 20, no. 3: 350–77.

Kinnard, Douglas. 1977. "President Eisenhower and the Defense Budget." *Journal of Politics* 39, no. 3: 596–623.

Kinzer, Stephen. 2017. "Saudi Arabia Is Destabilizing the World." *Boston Globe*, June 11.

Kinzer, Stephen. 2017. *The True Flag: Theodore Roosevelt, Mark Twain, and the Birth of American Empire*. New York: Henry Holt.

Kissinger, Henry. 1994. *Diplomacy*. New York: Simon & Schuster.

Kissinger, Henry. 2014. *World Order*. New York: Penguin.

Koh, Harold Hongju. 1997. "Why Do Nations Obey International Law?" *The Yale Law Journal* 106, no. 8: 2599–659.

Korinek, Anton. 2011. "The New Economics of Prudential Capital Controls: A Research Agenda." *IMF Economic Review* 59, no. 3: 523–61.

Kosack, Stephen and Jennifer Tobin. 2006. "Funding Self-Sustaining Development: The Role of Aid, FDI and Government in Economic Success." *International Organization* 60, no. 1: 205–43.

Krebs, Ronald R. 2005. "Correspondence: Selling the Market Short? The Marketplace of Ideas and the Iraq War." *International Security* 29, no. 4: 196–207.

Kreps, Sarah and Sarah Maxey. 2018. "Americans Feel a Moral Obligation to Help Humanitarian Victims (Like Those in Syria) with Military Force." *Washington Post*, April 10.

Kreps, Sarah and Sarah Maxey. 2018. "Sources of Support for Humanitarian Intervention," *Journal of Conflict Resolution* 62, no. 8: 1814–42.

Kroll, Andy. 2017. "How a Crew of Hardliners Hijacked Donald Trump's Cuba Policy." *Mother Jones*, June 16.

Krugman, Paul. 2011. "Keynes Was Right." *New York Times*, December 29.

Krugman, Paul. 2018. "Making Tariffs Corrupt Again." *New York Times*, September 20.

Kuklinski, James H., Paul J. Quirk, Jennifer Jerit, David Schweider, and Robert F. Rich. 2000. "Misinformation and the Currency of Democratic Citizenship." *Journal of Politics* 62, no. 3: 790–816.

Kupchan, Charles A. and Peter L. Trubowitz. 2015|2007. "Grand Strategy for a Divided America." In *American Foreign Policy*, edited by G. J. Ikenberry and P. L. Trubowitz, 583–89. Oxford: Oxford University Press.

Lacina, Bethany and Nils Petter Gleditsch. 2005. "Monitoring Trends in Global Combat: A New Dataset of Battle Deaths." *European Journal of Population/ Revue Européenne de Démographie* 21, nos. 2–3: 145–66.

LaFranchi, Howard. 2018. "Challenge to US Sovereignty? In Polls Public Accepts Constraints on Power." *Christian Science Monitor*, September 11.

Lai, Brian and Dan Slater. 2006. "Institutions of the Offensive: Domestic Sources of Dispute Initiation in Authoritarian Regimes, 1950–1992." *American Journal of Political Science* 50, no. 1: 113–26.

Lamothe, Dan and Josh Dawsey. 2019. "Trump Wanted a Big Cut in Troops in Afghanistan. New US Military Plans Fall Short." *Washington Post*, January 8.

Landler, Mark. 2016. "How Hillary Clinton Became a Hawk." *New York Times Magazine*. April 21.

Landler, Mark. 2018. "Trump Tells Ally US Will Leave Iran Deal." *New York Times*, May 8.

Landler, Mark and Peter Baker. 2019. "Trump Vetoes Measure to Force End to US Involvement in Yemen War." *New York Times*, April 16.

Landler, Mark and Michael R. Gordon. 2017. "As US Adds Troops in Afghanistan, Trump's Strategy Remains Undefined." *New York Times*, June 18.

Landler, Mark, Maggie Haberman, and Eric Schmitt. 2019. "Trump Tells Pentagon Chief He Does Not Want War with Iran." *New York Times*, May 16.

Langworth, Richard, ed. 2008. *Churchill by Himself: The Definitive Collection of Quotations*. New York: PublicAffairs.

Lawton. Kim. 2015. "Do Americans Care about Foreign Policy?" *PBS*, August 20.

Leeds, Brett Ashley. 2003. "Do Alliances Deter Aggression? The Influence of Military Alliances on the Initiation of Militarized Interstate Disputes." *American Journal of Political Science* 47, no. 3: 427–39.

Legro, Jeffrey W. 2015. "Sovereignty American Style: Protecting Apple Pie, Fixing Foreign Recipes." In *America, China, and the Struggle for World Order*, edited by G. J. Ikenberry, Zhu Feng, and Wang Jisi, 19–42. New York: Palgrave Macmillan.

Legro, Jeffrey W. 2015|2000. "Whence American Internationalism." In *American Foreign Policy*, edited by G. J. Ikenberry and P. L. Trubowitz, 323–52. Oxford: Oxford University Press.

Lemnitzer, Jan Martin. 2014. *Power, Law, and the End of Privateering*. London: Palgrave MacMillan.

Leverett, Flynt L. 2004. "Why Libya Gave Up on the Bomb." *Brookings*, January 23.

Levy, Aharon and Yossi Maaravi. 2018. "The Boomerang Effect of Psychological Interventions," *Social Influence* 13, no. 1: 39–51.

Levy, Jack. 1986. "Organizational Routines and the Causes of War." *International Studies Quarterly* 30, no. 2: 193–222.

Lewin, Tamar and Anemona Hartocollis. 2010. "Colleges Rethink ROTC after 'Don't Ask' Repeal." *New York Times*, December 21.

Liberman, Peter. 1996. *Does Conquest Pay? The Exploitation of Occupied Industrial Societies*. Princeton: Princeton University Press.

Liberman, Peter. 2006. "An Eye for an Eye: Public Support for War against Evildoers." *International Organization* 60, no. 3: 687–722.

Lieber, Keir and Daryl G. Press. 2013. "Why States Won't Give Nuclear Weapons to Terrorists." *International Security* 38, no. 1: 80–104.

Lillington, Karlin. 2016. "How Real Is the Threat of Cyberterrorism?" *Irish Times*, April 14.

Lincoln, Abraham. 1848. "Speech to Congress, January 12, 1848."

Lind, Michael. 2006. *The American Way of Strategy: US Foreign Policy and the American Way of Life*. Oxford: Oxford University Press.

Lipscy, Philip. 2015. "Explaining Institutional Change: Policy Areas, Outside Options, and the Bretton Woods Institutions." *American Journal of Political Science* 59, no. 2: 341–56.

Liptak, Kevin. 2017. "Trump: US Troops 'Fighting Like Never Before' in Iraq." *CNN*, March 29.

Lizza, Ryan. 2013. "State of Deception: Why Won't the President Rein in the Intelligence Community?" *The New Yorker*, December 16.

Lord, Kristin. 2014. "Soft Power Outage: The Revelations about the United States' Brutal Torture Program Have Damaged the Country's Best Asset Abroad." *Foreign Policy*, December 23.

Lorenzo, David J. 2016. *Debating War: Why Arguments Opposing American Wars and Interventions Fail*. London: Routledge.

Luard, Evan. 1989. *The Blunted Sword: The Erosion of Military Power in World Politics*. New York: New Amsterdam.

Luce, Edward. 2017. *The Retreat of Western Liberalism*. New York: Atlantic Monthly Press.

Ludvigsen, Jan Andre Lee. 2018. "The Portrayal of Drones in Terrorist Propaganda: A Discourse Analysis of Al Qaeda in the Arabian Peninsula's *Inspire*." *Dynamics of Asymmetric Conflict* 11, no. 1: 26–49.

Lupia, Arthur. 1994. "Shortcuts versus Encyclopedias: Information and Voting Behavior in California Insurance Reform Elections." *American Political Science Review* 88, no. 1: 63–76.

Lupu, Yonatan and Erik Voeten. 2012. "Precedent in International Courts: A Network Analysis of Case Citations by the European Court of Human Rights." *British Journal of Political Science* 42, no. 2: 413–39.

Luttwak, Edward N. 2009. *The Grand Strategy of the Byzantine Empire*. Cambridge: Belknap Press of the Harvard University Press.

MacAskill, Ewen and Julian Borger. 2007. "Cheney Pushes Bush to Act on Iran." *The Guardian*, July 15.

MacDonald, Paul K. and Joseph M. Parent. 2011. "Graceful Decline? The Surprising Success of Great Power Retrenchment." *International Security* 35, no. 4: 7–44.

Mack, Andrew. 1975. "Why Big Nations Lose Small Wars: The Politics of Asymmetric Conflict." *World Politics* 27, no. 2: 175–200.

MacKay, Joseph and Christopher David LaRoche. 2018. "Reactionary World Politics." *Duck of Minerva*, March 25.

MacKay, Joseph and Christopher David LaRoche. 2018. "Why Is There No Reac-

tionary International Theory?" *International Studies Quarterly* 62, no. 2: 234–44.

Malhotra, Deepak and Jeremy Ginges. 2010. "Preferring Balanced vs. Advantageous Peace Agreements: A Study of Israeli Attitudes toward a Two State Solution." *Judgement and Decision Making* 5, no. 6: 420–27.

Maloney, Suzanne. 2014. "Why 'Iran Style' Sanctions Worked against Tehran (And Why They Might Not Succeed with Moscow)." *Brookings*, March 21.

Mandelbaum, Michael. 1999. "A Perfect Failure: NATO's War against Yugoslavia," *Foreign Affairs* 78, no. 5: 2–8.

Mandelbaum, Michael. 2005. *The Case for Goliath: How America Acts as the World's Government in the Twenty-First Century*. New York: PublicAffairs.

Mandelbaum, Michael. 2016. *Mission Failure: America and the World Since the End of the Cold War*. Oxford: Oxford University Press.

Mankiw, N. Gregory. 1997. *Macroeconomics*. 3rd ed. New York: Worth.

Mansori, Kash. 2011. "Why Greece, Spain, and Ireland Aren't to Blame for Europe's Woes." *The New Republic*, October 11.

Maoz, Ifat, Andrew Ward, Michael Katz, and Lee Ross. 2002. "Reactive Devaluation of an 'Israeli' vs. 'Palestinian' Peace Proposal." *Journal of Conflict Resolution* 46, no. 4: 515–46.

Maoz, Zeev. 1983. "Resolve, Capabilities, and the Outcomes of Interstate Disputes, 1816–1976." *Journal of Conflict Resolution* 27, no. 2: 195–229.

Marinov, Nikolay. 2005. "Do Economic Sanctions Destabilize Country Leaders?" *American Journal of Political Science* 49, no. 3: 564–76.

Martin, David. 2016. "Russian Hack Almost Brought the US Military to its Knees." *CBS News*, December 15.

Martinez, Luis and Elizabeth McLaughlin. 2018. "What You Need to Know about US Military Involvement in Syria as Trump Orders Withdrawal." *ABC News*, December 20.

Mashal, Mujib. 2019. "US and Taliban Agree in Principle to Peace Framework, Envoy Says." *New York Times*, January 28.

Mashal, Mujib and Najom Rahim. 2016. "US Commander in Afghanistan Apologizes for Bombing of Hospital." *New York Times*, March 22.

Mason, Ra. 2017. "Why a Row over Military Bases on Okinawa Spells Trouble for US-Japan Relations." *The Conversation*, March 10.

Masters, James. 2017. "France Tops US in Global 'Soft Power' Rankings as Trump Factor Blamed." *CNN*, July 18.

Matfess, Hilary. 2015. "Boko Haram Is No al-Qaeda." *Washington Post*, January 13.

Mathews, Jessica T. 2019. "America's Indefensible Defense Budget." *New York Review of Books*, July 18.

Mathews, Sidney T. 1990. "General Clark's Decision to Drive on Rome." In *Command Decisions*, edited by K. R. Greenfield, 351–64. Washington: Center of Military History, Department of the Army.

Matishak, Martin. 2015. "Rangel: Reinstate the Draft." *The Hill*, March 19.

Mattingly, Garrett. 1988. *Renaissance Diplomacy*. New York: Dover.

Mazzetti, Mark. 2011. "US Aides Believe China Examined Stealth Copter." *New York Times*, August 14.

McBride, James. 2018. "How Does the US Spend Its Foreign Aid?" *Council on Foreign Relations*, October 1.

McCain, John. 2017. "Restoring the Vision: Overcoming Gridlock to Reassert Congress's Role in Deliberating National Security." *Texas National Security Review* 1, no. 1: 126–29.

McCartney, Paul T. 2004. "American Nationalism and US Foreign Policy from September 11 to the Iraq War." *Political Science Quarterly* 119, no. 3: 399–423.

McDonald, Patrick J. 2004. "Peace through Trade or Free Trade?" *Journal of Conflict Resolution* 48, no. 4: 547–72.

McDonald, Patrick J. 2009. *The Invisible Hand of Peace: Capitalism, the War Machine, and International Relations Theory*. Cambridge: Cambridge University Press.

McDougall, Walter A. 1997. *Promised Land, Crusader State*. Boston: Houghton Mifflin.

McEvedy, Colin. 1961. *The Penguin Atlas of Medieval History*. London: Penguin.

McEvedy, Colin. 1986. *The Penguin Atlas of Modern History (to 1815)*. London: Penguin.

McFadden, Cynthia, William M. Arkin, and Tim Uehlinger. 2017. "How the Trump Team's First Military Raid in Yemen Went Wrong." *NBC News*, October 2.

McGillivray, Mark, Simon Feeny, Niels Hermes, and Robert Lensink. 2006. "Controversies over the Impact of Development Aid: It Works; It Doesn't; It Can, but that Depends." *Journal of International Development* 18, no. 7: 1031–50.

McGregor, Janyce. 2018. "Pacific Rim Trade Deal to Kick in Dec. 30 including Canada, Australia." *CBC*, October 31.

Mead, Walter Russell. 2001. *Special Providence: American Foreign Policy and How It Changed the World*. London: Routledge.

Mearsheimer, John J. 2018. *Great Delusion: Liberal Dreams and International Relations*. New Haven: Yale University Press.

Mehta, Sarah. 2015. "There's Only One Country That Hasn't Ratified the Convention on Children's Rights: US." *ACLU*, November 20.

Mellnik, Ted and Aaron Williams. 2018. "Is Canada 'Ripping Us Off'? Or Is It the Best US Trade Partner?" *Washington Post*, September 21.

Mercer, Jonathan. 1996. *Reputation and International Politics*. Ithaca: Cornell University Press.

Mercer, Jonathan. 2010. "Emotional Beliefs." *International Organization* 64, no. 1: 1–31.

Michaels, Jim. 2016. "ROTC Welcomed Back at Ivy League Schools." *USA Today*, May 23.

Miklaszewski, Jim, Pete Williams, Robert Windrem, and Richard Esposito. 2013. "US Commandos Raid Terrorist Hideouts in Libya, Somalia, Capture Senior al Qaeda Official." *NBC News*, October 6.

Mill, John Stuart. 1997|1859. *On Liberty*. Upper Saddle River: Prentice Hall.

Miller, Greg. 2016. "Why CIA Drone Strikes Have Plummeted." *Washington Post*, June 16.

Miller, Paul D. 2016. *American Power & Liberal Order: A Conservative Internationalist Grand Strategy*. Washington: Georgetown University Press.

Mintz, Alex and Carly Wayne. 2015. *The Polythink Syndrome: US Foreign Policy Decisions on 9/11, Afghanistan, Iraq, Iran, Syria, and ISIS*. Palo Alto: Stanford University Press.

Mitchell, Sara McLaughlin and Paul Hensel. 2007. "International Institutions and Compliance with Agreements." *American Journal of Political Science* 51, no. 4: 721–37.

Moore, Gregory. 2015. *Defining and Defending the Open Door Policy: Theodore Roosevelt and China, 1901–1909*. Lanham: Lexington Books.

Moore, Michael T. and David M. Fresco. 2012. "Depressive Realism: A Meta-Analytic Review." *Clinical Psychology Review* 32, no. 6: 496–509.

Morello, Carol and Karen DeYoung. 2015. "Historic Deal Reached with Iran to Limit Nuclear Program." *Washington Post*, July 14.

Morgenthau, Hans J. 1952. "Another 'Great Debate': The National Interest of the United States." *American Political Science Review* 46, no. 4: 961–88.

Morrow, James. 2001. "The Institutional Features of Prisoners of War Treaties." *International Organization* 55, no. 4: 971–91.

Morse, Julia C. 2019. "Blacklists, Market Enforcement, and the Global Regime to Combat Terrorist Financing." *International Organization* 73, no. 3: 511–45.

Mueller, John. 1994. "The Catastrophe Quota: Trouble after the Cold War." *Journal of Conflict Resolution* 38, no. 3: 355–75.

Mui, Ylan Q. 2017. "Withdrawal from Trans-Pacific Partnership Shifts US Role in World Economy." *Washington Post*, January 23.

Mukherjee, Rohan. 2019. "Two Cheers for the Liberal World Order: The International Order and Rising Powers in a Trumpian World." *H-Diplo/ISSF*, February 22.

Myers, Steven. 2000. "Chinese Embassy Bombing: A Wide Net of Blame." *New York Times*, April 17.

Nacos, Brigitte L. 2014. "There Is a Need to Focus More on Building Bridges." In *Debating Terrorism and Counterterrorism*, 2nd ed., edited by S. Gottlieb, 212–25. Washington: CQPress.

Nacos, Brigitte L. 2016. *Terrorism and Counterterrorism*. 5th ed. London: Routledge.

National Security Council. 1950. *A Report to the National Security Council by the Executive Secretary on the United States Objectives and Programs for National Security—NSC 68*. Washington: United States Government.

Nazario, Sonia. 2016. "How the Most Dangerous Place on Earth Got Safer." *New York Times*, August 11.

Nephew, Richard. 2018. *The Art of Sanctions: A View from the Field*. New York: Columbia University Press.

Newport, Frank. 2003. "Seventy-Two Percent of Americans Support War against Iraq." *Gallup News Service*, March 24.

*New York Daily News*. 2017. "Here's a List of Terror Attacks and Foiled Plots in New York City since 2010." December 11.

Nexon, Daniel. 2018. "Toward a Neo-Progressive Foreign Policy: The Case for an Internationalist Left." *Foreign Affairs*, September 4.

Nordlinger, Eric A. 1995. *Isolationism Reconfigured: American Foreign Policy for a New Century*. Princeton: Princeton University Press.

Nye, Joseph S. 2002. "Limits of American Power." *Political Science Quarterly* 117, no. 4: 545–59.

Nye, Joseph S. 2008. "Public Diplomacy and Soft Power." *The Annals of the American Academy of Political and Social Science* 616, no. 1: 94–109.

Nye, Joseph S., Graham T. Allison, and Albert Carnesale. 1985. "Analytic Conclusions: Hawks, Doves, and Owls." In *Hawks, Doves, and Owls*, edited by G. T. Allison, A. Carnesdale, and J. S. Nye, 223–46. New York: W. W. Norton.

Nyhan, Brendan and Jason Reifler. 2010. "When Corrections Fail: The Persistence of Political Misperceptions." *Political Behavior* 32, no. 2: 303–30.

Nyhan, Brendan and Jason Reifler. 2015. "Does Correcting Myths about the Flu Vaccine Work? An Experimental Evaluation of the Effects of Corrective Information." *Vaccine* 33, no. 3: 459–64.

Nyhan, Brendan, Jason Reifler, Sean Richey, and Gary L. Freed. 2014. "Effective Messages in Vaccine Promotion: A Randomized Trial." *Pediatrics* 133, no. 4: e835–e842.

O'Connor, Marleen A. 2002. "The Enron Board: The Perils of Groupthink." *University of Cincinnati Law Review* 71: 1233–320.

O'Neill, Barry. 1999. *Honor, Symbols, and War*. Ann Arbor: University of Michigan Press.

Organski, A. F. K. 1968. *World Politics*. 2nd ed. New York: Alfred A. Knopf.

Ornstein, Norman J. and Thomas E. Mann. 2006. "When Congress Checks Out." *Foreign Affairs* 85, no. 6: 67–82.

Osgood, Robert Endicott. 1953. *Ideals and Self-Interest in America's Foreign Relations: The Great Transformation of the Twentieth Century*. Chicago: Chicago University Press.

Osiander, Andreas. 1994. *The States System of Europe, 1640–1990*. Oxford: Oxford University Press.

Osiander, Andreas. 2001. "Sovereignty, International Relations, and the Westphalian Myth." *International Organization* 55, no. 2: 251–87.

Ostrom, Elinor. 1990. *Governing the Commons: The Evolution of Institutions for Action*. Cambridge: Cambridge University Press.

Ostry, Jonathan D., Atish R. Ghosh, Marcos Chamon, Mahvash S. Qureshi. 2012. "Tools for Managing Financial-Stability Risks from Capital Inflows." *Journal of International Economics* 88, no. 2: 407–21.

Ostry, Jonathan D., Atish R. Ghosh, Karl Habermeier, Luc Laeven, Marcos Chamon, Mahvash S. Qureshi, and Annamaria Kokenyne. 2011. "Managing Capital Inflows: What Tools to Use?" *IMF Staff Discussion Notes* No. 11/06.

Owens, John. 2009. "Congressional Acquiescence to Presidentialism in the US 'War on Terror.'" *Journal of Legislative Studies* 15, nos. 2–3: 147–90.

Oxman, Bernard. 2006. "The Territorial Temptation: The Siren Song at Sea." *The American Journal of International Law* 100, no. 4: 830–51.

Oye, Kenneth A. 1986. *Cooperation under Anarchy*. Princeton: Princeton University Press.

Palfrey, Thomas R. and Keith T. Poole. 1987. "The Relationship between Information, Ideology, and Voting Behavior." *American Journal of Political Science* 31, no. 3: 511–30.

Pape, Robert. 1996. *Bombing to Win: Air Power and Coercion in War*. Ithaca: Cornell University Press.

Pape, Robert. 1997. "Why Sanctions Do Not Work." *International Security* 22, no. 2: 90–136.

Pape, Robert. 2004. "The True Worth of Air Power." *Foreign Affairs* 83, no. 2: 116–30.

Patrick, Stewart. 2015. "The United States, the United Nations, and Collective Security: Exploring Deep Sources of American Conduct." In *America, China, and the Struggle for World Order*, edited by G. J. Ikenberry, Zhu Feng, and Wang Jisi, 71–102. New York: Palgrave Macmillan.

Paul, Christopher and Rand Waltzman. 2018. "How the Pentagon Should Deter Cyber Attacks." *Rand Corporation*, January.

Perlroth, Nicole, David E. Sanger, and Scott Shane. 2019. "How Chinese Spies Got the NSA's Hacking Tools, and Used Them for Attacks." *New York Times*, May 6.

Petri, Peter A. and Michael G. Plummer. 2016. "The Economic Effects of the Trans-Pacific Partnership: New Estimates." *Peterson Institute for International Economics:* WP 16–2.

Pickrell, Ryan. 2017. "Mattis Gives Congress a Sobering View of What War with North Korea Would Look Like." *The Daily Caller*, June 16.

Pillar, Paul R. 2016. *Why America Misunderstands the World: National Experience and Roots of Misperception*. New York: Columbia University Press.

Pilling, David. 2017. "Chinese Investment in Africa: Beijing's Testing Ground." *Financial Times*, June 13.

Pinker, Steven. 2011. *The Better Angels of our Nature: A History of Violence and Humanity*. New York: Penguin.

Planck, Max. 1948. *Wissenschaftliche Selbstbiographie. Mit einem Bildnis und der von Max von Laue gehaltenen Traueransprache*. Leipzig: Johann Ambrosius Barth Verlag.

Plaw, Avery and Matthew S. Fricker. 2012. "Tracking the Predators: Evaluating the US Drone Campaign in Pakistan." *International Studies Perspectives* 13, no. 4: 344–65.

Posen, Barry R. 2003. "Command of the Commons: The Military Foundation of US Hegemony." *International Security* 28, no. 1: 5–46.

Posen, Barry R. 2014. *Restraint: A New Foundation for US Grand Strategy*. Ithaca: Cornell University Press.

Postan, M. M. 1964. "The Costs of the Hundred Years' War." *The Past and Present Society* 27: 34–53.

Prange, Gordon William. 1981. *At Dawn We Slept: The Untold Story of Pearl Harbor*. With D. M. Goldstein and K. V. Dillon. New York: Penguin.

Preble, Christopher A. 2009. *The Power Problem: How American Military Dominance Makes Us Less Safe, Less Prosperous, and Less Free*. Ithaca: Cornell University Press.

Press, Daryl G. 2005. *Calculating Credibility: How Leaders Assess Military Threats*. Ithaca: Cornell University Press.

Prince, J. Dyneley. 1904. "Review: The Code of Hammurabi." *The American Journal of Theology* 8, no. 3: 601–9.

Prorok, Alyssa K. and Benjamin J. Appel. 2014. "Compliance with International Humanitarian Law: Democratic Third Parties and Civilian Targeting in Interstate War." *Journal of Conflict Resolution* 58, no. 4: 713–40.

Purkiss, Jessica and Jack Serle. 2017. "Obama's Covert Drone War in Numbers: Ten Times More Strikes than Bush." *The Bureau of Investigative Journalism*, January 17.

Putnam, Tonya. 2014. "An $8.9 Billion Fine Shows that Foreign Banks Evade US Laws at Their Peril." *Washington Post*, June 30.

Quealy, Kevin. 2017. "The Lowest-Profile State Department in 45 Years, in 2 Charts." *New York Times*, October 4.

Quester, George H. 1982. *American Foreign Policy: The Lost Consensus*. Westport: Praeger.

Rappeport, Alan and Glenn Thrush. 2017. "Pentagon Grows, While EPA and State Dept. Shrink in Trump's Budget." *New York Times*, March 16.

Rashbaum, William K. and David Johnston. 2009. "US Agents Arrest Father and Son in Terror Inquiry." *New York Times*, September 19.

Reagan, Ronald. 1984. "Acceptance Speech, Republican National Convention." August 23.

Reiter, Dan. 2009. *How Wars End*. Princeton: Princeton University Press.

Rey, Hélène. 2018. "Dilemma not Trilemma: The Global Financial Cycle and Monetary Policy Independence." *NBER Working Paper* No. 21162.

Richardson, Louise. 1999. "The Concert of Europe and Security Management in the Nineteenth Century." In *Imperfect Unions*, edited by H. Haftendorn, R. O. Keohane, and C. A. Wallander, 48–79. Oxford: Oxford University Press.

Rieffel, Lex and James W. Fox. 2008. "Strengthen the Millennium Challenge Corporation: Better Results Are Possible." *Brookings*, December 10.

Ritov, Ilana and Jonathan Baron. 1994. "Judgements of Compensation for Misfortune: The Role of Expectation." *European Journal of Social Psychology* 24, no. 5: 525–39.

Roach, J. Ashley. 2010. "Countering Piracy off Somalia: International Law and International Institutions." *The American Journal of International Law* 104, no. 3: 397–416.

Roberts, Cynthia. 2019. "Avoid Allowing Opponents to 'Beat America at its Own Game:' Ensuring US Financial and Currency Power." In *Chinese Strategic Intentions: A Deep Dive into China's Worldwide Activities*, edited by. N. Peterson, 145–55. Washington: Department of Defense.

Roberts, Cynthia, Leslie Armijo, Saori Katada. 2017. *The BRICS and Collective Financial Statecraft*. Oxford: Oxford University Press.

Roberts, J. Timmons, Bradley C. Parks, Michael J. Tierney, and Robert L. Hicks. 2009. "Has Foreign Aid Been Greened?" *Environment* 51, no. 1: 8–21.

Rohde, David. 2013. *Beyond War: Reimagining America's Role and Ambitions in a New Middle East*. New York: Penguin.

Roosevelt, Theodore. 1905. "Speech at Capitol Square, Richmond, Virginia." October 18.

Rosato, Sebastian and John Schuessler. 2015|2011. "A Realist Foreign Policy for the United States." In *American Foreign Policy*, edited by G. J. Ikenberry and P. L. Trubowitz, 115–36. Oxford: Oxford University Press.

Ross, Blair A. 2005. "The US Joint Task Force Experience in Liberia." *Military Review* 85, no. 3: 60–67.

Ross, Lee. 1995. "Reactive Devaluation in Negotiation and Conflict Resolution." In *Barriers to Conflict Resolution*, edited by K. J. Arrow, R. H. Mnookin, L. Ross, A. Tversky, and R. B. Wilson, 26–42. New York: W. W. Norton.

Ross, Lee and Constance Stillinger. 1991. "Barriers to Conflict Resolution." *Negotiation Journal* 7, no. 4: 389–404.

Rothkopf, David. 2014. "Obama's 'Don't Do Stupid Shit' Foreign Policy." *Foreign Policy*, June 4.

Ruggie, John Gerard. 1998. "What Makes the World Hang Together? Neo-Utilitarianism and Social Constructivist Challenge." *International Organization* 52, no. 4: 855–85.

Russett, Bruce and John Oneal. 2000. *Triangulating Peace: Democracy, Interdependence, and International Organizations*. New York: W. W. Norton.

Sachs, Jeffrey. 2018. *A New Foreign Policy: Beyond American Exceptionalism*. New York: Columbia University Press.

Safire, William. 2006. "Whack-A-Mole." *New York Times*, October 29.

Sahay, Usha. 2013. "Syria, Signaling, and Operation Infinite Reach." *War on the Rocks*, September 5.

Salehyan, Idean. 2010. "The Delegation of War to Rebel Organizations." *Journal of Conflict Resolution* 54, no. 3: 493–515.

Sanger, David E. 2019. "As NATO Envoys Celebrate, Signs of Fracturing from Within." *New York Times*, April 4.

Sanger, David E. and Jane Perlez. 2017. "Trump Hands the Chinese a Gift: The Chance for Global Leadership." *New York Times*, June 1.

Sartori, Anne E. 2002. "The Might of the Pen: A Reputational Theory of Communication in International Disputes." *International Organization* 56, no. 1: 121–49.

Sartori, Anne E. 2005. *Deterrence by Diplomacy*. Princeton: Princeton University Press.

Savic, Ivan and Zachary C. Shirkey. 2017. *Uncertainty, Threat, and International Security: Implications for Southeast Asia*. London: Routledge.

Schaefer, Brett D. 2018. "Reforming US Food Aid Can Feed Millions More at the Same Cost." *National Review*, May 14.

Schelling, Thomas. 1966. *Arms and Influence*. New Haven: Yale University Press.

Schmidt, Brian C. and Michael C. Williams. 2008. "The Bush Doctrine and the Iraq War." *Security Studies* 17, no. 2: 191–220.

Schmitt, Eric. 2017. "US Commando Killed in Yemen in Trump's First Counterterrorism Operation." *New York Times*, January 29.

Schmitt, Eric and Saeed al-Batati. 2017. "The US Has Pummeled al Qaeda in Yemen. But the Threat Is Barely Dented." *New York Times*, December 30.

Schmitt, Eric and Julian E. Barnes. 2019. "White House Reviews Military Plans against Iran, in Echos of Iraq War." *New York Times*, May 14.

Schmitt, Eric and Mark Landler. 2019. "Pentagon Officials Fear Bolton's Actions Increase Risk of Clash with Iran." *New York Times*, January 13.

Schmitt, Eric, Alissa Rubi, and Thomas Gibbons-Neff. 2019. "ISIS Is Regaining Strength in Iraq and Syria." *New York Times*, August 10.

Schroeder, John H. 1973. *Mr. Polk's War: American Opposition and Dissent, 1846–1848*. Madison: University of Wisconsin Press.

Scowcroft, Brent. 2002. "Don't Attack Saddam." *The Wall Street Journal*, August 15.

Sechser, Todd. 2004. "Are Soldiers Less War Prone than Statesmen?" *Journal of Conflict Resolution* 48, no. 5: 746–74.

Shalal-Esa, Andrea. 2011. "Helicopter Loss in bin Laden Raid Highlights Risks." *Reuters*, May 3.

Shane, Scott. 2015. "Drone Strikes Reveal Uncomfortable Truth: US Is Often Unsure about Who Will Die." *New York Times*, April 23.

Shane, Scott. 2016. "Drone Strike Statistics Answer Few Questions, Raise Many." *New York Times*, July 3.

Shear, Michael D., Helene Cooper, and Eric Schmitt. 2019. "Trump Says He Was 'Cocked and Loaded' to Strike Iran, but Pulled Back." *New York Times*, June 21.

Shimko, Keith. 2017. *The Foreign Policy Puzzle: Interests, Threats, and Tools*. Oxford: Oxford University Press.

Shirkey, Zachary C. 2012. *Joining the Fray: Outside Military Intervention in Civil Wars*. Aldershot: Ashgate.

Shirkey, Zachary C. 2013. "America Can't Escape the Middle East." *National Interest*, July 29.

Shirkey, Zachary C. 2014. "A Better Way to Combat Terrorism." *National Interest*, August 21.

Shirkey, Zachary C. 2014. "International Organizations Are Limited in Their Ability to Combat Terrorism." In *Debating Terrorism and Counterterrorism*, 2nd ed., edited by S. Gottlieb, 279–91. Washington: CQPress.

Shoesmith, Ian and Jon Kelly. 2010. "The Coventry Blitz 'Conspiracy.'" *BBC News*, November 12.

Simmons, Beth. 2000. "International Law and State Behavior: Commitment and Compliance in International Monetary Affairs." *American Political Science Review* 94, no. 4: 819–35.

SIPRI. 2017. "Trends in World Military Expenditure, 2016." Stockholm: SIPRI.

Slantchev, Branislav. 2003. "The Principle of Convergence in Wartime Negotiations." *American Political Science Review* 97, no. 4: 621–32.

Slantchev, Branislav and Ahmer Tarar. 2011. "Mutual Optimism as a Rationalist Explanation of War." *American Journal of Political Science* 55, no. 1: 135–48.

Slaughter, Anne Marie. 2005. *A New World Order*. Princeton: Princeton University Press.

Smeltz, Dina, Ivo H. Daalder, Karl Friedhoff, and Craig Kafura. 2017. "What Americans Think about America First." *The Chicago Council on Global Affairs*, October 2.

Smith, Adam. 1937|1776. *The Wealth of Nations*. New York: Modern Library.

Snidal, Duncan. 1991. "Relative Gains and the Pattern of International Cooperation." *American Political Science Review* 85, no. 3: 701–26.

Snow, Donald M. 2000. *When America Fights: The Use of US Military Force*. Washington: CQ Press.

Snow, Donald M. 2009. *What after Iraq?* New York: Pearson Longman.

Snow, Donald M. 2015. *The Case against Military Intervention: Why We Do It and Why It Fails*. London: Routledge.

Snyder, Jack. 1984. "Civil-Military Relations and the Cult of the Offensive, 1914." *International Security* 9, no. 1: 108–46.

Snyder, Jack. 2009. "Imperial Myths and Threat Inflation." In *American Foreign Policy and the Politics of Fear*, edited by A. T. Thrall and J. K. Cramer, 40–53. New York: Routledge.

Snyder, Jack and Karen Ballentine. 1996. "Nationalism and the Marketplace of Ideas." *International Security* 21, no. 2: 5–40.

Spaeth, Ryu. 2014. "Can Obama Make a Dovish Foreign Policy Popular?" *The Week*, June 25.

Specia, Megan and David E. Sanger. 2018. "Why North Korea Is Angered by 'Libya Model' in Nuclear Talks." *New York Times*, May 17.

Specter, Arlen. 2009. "The Need to Roll Back Presidential Power Grabs." *The New York Review of Books*, May 14.

Stanley, Elizabeth. 2018. "War Duration and the Micro-Dynamics of Decision Making under Stress." *Polity* 50, no. 2: 178–200.

Stares, Paul B. 2018. *Preventive Engagement: How America Can Avoid War, Stay Strong, and Keep the Peace*. New York: Columbia University Press.

Stein, Arthur. 1982. "Coordination and Collaboration: Regimes in an Anarchic World." *International Organization* 36, no. 2: 294–324.

Steinhauer, Jennifer. 2015. "Republicans Have Minds Made Up as Debate Begins on Iran Nuclear Deal." *New York Times*, July 23.

Stern, Roger J. 2010. "United States Cost of Military Force Projection in the Persian Gulf, 1976–2007." *Energy Policy* 38, no. 6: 2816–25.

Stone, Christopher. 2004. "Common but Differentiated Responsibilities in International Law." *American Journal of International Law* 98, no. 2: 276–301.

Sullivan, Jake. 2019. "More, Less, or Different? Where US Foreign Policy Should—and Shouldn't—Go from Here." *Foreign Affairs* 98, no. 1: 168–75.

Sunstein, Cass R. 2016. "Beyond Cheneyism and Snowdenism." *University of Chicago Law Review* 83: 271–93.

Svenson, Ola. 1981. "Are We All Less Risky and More Skillful than Our Fellow Drivers?" *Acta Psychologica* 47, no. 2: 143–48.

Tams, Carsten. 1999. "The Functions of a European Security and Defense Identity and Its Institutional Form." In *Imperfect Unions*, edited by H. Haftendorn, R. O. Keohane, and C. A. Wallander, 80–106. Oxford: Oxford University Press.

Taylor, Adam and Laris Karklis. 2016. "This Remarkable Chart Shows How US Defense Spending Dwarfs the Rest of the World." *Washington Post*, February 9.

Taylor, Andrew. 2017. "House Republicans Seek Cuts to Foreign Aid, Support for US-Mexico Wall." *Associated Press*, July 12.

Tetlock, Philip E. 1985. "Accountability: A Social Check on the Fundamental Attribution Error." *Social Psychology Quarterly* 48, no. 3: 227–36.

Tetlock, Philip E. and Charles B. McGuire, Jr. 2015|1985. "Cognitive Perspectives on Foreign Policy." In *American Foreign Policy*, edited by G. J. Ikenberry and P. L. Trubowitz, 489–502. Oxford: Oxford University Press.

Tharoor, Ishaan. 2013. "Viewpoint: Why Was the Biggest Protest in World History Ignored?" *Time*, February 15.

Thibodeau, Ian and Jim Lynch. 2017. "Trump Steel Tariffs Could Hurt US Autos." *Detroit News*, July 16.

Thrall, A. Trevor. 2007. "A Bear in the Woods? Threat Framing and the Marketplace of Values." *Security Studies* 16, no. 3: 452–88.

Thrush, Glenn. 2018. "Trump Embraces Foreign Aid to Counter China's Global Influence." *New York Times*, October 14.

Thucydides. 1993|c. 400 BC. *History of the Peloponnesian War*. London: Everyman.

Tierney, Dominic. 2010. *How We Fight: Crusades, Quagmires, and the American Way of War*. Boston: Little, Brown.

Tierney, Dominic. 2015. *The Right Way to Lose a War: America in an Age of Unwinnable Conflicts*. Boston: Little, Brown.

Tompkins, E. Berkeley. 1970. *Anti-Imperialism in the United States: The Great Debate, 1890–1920*. Philadelphia: University of Pennsylvania Press.

Trager, Robert F. and Dessislava P. Zagorcheva. 2005/2006. "Deterring Terrorism: It Can Be Done." *International Security* 30, no. 3: 87–123.

*Treaty of Amity Commerce and Navigation, between His Britannick Majesty; and The United States of America, by Their President, with the Advice and Consent of Their Senate*, Br-US, November 19, 1794.

*Treaty of Friendship, Limits, and Navigation between Spain and the United States*, Sp-US, October 27, 1795.

Tuchman, Barbara W. 1961. *The Guns of August*. New York: Macmillan.

Tuschhoff, Christian. 1999. "Alliance Cohesion and Peaceful Change in NATO." In *Imperfect Unions*, edited by H. Haftendorn, R. O. Keohane, and C. A. Wallander, 140–61. Oxford: Oxford University Press.

Tyson, Alec. 2016. "Americans Still Favor Ties with Cuba after Castro's Death, US Election." *Pew Research Center*, December 13.

United Nations. 1948. *Universal Declaration of Human Rights: General Assembly Resolution 217*. Paris: United Nations.

United Nations. 2017. *2017 Revision of World Population Prospects*. New York: United Nations.

USAID. 2016. *Shared Progress, Shared Future: Agency Financial Report Fiscal Year 2016*. Washington: USAID.

US Department of Defense. 2017. "About the Department of Defense." Washington: US Department of Defense.

US Department of Defense. 2019. "Casualty." Washington: US Department of Defense.

US Department of State. 2015. *Congressional Budget Justification: Department of State, Foreign Operations, and Related Programs: Fiscal Year 2016*. Washington: US Department of State.

Van Evera, Stephen. 1984. "The Cult of the Offensive and the Origins of the First World War." *International Security* 9, no. 1: 58–107.

Van Evera, Stephen. 1999. *Causes of War: Power and the Roots of Conflict*. Ithaca: Cornell University Press.

Van Natta, Don, Jr. and Desmond Butler. 2004. "How Tiny Swiss Cellphone Chips Helped Track Global Terror Web." *New York Times*, March 4.

Vayrynen, Raimo. 2013. *The Waning of Major War: Theories and Debates*. London: Routledge.

Vegetius Renatus, Publius Flavius. 2001|c. 383. *Vegetius: Epitome of Military Science*. Translated by N. P. Milner. Liverpool: Liverpool University Press.

Verdier, Pierre-Hughes and Erik Voeten. 2014. "Precedent, Compliance, and Change in Customary International Law: An Explanatory Theory." *The American Journal of International Law* 108, no. 3: 389–434.

Voeten, Erik. 2010. "Borrowing and Nonborrowing among International Courts." *The Journal of Legal Studies* 39, no. 2: 547–76.

Wagner, R. Harrison. 2000. "Bargaining and War." *American Journal of Political Science* 44, no. 3: 469–84.

Wagner, R. Harrison. 2007. *War and the State*. Ann Arbor: University of Michigan Press.

Walsh, Declan. 2019. "Amid US Silence, Gulf Nations Back the Military in Sudan's Revolution." *New York Times*, April 26.

Walsh, Kenneth T. 2008. "Bush's Legacy: Waging Preventive War in Iraq." *US News and World Report*, December 9.

Walt, Stephen. 2000. "Two Cheers for Clinton's Foreign Policy." *Foreign Affairs* 79, no. 2: 63–79.

Walt, Stephen. 2002. "Keeping the World 'Off Balance:' Self Restraint and US Foreign Policy." In *America Unrivaled*, edited by G. J. Ikenberry, 121–54. Ithaca: Cornell University Press.

Walt, Stephen. 2006. *Taming American Power: The Global Response to US Primacy*. New York: Norton.

Walt, Stephen. 2011. "Overcommitment, Inc." *Foreign Policy*, July 1.

Walt, Stephen. 2013. "Who Was Right about Invading Iraq?" *Foreign Policy*, March 6.

Walt, Stephen. 2018. *The Hell of Good Intentions: America's Foreign Policy Elite and the Decline of U.S. Primacy*. New York: Farrar, Strauss, and Giroux.

Walter, Barbara. 2006. "Building Reputation: Why Governments Fight Some Separatists but Not Others." *American Journal of Political Science* 50, no. 2: 313–30.

Walzer, Michael. 1977. *Just and Unjust Wars*. New York: Basic Books.

Watson, Adam. 1992. *The Evolution of International Society*. London: Routledge.

Watts, Joe. 2017. "Nine Terror Plots Foiled in the UK in the Past Year, MI5 Chiefs Reveal." *Independent*, December 5.

Webb, James. 2013. "Congressional Abdication." *National Interest* 124: 8–15.

Webster, Daniel. 1983. "Letter to Henry Stephen Fox." In *The Papers of Daniel Webster*, edited by K. E. Shewmaker. Hanover: Dartmouth University Press.

Weiser, Benjamin. 2014. "Some Captured Terrorists Talk Willingly and Proudly, Investigators Say." *New York Times*, October 13.

Weisiger, Alex. 2013. *Logics of War: Explanations for Limited and Unlimited Conflicts*. Ithaca: Cornell University Press.

Weisiger, Alex, and Keren Yarhi-Milo. 2015. "Revisiting Reputation: How Past Actions Matter in International Politics." *International Organization* 69, no. 2: 473–95.

Weiss, Jeremy. 2013. "E. H. Carr, Norman Angell, and Reassessing the Realist-Utopian Debate." *The International History Review* 35, no. 5: 1156–84.

Whipple, A. B. C. 1991. *To the Shores of Tripoli: The Birth of the US Navy and Marines*. New York: William Morrow.

Wike, Richard. 2012. "Does Humanitarian Aid Improve America's Image?" *Pew Research Center: Global Attitudes & Trends*, March 6.

Winthrop, John. 1838|1630. "A Modell of Christian Charity." *Collections of the Massachusetts Historical Society* (Boston), 3rd series, 7: 31–48.

Wolfers, Arnold. 1962. *Discord and Collaboration: Essays on International Politics*. Baltimore: John Hopkins University Press.

Wolfers, Justin. 2014. "What Debate? Economists Agree the Stimulus Lifted the Economy." *New York Times*, July 29.

Wong, Edward and Nicholas Casey. 2019. "US Targets Venezuela with Tough Oil Sanctions during Crisis of Power." *New York Times*, January 28.

World Conference on Human Rights. 1993. *Vienna Declaration and Programme of Action*. Vienna: World Conference on Human Rights.

*World Public Opinion*. 2011. "Review of Polling Finds International and American Support for World Order Based on International Law, Stronger UN." December 11.

Wright, Thomas J. 2016. "Trump's 19th Century Foreign Policy." *Politico*, January 20.

Wright, Thomas J. 2017. *All Measures Short of War: The Contest for the 21st Century and the Future of American Power*. New Haven: Yale University Press.

Wroughton, Lesley and Patricia Zengerle. 2019. "As Promised, Trump Slashes Aid to Central America over Migrants." *Reuters*, June 17.

Yaffa, Joshua. 2016. "Putin's Dragon: Is the Rule of Chechnya Out of Control?" *The New Yorker* 92, no. 1: 72.

Yale Program on Climate Change Communication. 2016. "Most Registered Voters Say the US Should Participate in the Paris Climate Agreement." November.

Yemma, John. 1981. "Begin and Sadat Settling Their Camp David Accounts." *Christian Science Monitor*, August 27.

Young, Joseph and Lionel Beehner. 2015. "Al-Shabab Poses No Threat to US Interests." *USA Today*, April 5.

Zacher, Mark W. 2001. "The Territorial Integrity Norm: International Boundaries and the Use of Force." *International Organization* 55, no. 2: 215–50.

Zakaria, Fareed. 2017. "Failing to Deliver." *New York Times*, July 25.

Zenko, Micah. 2013. "Reforming US Drone Strike Policies." *Council on Foreign Relations Special Report* 65.

Zenko, Micah. 2017. "Obama's Final Drone Strike Tally." *Council on Foreign Relations*, January 20.

Zenko, Micah and Michael A. Cohen. 2012. "Clear and Present Safety: The United States Is More Secure than Washington Thinks." *Foreign Affairs* 91, no. 2: 79–93.

Zenko, Micah and Rebecca Friedman Lissner. 2017. "Trump Is Going to Regret Not Having a Grand Strategy." *Foreign Policy*, January 13.

# Index